P9-CKX-285

DATE DUE

DEMCO 38-296

SEXUALITY AND THE ELDERLY

Recent Titles in
Bibliographies and Indexes in Gerontology

Long Term Care: An Annotated Bibliography
Theodore H. Koff and Kristine M. Bursac, compilers

Employment of the Elderly: An Annotated Bibliography
John C. Rife, compiler

Alcoholism and Aging: An Annotated Bibliography and Review
Nancy J. Osgood, Helen E. Wood, and Iris A. Parham, compilers

Counseling Older Persons: An Annotated Bibliography
Valerie L. Schwiebert and Jane E. Myers, compilers

Research on Religion and Aging: An Annotated Bibliography
Harold G. Koenig, compiler

Psychology of Aging: An Annotated Bibliography
Bert Hayslip, Jr., Heather L. Servaty, and Amy S. Ward, compilers

Literature and Gerontology: A Research Guide
Robert E. Yahnke and Richard M. Eastman

Injury Prevention for the Elderly: A Research Guide
Bonnie L. Walker, compiler

Aging Well: A Selected, Annotated Bibliography
W. Edward Folts, Bette A. Ide, Tanya Fusco Johnson,
Jennifer Crew Solomon, compilers

Men and Aging: A Selected, Annotated Bibliography
Edward H. Thompson, Jr., compiler

Group Work with the Elderly: An Annotated Bibliography
Ronald H. Aday and Kathryn L. Aday

Folklore, Culture, and Aging: A Research Guide
David P. Shuldiner

SEXUALITY AND THE ELDERLY

A Research Guide

Compiled by
Bonnie L. Walker

Bibliographies and Indexes in Gerontology,
Number 35
Erdman B. Palmore, Series Adviser

GREENWOOD PRESS
Westport, Connecticut • London

Riverside Community College
Library
'98
4800 Magnolia Avenue
APR
Riverside, California 92506

HQ30.S43 1997
Sexuality and the elderly :
a research guide

Library of Congress Cataloging-in-Publication Data

Sexuality and the elderly : a research guide / compiled by Bonnie L.
  Walker.
     p.   cm.—(Bibliographies and indexes in gerontology, ISSN
  0743–7560 ; no. 35)
    Includes bibliographical references and index.
    ISBN 0–313–30133–6 (alk. paper)
    1. Aged—Sexual behavior—Bibliography.   I. Walker, Bonnie L.
  II. Series.
  Z7164.S42S42   1997
  [HQ30]
  016.3067′084′6—dc21   96–52496

British Library Cataloguing in Publication Data is available.

Copyright © 1997 by Bonnie L. Walker

All rights reserved. No portion of this book may be
reproduced, by any process or technique, without the
express written consent of the publisher.

Library of Congress Catalog Card Number: 96–52496
ISBN: 0–313–30133–6
ISSN: 0743–7560

First published in 1997

Greenwood Press, 88 Post Road West, Westport, CT 06881
An imprint of Greenwood Publishing Group, Inc.

Printed in the United States of America

The paper used in this book complies with the
Permanent Paper Standard issued by the National
Information Standards Organization (Z39.48–1984).

10 9 8 7 6 5 4 3 2 1

Portions of this book were prepared pursuant to the National Institute for the Aging
1R43AG140007-01. The statements and conclusions herein are those of Bonnie Walker &
Associates and do not necessarily reflect the views or policies of the sponsoring agencies.

To my friends,
Mary Byers and Robert Smith

Contents

Series Foreword

The annotated bibliographies in this series provide answers to the fundamental question, "What is known?" Their purpose is simple, yet profound: to provide comprehensive reviews and references for the work done in various fields of gerontology. They are based on the fact that it is no longer possible for anyone to comprehend the vast body of research and writing in even one sub-specialty without years of work.

This fact has become true only in recent years. When I was an undergraduate (Class of '52) I think no one at Duke had even heard of gerontology. Almost no one in the world was identified as a gerontologist. Now there are over 6,000 professional members of the Gerontological Society of America. When I was an undergraduate there were no courses in gerontology. Now there are thousands of courses offered by most major (and many minor) colleges and universities. When I was an undergraduate there was only one gerontological journal (the *Journal of Gerontology*, begun in 1945). Now there are over forty professional journals and several dozen books in gerontology published each year.

The reasons for this dramatic growth are well known: the dramatic increase in numbers of aged, the shift from family to public responsibility for the security and care of the elderly, the recognition of aging as a "social problem," and the growth of science in general. It is less well known that this explosive growth in knowledge has developed the need for new solutions to the old problem of comprehending and "keeping up" with a field of knowledge. The old indexes and library card catalogues have become increasingly inadequate for the job. On-line computer indexes and abstracts are one solution but make no evaluative selections nor organize sources logically as is done here. The annotated bibliographies in our series are also more widely available than on-line computer indexes.

In the past, the "review of literature" has often been haphazard and was rarely comprehensive, because of the large investment of time (and money) that would be required by a truly comprehensive review. Now, using these bibliographies, researchers, teachers, students, and others concerned with a topic can be more confident that they are not duplicating past efforts and "reinventing the wheel." It may well become standard and expected practice for researchers to consult such bibliographies, even before they start their research.

In recent decades there has been a growing interest in sexuality in the elderly. This is attested to by the 457 references in this bibliography. It has become more and more evident that most elders are not asexual, but have sexual interests just as other ages do, even though various sexual problems may develop in later years. There is also evidence that many of these problems may be prevented and/or ameliorated with better understanding, counseling, and medical care.

The main purpose of this bibliography is to provide information that will be useful to anyone concerned with sexuality in the elderly, including younger researchers, teachers, policy analysts, health professionals, counselors, and relatives.

The author has done an outstanding job of covering the literature and organizing it into easily accessible form. You may access the information in three ways: (1) browse through the relevant chapter; (2) look up the topic in the subject index; or (3) look up a given author in the author index. This bibliography is unusual in the large number of references it contains and the extensive information that is contained in each reference.

So it is with great pleasure that we add this bibliography to our series. We believe that you will find this volume to be the most useful, comprehensive, and easily accessible reference work in its field. I will appreciate any comments you care to send to me.

Erdman B. Palmore
Center for the Study of Aging and Human Development
Box 3003
Duke University Medical Center
Durham, NC 27710

Preface

This literature review was undertaken in order to determine what caregivers needed to know about elderly sexuality, to determine the needs of elderly people related to their sexuality, and to determine how best caregivers could assist them in meeting those needs.

In selecting materials for this book, the first priority was given to empirical studies. As the search continued, however, it became apparent that commentaries by individuals such as Robert N. Butler and Domeena C. Renshaw, trade market books such as Alex Comfort's *The Joy of Sex* and David Reuben's *Everything You Always Wanted to Know about Sex*, and the literature reviews of Martin Berezin and more recently Fran Kaiser, were extremely important. In the area of sexuality, what society, caregivers, and the elderly believe is true and important may be just as influential and important as what has been scientifically demonstrated to be true.

In addition to acquiring knowledge about sexuality and understanding attitudes about sexuality, this literature review also sought to investigate measurement issues and measurement instruments. Any project designed to educate or train caregivers about elderly sexuality requires an instrument to assess the knowledge and attitudes toward sexuality of elderly people. An instrument designed to assess the knowledge and attitudes of the elderly toward sexuality is also needed.

The literature review also uncovered information about what experts believe should be included in the curriculum of people who care for the elderly. Such a curriculum needed to include information about the effects of aging on sexuality, sexual behavior of the elderly, attitudes toward sexuality, health problems that affect sexuality, and information about marriage, divorce, living arrangements, and alternative life styles among elderly people.

The information in this book is arranged by topics that were identified as a result of the author's literature search and through discussions with experts in gerontology, sexuality, and long-term care administration. There is some overlap among the chapters. Much of what is known about elderly sexual behavior is reported in the materials included in Chapter 1, "Major Studies" even though Chapter 9 also includes many less comprehensive and perhaps less influential reports and discussions of this topic. Chapter 2 includes the most widely cited literature reviews. These reviews typically cover most of the topics included in the other chapters such as societal attitudes and mythology, effects of aging on sexuality, sexual behavior of the elderly, dysfunctions, and the social impact of aging and changes in sexuality. The other chapters also include literature reviews which focus on specific, more narrowly defined topics.

This literature review includes two topics that are receiving increased attention in the 90s — alternative life styles (gay, lesbian, and bisexual) and AIDS. Of the 19 articles located about gay, lesbian, and bisexual elderly, three were published in the late 70s, seven in the 80s, and seven in the 90s. Of the eight articles about the elderly and the risk of AIDS, four were published in the late 80s and four were published in the 90s.

The process of locating the most important and most current research was circular and involved literature searches, discussions of findings, analysis of reference lists in those articles and books, more literature searches, and more discussions.

Searches of on-line data bases provided a solid start for this project. From the articles listed in Med-Line, Articles1st, and ERIC, the compiler identified more than 300 additional references listed in the bibliographies of those articles. In order to identify the most current references, letters were sent to the authors of published materials to request information about other materials they had published, or papers in preparation. Several authors responded with copies of publications and copies of their own bibliographies. Help was also sought from many professional colleagues in the field of gerontology and sociology. Also included in this collection are a sampling of newspaper articles and magazine pieces appearing in the popular press on the subject of elderly sexuality.

Acknowledgments

The following individuals assisted the author at various stages of this project in locating and identifying materials that are included in this book: Robert N. Butler, M.D., Joseph A. Catania, Ph.D., Elizabeth Flanagan, Ph.D., Jennifer Hillman, Ph.D., Nathan Kogan, Ph.D., Joseph LoPiccolo, Ph.D., Adrianne Marcus, Thomas Mulligan, M.D., Erdman Palmore, Ph.D., Domeena C. Renshaw, M.D., Jodi Teitelman, Ph.D., and Gordon S. Walbroehl, M.D.

The following individuals assisted the author in locating materials, preparing the manuscript, and editing the text: Christine Hambach, Lise M. Holliker, B.A., Nancy J. Osgood, Ph.D., Darrick Sparks, B.S., and Katherine Wood.

1

Major Studies

Modern research in human sexuality began with the 1948 report on male sexuality and the 1950 report on female sexuality by Alfred Kinsey and his colleagues. Nearly every empirical study referenced in this work used one or both of these studies as a jumping off point. While the Kinsey studies provide researchers with the most comprehensive look at human sexual behaviors in the United States, the studies by Masters and Johnson provide us with information about the sexual response itself. No other major study has attempted to study sexual behavior "up close." Nearly every other person whose work is listed in this book references these studies. Shere Hite's 1976 report on female sexuality also provides information about sexual behavior and response and relies on questionnaire data. Hite's work is cited by many other investigators of female sexuality. The only other major study of sexuality in recent years is the 1993 *Janus Report*.

Also included in this chapter are books which, although not scientific studies, have had a major impact on the way people in the United States think about sexual expression and therefore have influenced both the design and findings of scientific studies. Two of these books are Alex Comfort's *The Joy of Sex* and David Reuben's *Everything You Always Wanted to Know about Sex*. Widely read by the general public, and still sold in book stores, these works often appear in the reference list of writers whose works appear in scientific journals. A third book, frequently cited by other writers although not based on a specific study and not read by the general public is Walz and Blum's 1987 book on sexual health in later life.

A few major research studies have specifically investigated the sexual behavior of the elderly and changes in sexuality associated with aging. These studies are placed here instead of in the chapters which focus on those topics because they have been widely used as benchmarks for nearly every other study conducted after them. Rarely does a researcher design a study related to elderly sexuality without examining the findings of the Duke Longitudinal Studies on Aging. Several books and articles based on the data from those studies are included here. Also important, but less frequently cited, are the reports from the Baltimore Longitudinal Study on Aging.

In addition to those large scale longitudinal studies, several other researchers have surveyed the elderly population to learn about its sexual behavior and attitudes. Those studies which have produced findings of interest to the scientific community as indicated by their being included on many reference lists are the *Starr and Weiner Report* (1981), the Brecher study (1984), and Marsiglio and Donnelly's national study of married persons (1991).

001   Brecher, Edward M., & The Editors of Consumer Reports Books. (1984). *Love, sex, and aging: A Consumers Union report.* Boston: Little, Brown and Company.

This book reports the findings of a 1978-1979 study by the Consumers Union in which 1,844 women and 2,402 men ages 50 to 93 completed surveys on the subject of love and sex. They reported their experiences, attitudes, opinions, hopes, and concerns. The report includes summary data as well as selected comments of the participants. The majority of faithful wives (87%) and husbands (91%) rated their marriages as happy. A substantial number of unfaithful wives (72%) and husbands (75%) also rate their marriages as happy. Most single men and women appeared happy. Chronic loneliness was not a problem for the majority of the respondents. Close friendships were important to many of the single respondents, especially women. Only a minority of the respondents reported homosexual experiences and even fewer reported such experiences since age 50. A small majority of women (58%) and a minority of men (46%) tended to hold to Victorian sexual views. Subjects tended to have a liberal viewpoint on homosexuality, masturbation, and sex without marriage. Impaired health was found to have a measurably adverse effect on the proportion of women and men who remained sexually active. A large majority of the respondents were sexually active and reported a high enjoyment of sex. The authors reviewed the pros and cons of estrogen use after menopause and concluded that there was no clear evidence as to whether the benefits outweighed the risk. Decline of sexual activity associated with aging was related to frequency rather than enjoyment. The respondents reported a broad range of methods by which they compensate for sexual changes associated with aging. Those methods include manual and oral stimulation of the breast and genitals, use of vaginal lubricant, use of vibrator, use of variety of coital positions, use of fantasy, and others. The author concluded that the respondents were very much the marrying kind and that most were overwhelmingly happy with their marriage—80% were married to their first and only spouse. Those who were happy were most likely to maintain excellent communication with their spouses. Declines associated with aging were sexual desire, ease of sexual arousal, and enjoyment of sex. For respondents who masturbate, there was a decline in numbers and frequency.

002   Busse, Ewald W., & Maddox, George L. (1985). *The Duke Longitudinal Studies of Normal Aging 1955-1980: Overview of history, design, and findings.* New York: Springer Publishing Company.

This book describes the design and reports the findings of the first and second studies of the Duke Longitudinal Studies. The authors present their methodology and results related to the aging central nervous system including psychiatric, medical findings, cognitive functioning and behavior, psychometric and behavioral findings. They report experimental evidence from ancillary studies on cognitive changes with age and their psychophysiological correlates. They also report their findings related to social factors. They found that the majority of older persons did tend to decrease sexual activity, partly because of widowhood and partly because of declining health. But there was a substantial minority who maintained or even increased their sexual activity. More comprehensive reports on the findings related to sexuality and the elderly were produced by Pfeiffer, Verwoerdt and Wang, 1968; Verwoerdt, Pfeiffer and Wang, 1969; Pfeiffer, 1969; and Pfeiffer, Verwoerdt and Davis, 1972; and George and Weiler, 1980.

003   Comfort, Alex. (1972). *The joy of sex: A cordon bleu guide to love making.* New York: Crown.

Comfort's book, written as a guide for sexual partners, provides explicit sexual information related primarily to intercourse between heterosexual partners. Comfort is the author of an earlier volume, *The Joy of Sex*, published in the late 1950s.

004   **George, Linda K., & Weiler, Stephen J. (August, 1981). Sexuality in middle and late life: The effects of age, cohort, and gender. *Archives of General Psychiatry, 38*(6), 919-923.**

The authors investigated sexual activity in middle and late life. The literature had suggested a decline in sexual activity during the last half of adulthood. The data used in this analysis are those from the second Duke Longitudinal Study. Longitudinal data were collected on the sexual activity of 278 married men and women, initially ages 46 to 71 years. The research design included four test dates at 2 year intervals. These data suggested that levels of sexual activity remain more stable over time than previously believed. The authors point out that it is crucial to distinguish between aggregate trends and intraindividual change. They concluded, although stable levels of sexual activity are typical, aggregate statistics can blur distinct patterns of change exhibited by individuals. They paid special attention to the relative influences of age, cohort, and gender on sexual activity during middle and late life.

005   **Hite, Shere. (1976). *The Hite report: A nationwide study on female sexuality.* New York: Macmillan Publishing Co., Inc.**

Hite reports findings from an investigation of what women feel, like, and think about sex. Subjects were 3,000 women who returned one of the 100,000 questionnaires distributed to a variety of women's groups throughout the United States between 1972 and 1976. Questionnaires were also published in magazines, newsletters and a book written by Hite. The report is based on 1,844 tabulated results from three questionnaires. Ages of subjects were available for two of the surveys. On those surveys, there were 19 women reporting their age as 60 and older. The open-ended instrument asked questions about orgasm, sexual activities, relationships, life stages, and general attitudes. The ages of the subjects were 14 to 73. About a third were married; the others were single. About 10% of the single women were living with a lover. Hite tabulated responses by providing direct quotations from the questionnaires which she grouped by subtopic. She reported that 82% of the subjects masturbated. Many had problems of guilt, felt foolish, and had other negative feelings about it. In her chapter on older women, she reports that for most, sexual pleasure increased with age, especially postmenopausal. Most still were sexually active and had sexual desire. They reported problems finding partners. Their lovers included same age men, other women, and younger men.

006 **Janus, Samuel S., & Janus, Cynthia L. (1993).** *The Janus report on sexual behavior.* **New York: John Wiley & Sons.**

This book reports the findings from a cross-sectional national survey conducted in 1988 and 1992. The purpose of this study was to identify, track, and clarify Americans' sexual practices, attitudes toward sex, and patterns of sexual behavior. Data were gathered through questionnaires and interviews. A copy of the questionnaire is included as an appendix to the book. The final sample population consisted of 2,765 subjects between the ages of 18 and over 65. Subjects were married (57%), divorced (9%), single (30%), widowed (4%), the rest unidentified. The majority of subjects had completed high school (48%), 24% had some college, 15% were college graduates, 11% had postgraduate education, the rest were unidentified. Subjects lived in the Northwest (20%), Midwest (24%), South (34%), West (21%), with 1% unidentified. There were 1,347 men and 1,418 women. The authors distributed 4,550 questionnaires and received 3,260 back. They discarded 495 responses due to major omissions in data. To supplement the questionnaires, they conducted 125 in depth interviews between 1988 and 1992.

The sample included 464 (17%) people ages 51 to 64 and 441 (16%) people ages 65 and older. Although sexual behaviors of the elderly were not the focus of this study, the authors report some findings related to older people. They found that 14% of men ages 65 and over reported daily sexual activity, compared to only 1% of women in that age group. However, among people over 65, 53% of the men and 41% of the women were considered sexually active. Those who had sex at least weekly were 69% of men and 74% of women, 97% of men and 87% reported having orgasms during lovemaking at least sometimes. Although people over 65 reported less masturbation than younger groups, 17% of men and 2% of women reported masturbating several times a week or more. Among the subjects 65 and older, 50% of the men reported masturbating at least monthly and 27% of the women. The authors found that 74% of men and 56% of women said they were more cautious about sex in the past few years. They reported that 29% of men and 39% of women reported increased sexual activity as compared to 3 years earlier; 34% of men and 40% of women reported decreased sexual activity as compared to 3 years earlier. In the over 65 group, 17% of men and 1% of women said they had been sexually active by age 14; 40% of men and 59% of women were sexually active after age 18.

007   **Kinsey, Alfred C., Pomeroy, Wardell B., & Martin, Clyde E. (1948). Age and sexual outlet. In Alfred C. Kinsey, Wardell B. Pomeroy, & Clyde E. Martin, *Sexual behavior in the human male* (pp. 218-262). Philadelphia: W. B. Saunders Company.**

Chapter 7 of this landmark study discusses the relationship of aging and sexual outlet. The authors state that there is no other single factor which affects frequency of sexual outlet as much as age. This chapter has these subheadings: "Adolescent Sexual Activity," "Old Age and Impotence," "Masturbation and Age," "Nocturnal Emissions and Age," "Petting to Climax and Age," "Premarital Intercourse and Age," "Marital Intercourse and Age," "Extramarital Intercourse and Age," "Homosexual Activity and Age," "Animal Contacts and Age," and "Post-Marital Outlets and Age." Kinsey and colleagues conclude that the most important generalization to be drawn from older groups is that they carry on directly the pattern of gradually diminishing activity which started with 16-year-olds. Even in the most advanced ages, there is no sudden elimination of any large group of individuals from the picture. They say that each male may reach the point where he ·is physically no longer capable of sexual performance, where he loses all interest in further activity, but the rate at which males slow up in these last decades does not exceed the rate at which they have been slowing up and dropping out in previous age groups. They report that the average frequency of older active white males ranges from once a week in the 65-year-old group to .3 times per week in the 75-year-old group, and less than .01 times per week in the 80-year-old group. Heterosexual intercourse continues longer than any other outlet but masturbation still occurs in men in the sample between ages 71 and 86. Nocturnal dreams continue into the 76- to 80-year period. Kinsey found true ejaculatory impotence to be a rare phenomena, only 6 out of 4,108 cases. He found 66 cases of permanent erectile impotence. By 70 years of age, about one quarter of white males have become impotent and about 75% in the males over 80. Kinsey found homosexuality to be "much more frequent than is generally thought." However, by age 50 only one percent of still married males reported homosexual activity. The highest incidence of masturbation was among young single males (about 88%). By 50 there is about half as much masturbation among single males as in the younger adolescents.

008 **Kinsey, Alfred C., Pomeroy, Wardell B., & Martin, Clyde E. (1948).** *Sexual behavior in the human male.* **Philadelphia: W. B. Saunders Company.**

This investigation was the first of the large scale modern studies about human sexuality. The subjects were 5,300 white American males. Kinsey and his colleagues found that 83% of his respondents had had sexual intercourse before marriage. Half of the married men had had extramarital sexual relationships. Almost all men surveyed had masturbated until they reached orgasm. More than a third had had at least one homosexual experience after puberty, generally during their adolescent years. This book's detailed description of the methodology followed is especially helpful for anyone planning to conduct research in the area of sexuality. Kinsey and colleagues include a helpful chapter on interview techniques including a report of a decision to make notes, even if it made subjects uncomfortable, to assure accuracy. This book also includes a description of several other studies which had been previously conducted and the authors analyses of their strengths and weaknesses. In the chapter on validity of the data, the authors discuss "immediate versus remote recall" which is relevant to reports from older people in the study. The authors devote one chapter to findings related to relationships between age and various types of sexual outlets. (A discussion of the findings in that chapter is presented in the reference listed above.)

009 **Kinsey, Alfred C., Pomeroy, Wardell B., Martin, Clyde E., & Gebhard, Paul H. (1953).** *Sexual behavior in the human female.* **Philadelphia: W. B. Saunders Company.**

In this landmark study of sexual behavior in females, Kinsey and his colleagues interviewed 7,789 females. The data analyses are based on findings from 5,940 white, nonimprisoned subjects interviewed prior to January 1, 1950. Of those there were 56 subjects between the ages of 61 and 90. Discussion of aging effects on sexuality or sexual behavior of older women is limited. The authors concluded that male aging rather than female loss of interest or capacity was responsible for the observed age-related decline in female sexual activity. They found that female sexual activities not dependent on males such as masturbation remained constant from youth to old age. They found that (unlike males), for females at all ages, a considerable portion of their sexual activity did not result in orgasm. Kinsey and his colleagues include several detailed chapters describing the data collection and data analysis procedures.

010   **Marsiglio, William, & Donnelly, Denise. (1991). Sexual relations in later life: A national study of married persons. *Journal of Gerontology, 46*(6), S338-S344.**
        This article reports the results of a large cross-sectional study of sexual behavior among married people ages 60 and older. Data are from the National Survey of Families and Households (NSFH) conducted in 1987-1988 by the Center for Demography and Ecology, University of Wisconsin-Madison. The survey included face-to-face interviews and a self-administered questionnaire with a national probability sample of 13,017 U.S. adults ages 19 and older. The analysis reported in this article used data from 807 respondents who were 60 years of age or older and who answered the sexual frequency question on the survey. The dependent variable, sexual frequency, was based on the answer to the question: "About how often did you and your husband/wife have sex during the past month?" Independent variables included: age, gender, race, formal education, health status, self-worth and personal efficacy, general well-being, religious fundamentalism, shared activities, and relationship satisfaction. Analyses included descriptive data, as well as logistic regression. Several interesting findings were reported. No differences in sexual frequency were found by race or gender. Age did have an effect. About 53% of all married persons age 60 and older reported having sex at least once in the past month, and this figûre varied considerably by age, with only 24% of respondents ages 76 and older having engaged in sexual relations during the past month. Analysis also revealed that health status of a person's partner and his or her own sense of self-worth and competence were significantly and positively related to the incidence of sexual relations within the past month. Among those who were sexually active in the past month, whites, persons who had attended but not graduated from college, persons who had been married for less time, and those who shared the most activities reported higher levels of sexual activity for the past month.

011 Masters, William H., & Johnson, Virginia E. (1970). *Human sexual inadequacy*. Boston: Little, Brown and Company.

In this book the authors report their investigations of sexual dysfunction.

012 Masters, William H., & Johnson, Virginia F. (1966). *Human sexual response*. Boston: Little, Brown and Company.

In this landmark study, Masters and Johnson investigated what happens physiologically when people become sexually aroused and experience orgasm. Among other findings, they report that the elderly woman who engages in regular sexual activity will retain a higher capacity for sexual performance than the woman who does not have sexual relations regularly. They note that the psyche plays a part at least equal to that of an unbalanced endocrine system in determining the sex drive of a postmenopausal woman. Sexual drive is related to a woman's self-concept. Physical changes with aging influence the aging woman's concept of herself as a sexual person.

013 National Institute on Aging. (October, 1993). *With the passage of time: The Baltimore Longitudinal Study of Aging*. Washington, DC: NIH Publication No. 93-3685.

This volume is the most current report from the Baltimore Longitudinal Study of Aging. It describes the methodology of the study, recent findings, and provides a list of selected books and articles which have provided reports from the project.

014 Palmore, Erdman. (1981). *Social patterns in normal aging: Findings from the Duke Longitudinal Study*. Durham, NC: Duke University Press.

The purpose of the Duke Longitudinal Studies on Aging (DLSA) was to measure changes in the same individuals as they aged and to study patterns of adaptation to the normal stresses of middle age such as widowhood, retirement, and changes in living arrangements. In this book the author reviews previous theories and findings on social patterns in normal aging and presents findings from those studies relevant to these theories. The focus is on normal or typical aging rather than on unusual or pathological aging. The major theories discussed are: disengagement, activity, and continuity theories; age stratification; minority group theory; life events and stress; and homogeneity versus heterogeneity.

The first study began in 1955 with a group of 270

community-dwelling males and females ages 60 to 94. Data collections were repeated 11 times between 1955 and 1976. The second study added people of younger ages (46 to 70) and consisted of 502 individuals ages 46 to 70. The research focused on patterns of adaptation to the normal stresses of middle age such as widowhood, retirement, and changes in living arrangement. The study was designed to allow cross-sequential types of analysis in order to partial out the effects of aging from differences between periods of measurements. Researchers continued to look at normal process of physical, psychological, and social aging.

Chapter 6 of this book reports the findings related to sexual behavior. In this study "sexually active" refers to those subjects who report any intercourse. Findings suggest a gradual decline with age in sexual activity. Part of the decline is due to widowhood but decline is also seen among married men and women. Some age cohorts, however, did not show a decline.

About half of the married women remained sexually active through their 60s; half of the married men remained active through their mid-70s. Also some married couples reported stable or even increased sexual activity from earlier to later examinations. Sexual interest and sexual enjoyment followed similar patterns. Life satisfaction and health were both significant consequences of frequency of sex relations among men in the first study. Longevity had no apparent relationship to sexual activity. In the second study there were several significant indications that sexual activity tends to maintain or enhance both health and happiness among men and women.

At the time of the last data collection in the second study 44 of the original participants remained.

015   **Pfeiffer, Eric, & Davis, Glenn C. (April, 1972). Determinants of sexual behavior in middle and old age.** *Journal of the American Geriatrics Society, 20*(4), 151-158.

This paper reports the multiple determinants of sexual behavior in middle and late life and the amount of the variance in sexual behavior contributed by each factor. The data were obtained at the Duke University Center for the Study of Aging and Human Development. The subjects were 502 persons (261 white men and 241 white women, ages 45 to 69). A separate study with black subjects was also conducted at the Center. The majority of men (98%) were married. Among women, 71% were married and 18% were widowed. Data on sexual behavior were gathered as a part of a self-administered medical history questionnaire. Areas of sexual behavior studied were enjoyment of sex relations in young years and at the present time; sexual feelings in younger years and at the present time; frequency of sex relations in younger years and at the present time; awareness of any decline in sexual interest or activity; age at which sex relations stopped; reason for stopping sex relations. Previous sexual experience was highly related to present sexual behavior. Other factors were sex, age, present health status, past health status, and expectation of future life satisfaction were prominent contributors to the total variance. Pfeiffer and Davis concluded that sex continues to play an important role in the lives of the majority of middle-aged people and in the lives of many old people. There is a wide range of differences among the people in this group. Many diverse factors influence the extent of sexual activity and interest among the men studied. The most important factor is past sexual experience, age, health factors and social class. Fewer factors determine the extent of sexual activity and interest among women. They are principally marital status, age, and enjoyment derived from sexual experience in younger years. The authors state that with advancing age, fewer and fewer women have a sexual partner available. "The remedy would seem to lie in efforts directed at prolonging vigor and extending the life span of men."

016   Pfeiffer, Eric, Verwoerdt, Adriaan, & Davis, Glenn C. (1972). Sexual behavior in middle life. *American Journal of Psychiatry, 128*(10), 1262-1267.

The purpose of this study was to examine the interest of middle-aged people in sexual behavior. The authors gathered data on sexual behavior from 261 white men and 241 white women ages 45 to 69. They interviewed subjects randomly selected from members of a medical group insurance plan. Subjects also completed a self-administered medical history questionnaire to gather more data than was possible from the interview. The data suggest that older men generally had greater interest in sexual behavior than women. The authors concluded that there was a noticeable decrease in sexual interest and activity; however, sex still played an important role in the lives of the subjects.

017   Pfeiffer, Eric, Verwoerdt, Adriaan, & Wang, Hsioh-Shan. (1969). The natural history of sexual behavior in a biologically advantaged group of aged individuals. *Journal of Gerontology, 24*(2), 193-198.

The authors investigated a small subgroup of subjects who were involved in the Duke Longitudinal Studies on Aging. Among the original 254 subjects included in the larger study, there were 39 subjects for whom data on both sexual interest and sexual activity were available in each of the four data collections which took place over a 10-year period of time. The average age of the subjects increased from approximately 67 to 77. Sexual interest refers to the subjects' responses to the question, "How would you describe your sexual feelings at the present time?" Responses were categorized as strong, moderate, weak, or none. Sexual activity in this study refers to the subjects' responses to the question, "How often, on the average, do you have sexual intercourse at the present time?" Replies were categorized as more than once a week, once a week, once every two weeks, once a month, or none. They found that sexual interest remained stable but that sexual activity declined for the group as a whole. Looking at data for men and women separately they found that for the women, all percentages in regard to interest and activity were lower than men in all four studies. Changes over time for both interest and activity were slight. For men, while interest remained high, sexual activity declined significantly with advancing age. The authors discuss implications of the subject selection procedure and conclude that their subgroup was not representative of older people in general. This group of men were much more likely to be married than the general population as were the women. The authors offer a number of explanations as to why the women's interest and activity are low in old age and refer to results of the future studies underway at Duke that might provide additional information.

018   Pfeiffer, Eric, Verwoerdt, Adriaan, & Wang, Hsioh-Shan. (December, 1968). Sexual behavior in aged men and women: I. Observations on 254 community volunteers. *Archives of General Psychiatry, 19*(6), 753-758.

This paper is one in a series of reports from the Duke Longitudinal Studies on Aging. One aspect of the study was an investigation of the sexual behavior of aged individuals who had been studied at three occasions over an extended period of time. Subjects were 254 community volunteers. The data on sexual behavior constituted only a small part of the overall study and were gathered as part of the medical history and were elicited during a structured interview. Interview questions asked about enjoyment of intercourse in younger years, sexual feelings in younger years, enjoyment of intercourse at present time, sexual feelings at present time, present frequency of intercourse, if intercourse has stopped, when stopped, and reason for stopping intercourse. Included in the panel of subjects was a subgroup of 31 intact couples, average age about 69 at the time of the first study. The data showed that average frequency of intercourse declined with advancing age. The proportion of subjects still sexually active declined significantly over time but the magnitude of the decline lessened at the time of the third data collection. Level of sexual interest declined with age. The most common reason for stopping intercourse was death of the partner. The study involved intact couples, which provided an opportunity for studying congruence between marriage partners. Additional findings are reported in other papers.

019   Reuben, David. (1971). *Everything you always wanted to know about sex but were afraid to ask.* New York: McKay Publishing.
      This book was written for the lay population and provides frank, detailed responses to questions about sexuality.

020   Shock, Nathan W., Greulich, Richard C., Costa, Paul T., Jr., Andres, Reubin, Lakatta, Edward G., Arenberg, David, & Tobin, Jordan D. (November, 1984). *Normal human aging: The Baltimore longitudinal study of aging.* Washington, DC: U.S. Department of Health and Human Services.
      The Baltimore Longitudinal Study of Aging (BLSA) is being conducted in Baltimore, Maryland at the Nathan W. Shock Research Laboratories, at the Gerontological Research Center. The purpose of the study is to examine the physical, mental, and emotional effects of aging in healthy people. The subjects are more than 1,500 males who entered the study in 1958 at the age of 17 to 96. In 1978, 700 women were enrolled. The researchers report age related changes in appearance, dental changes, weight and metabolic changes, changes in the cardiovascular system, changes in reaction time, cognitive changes, personality changes, changes in sexual activity, changes in the senses, physiological changes, changes in strength, and gender differences in aging. The authors reported that sexual activity decreases with age despite maintenance of normal levels of sex hormones. They did

not find a difference in testicular size with age. Sperm counts per ejaculation are the same but the proportion of immature sperm increases. Enlargement of the prostate gland is common in men over sixty. Prostate gland enlargement is not related to amount of sexual activity, number of sexual partners, or length or stability of marriage. They also found that sexual daydreams decline in frequency and in intensity with age until age 65 when they seem to cease completely. They also found that sexual activity is correlated with frequency of sexual daydreams in men. Relative frequency of sexual activity does not change with age. Men who were most sexually active in their 70s were highly active in their 20s.

021   **Starr, Bernard D., & Weiner, Marcella Bakur. (1981).** *On sex and sexuality in the mature years.* **New York: Stein and Day.**
        This book reports information from a survey of 800 older adults who were asked how they felt about sexual activities in which they did or did not participate. The questionnaire consisted of 50 open-ended questions related to sexuality. The emphasis of the study was on changes that occur over time. Topics covered in the report were: interest in sex, masturbation, female orgasm, sexual experimentation, intimate conversations, older women alone, and recommendations for improving sexuality. The authors suggest that education about the facts related to sex and aging is important but that it also becomes significant to work toward greater acceptance of the range and variability of sexual expression and that the attitudinal barriers are the real determinants of continuing sexual expression. Their findings indicate that older people can define and express their sexuality in more diffuse and varied terms and that they can be less goal-oriented in their sexual expressions, and that they can perceive the experience less in quantifying terms and more on significance and quality of the experience to them. Detailed results of the data analysis are included as an appendix along with a comprehensive reference list. A copy of the questionnaire and demographic items is also included.

022   **Verwoerdt, Adriaan, Pfeiffer, Eric, & Wang, Hsioh-Shan. (February 29, 1969). Sexual behavior in senescence: II. Patterns of sexual activity and interest.** *Geriatrics,* **24(2), 137-154.**
        This paper reports data gathered from the Duke Longitudinal Studies on Aging. The authors report on individual patterns of change in sexual behavior and the effects of age, sex,

and marital status on degree, incidence, and patterns of sexual activity and interest. Subjects were 260 community volunteers who were ages 60 to 94 at the beginning of the project. At that time 39% of the women and 82% of the men were married. The difference in marital status between men and women was largely due to the high proportion of widowed women as compared to widowed men. The group consisted of 67% Caucasians and 33% African Americans. Initial studies were carried out between 1955 and 1957. The same studies were repeated between 1959 and 1961 and again in 1964. The number of subjects declined to 190 subjects in the second study and 126 in the third primarily due to death or serious illness. Data on sexual behavior were gathered as part of each subject's medical history and were elicited during a structured interview. Subjects were asked about enjoyment of intercourse in younger years, sexual feelings in younger years, enjoyment of intercourse at the present time, sexual feelings at the present time, present frequency of intercourse, if intercourse had stopped, when, and reasons for stopping intercourse. The researchers found a tendency toward gradual decline of sexual activity with advancing age. This tendency was statistically significant only in the third study. Among male subjects in their 80s and 90s, about one fifth report continued sexual activity once a month or less. Interest in sexual intercourse declined significantly with age. They concluded that the sexual activity of aging women is determined by the availability of a husband or sexual partner and his sexual capacity. Unmarried women in the sample had a low incidence of sexual activity but differences between sexual interest among married and unmarried women was small. This study was supported by National Institute of Mental Health (NIMH) grants. The authors concluded that "age and the degree of sexual activity are not related in a strictly linear fashion and that one or more intervening variables exist, probably age-related infirmities or physical illness or both."

023   Walz, Thomas H., & Blum, Nancee S. (1987). *Sexual health in later life.* Lexington, MA: Lexington Books.
        This widely cited work discusses the importance of sexual health in later life. The authors offer several benefits. Sex can act as an antidote to the idea of body as a repository of pain in old age. Sex can be a way of preventing social disengagement in old age. Sex can be a means for promoting and maintaining intergenerational understanding. Sex can be a safe and valuable form of physical exercise. Sex can be a way of maintaining a

healthy self-image in old age. Sex can be a support in managing personal anxieties. Sexual health, according to Walz and Blum, is an attitude of mind as well as a bodily function; a comfortable accommodation with one's sexuality in later years of life is considered an important part of general physical and mental health. The authors also discuss same sex relationships. They use the term "partner" rather than "spouse." They also refer to sexuality as something more than genital contact or intercourse. Sex education for the elderly in the form of small group education/intervention sessions appears to be an appropriate vehicle for increasing sexual health since this format has been used in workshops related to sexual issues for other age groups. These workshops could be presented by gerontologists, nurses, family educators, or therapists. This book includes a copy of the *Adult Sexuality Knowledge and Attitude Test* (ASKAT). A copy of the ASKAT and permission to use it may be obtained by writing the first author at the University of Iowa.

2

Reviews of the Literature and Bibliographies

This chapter includes important reviews of the literature and previously compiled bibliographies on sexuality and the elderly. Only those reviews which cover the topic of elderly sexuality in a comprehensive manner are included in this chapter. Literature reviews related to specific topics are included with the related chapter.

Literature reviews on elderly sexuality follow a consistent pattern. They nearly always begin with a discussion of common myths, followed by a discussion what is known about the sexual behavior and age related changes of females and males mostly drawn from the findings in the Kinsey reports, the Masters and Johnson studies, and the Duke Longitudinal Studies on Aging. A few recent reviews reference the Baltimore Longitudinal Study on Aging. Depending on the publication date, reviewers usually cite all or most of the references identified as major studies in Chapter 1 and many of the texts included in Chapter 3. The reviews of the literature most often cited by other writers are those prepared by Martin Berezin in 1969 and 1976. The most recent comprehensive literature review to appear in the professional literature was prepared by Fran Kaiser.

Only a few bibliographies have appeared in the literature prior to this volume and they are included here. Also included in this list are two literature reviews in which the authors have surveyed attitudes toward the elderly (McTavish, 1971; Green, 1981). These reviews include attitudes toward elderly sexuality and also provide information about methodology concerns regarding studies involving older people.

Bibliographies on sexuality and aging have been prepared by the American Association for Retired Persons and the Sexuality Information and Education Council of the United States (1992), Brewer and Wright (1979), Teitelman (1987), and by Wharton (1978).

024   **American Association for Retired Persons. (*Circa* 1992).** ***Sexuality and late life: Bibliography.* Washington, DC: American Association of Retired Persons.**

This publication is a bibliography developed by the Sexuality Information and Education Council of the United States (SIECUS) and the American Association for Retired Persons (AARP). This annotated bibliography includes 39 references to recent publications related to sexuality and the elderly.

025   **Anderson, Catherine J. (November-December, 1975). Sexuality in the aged.** *Journal of Gerontological Nursing, 1*(5), 6-10.

This literature review examines the reasons why societal attitudes consistently deny the sexual needs of the elderly and maintain the myth of sexlessness among that population. Anderson found that most writers point to the loss of procreative power or the decline in fecundity or fertility as the main factor due to the emphasis on sex and procreation in Judeo-Christian teaching. Johnson credits changes in how sexuality and aging are viewed to findings from the studies of Kinsey in the 1950s, Masters and Johnson in the 1960s and Duke University in the 1970s. Those findings briefly summarized are that sex continues to play a role in the lives of elderly people, there is a tendency for sexual activity and interest to decline as people age. While physical decline is a factor for some elderly males, it is not true for the majority. People who have experienced a high level of sexual activity in younger years tend to have a higher level in later years. Elderly men and women are different in reported sexual behaviors. For men, the degree of sexual activity is related to past experience, age, health, and social class. For women it is related to the availability of a partner, age, and enjoyment from past experiences. Anderson examines the relationship between emotional problems and sexual activity and the sex need for counseling for elderly patients. Anderson also discusses the factor of sexuality in nursing assessments of geriatric patients and says that the factor of sexuality must be taken into the assessment of patients facing medical or surgical procedures. She concludes that there is a need to improve health attitudes related to sexuality in the elderly and that nurses must take the lead in bringing about this improvement.

026 **Bates-Jensen, Barbara M. (July-August, 1989). Sexuality and the elderly.** *Journal of Enterostomal Therapy, 16*(4), 158-163.

This article explores the developmental issue of sexuality and the elderly. Bates-Jensen, a gerontology clinical nurse specialist, acknowledges that the elderly are prone to chronic illnesses that affect sexuality but the effects of these illnesses are not presented in this discussion. The author begins with a review of the pioneer research of Kinsey, Masters and Johnson, and others which led to a more enlightened view of elderly sexuality including changes in federal guidelines for long-term care facilities assuring privacy for married couples. She discusses the current status of sexuality and the elderly focusing on the biologic and physical changes in sexual functioning and exploring the psychological and social factors influencing sexuality in the elderly. The main biologic factors that influence the act of intercourse are listed. She also points out that sensual functions such as smell, taste, hearing, and seeing decline with age and may affect methods of sexual expression. Physiological changes in aging women such as vaginal changes and others are explained as well as changes in aging men. The author also provides a thorough discussion of psychological aspects of sexuality and aging involving gender identify and sexual self-concept and sociologic aspects of sexuality and aging related to gender or sexual role behavior. Bates-Jensen concludes with a review of current research citing the Brecher Study, the Duke University Longitudinal Studies, and the *Starr-Weiner Report.* She recommends that health professionals take a stronger role in informing and educating the public about sexuality and the elderly.

027 **Berezin, Martin A. (1969). Sex and old age: A review of the literature.** *Journal of Geriatric Psychiatry, 2,* 131-149.

This widely cited review of the literature surveyed literature on elderly sexuality prior to 1969.

028 **Berezin, Martin A. (1976). Sex and old age: A further review of the literature.** *Journal of Geriatric Psychiatry, 9*(2), 189-209.

This widely cited article surveyed the literature between 1967 and 1976 and was a follow up to the author's 1969 review. Studies cited by the author repeatedly indicated that the most consistent factor in the consideration of sex and old age was the individual's comparative level of sexual activity in youth. Those who are sexually active when young are sexually active when old and vice versa. One significant change, Berezin noted since his first review, was an increase in the number of articles on sex and old age in the popular literature. These articles demand that elderly people have the right to a sex life without being stigmatized by society. Berezin cited examples of elderly sexuality appearing in films and television as evidence of changing mores. Although Berezin observed a continuing defensiveness in the literature, he believed the general public was becoming more aware of the myths and misconceptions about sex in old age. He said that what continues to be missing in the literature is the sense that older people's sexual behavior is connected to love relationships. He observed that studies continue to focus on the physical aspects of sex, such as sexual intercourse or masturbation. Berezin cited studies which discuss the physician's role in helping people with sexual problems, a point in which he concurred. He reported findings from the Duke University Center for the Study of Aging and Human Development. Their focus, he said, was on sexual activity and sexual interest. Berezin summarized the findings of these and other studies discussed in the article. Berezin found that studies on the aging homosexual were extremely rare. (*See also*, articles by Greenblatt and Leng, 1972; Comfort, 1974; de Nigola and Peruzza, 1974; Pfeiffer, 1974; Christenson and Johnson, 1973; Finkle, 1973 which are annotated in this publication.)

029   **Brewer, Joan Scherer, & Wright, Rod W. (1979).** *Sex research: Bibliographies from the Institute for Sex Research.* **Phoenix, AR: Oryx Press.**

   The literature of this sex research includes works from a wide variety of disciplines including anthropology, sociology, psychology, psychiatry, biology, medicine, social work, and education. Publications cited include catalogs, directories, encyclopedias, monographs, edited books, and periodicals. Sexual behavior of all ages and groups is included. There are 76 references related to sexual behavior of the aged published between 1954 and 1977.

030   **Byers, Joan P. (September-October, 1983). Sexuality and the elderly.** *Geriatric Nursing,* **4(5), 293-297.**

   This review of the literature discusses research in the area of sexuality through the early 1980s. Byers attempts to dispel myths by offering facts. She says that privacy and encouragement can foster sexual enjoyment into advanced old age. She points out positive changes in the culture. She notes that current federal guidelines for nursing homes assure married couples privacy for visits by the spouse and permit them to share a room unless doing so is medically contraindicated. She summarizes research findings which reveal a greater desire for sexual activity among the elderly than is generally assumed by both young and old. She notes that actual activity is less than what desired. Byers discusses effects of aging on sexual functioning and lists barriers to sexuality. She believes that nursing home staff can and should foster sexual enjoyment for the elderly by dispelling myths and by offering facts, privacy and encouragement.

031   Green, Susan K. (1981). Attitudes and perceptions about the elderly: Current and future perspectives. *International Journal of Aging and Human Development, 13*(2), 99-119.

This article is a comprehensive review of the literature of perceptions of older people beginning with studies appearing during the 1970s and builds on the review conducted by McTavish (1971). The author discusses the methodologies used in different studies, as well as research findings. She points out that studies differ by source of data, instruments used, cultural areas investigated, and extent of analysis of attitudes with other variables. Research on attitudes and perceptions of the aged is critically reviewed. Recent studies are examined with characteristics of the stimuli and contexts, and characteristics of the perceivers employed in them. The author suggestions are made for future research in which the use of multiple measures in specific contexts is emphasized.

032   Kaiser, Fran E. (February, 1996). Sexuality in the elderly. *Urologic Clinics of North America, 23*(1), 99-109.

This review of the literature references research from 1948 to 1995. Kaiser begins by saying that "the persistent myth that aging and decline in sexual function are inexorably linked has led health care providers to overlook one of the most important quality of life issues in older adults, that of sexuality." Kaiser begins the review with a discussion of prevalence of sexual activities in older populations, citing early studies such as Kinsey and the Duke University studies (*See* Chapter 1) and more recent findings of Bretschneider and McCoy (1988) that show that many people continue sexual activities throughout old age. He discusses the main causes of sexual decline: loss of partner, issues of health, impotence, loss of privacy, and others. Kaiser next discusses physiologic changes with age citing findings of Masters and Johnson and other researchers and describing findings in detail. Kaiser then discusses psychosocial factors which impact on sexual beliefs, attitudes, and behaviors. He says the "cult of youth" is not an acceptable role model for sex and sexuality in old age and likely contributes to many dysfunctional behaviors. Next Kaiser discusses sexual dysfunction in older adults including erectile dysfunction, (he provides a long list of problems that can cause impotence), sexual dysfunction in women, and specific disease conditions such as diabetes, cardiovascular disease, genitourinary conditions, arthritis, and cancer. Kaiser says that a careful history is vital in detecting sexual function and that health care professionals should take care to build a relationship where people can talk freely. In his view, sex and sexuality are important quality of life issues and that "health care providers can assist not in just adding years to life but adding life to those years."

033   **Kay, Billye, & Neelley, James N. (Spring, 1982). Sexuality and aging: A review of current literature.** *Sexuality and Disability,* **5(1), 38-47.**

This paper reviews literature published in the 1960s and 1970s concerning the biological, psychological, and social ramifications of sexuality and the elderly. The article includes information about sexual changes and sexual needs in the elderly. Based on the literature review, the authors make suggestions to improve the atmosphere of the aged person in regard to sexuality. They support the view that "the geriatric patient can and should enjoy a satisfying sex life." They conclude that "sexual activity in the aged is not exceptional and may give serenity to aging."

034   **Ludeman, Kate. (February, 1981). The sexuality of the older person: Review of the literature.** *The Gerontologist,* **21(2), 203-208.**

The author's research refutes the pervasive cultural myth of an asexual old age. Men and women continue to be physiologically capable of sexual functioning throughout old age, although interest in and actual sexual activity decline with age in most older persons. She discusses the finding that older men are more interested in sex and more active sexually than older women. She also says that older women, particularly postmarital women, report masturbating, with frequency declining with age. Homosexual relationships have been suggested for older women, since unmarried women over 65 outnumber men of the same age by four to one. This alternative has not been adequately explored through research. Ludeman noted gaps in research on the sexuality of older persons. For example, in many studies researchers define sexual activity and interest as the same thing, often there is no use of statistical tests, and in general study groups are not random samples. She suggests that research studies on this topic need a uniform basis to interpret data collected from questionnaires or interviews.

035 **McTavish, Donald G. (Winter, 1971). Perceptions of old people: A review of research, methodologies, and findings.** *The Gerontologist, 11*(4), 90-101.

This article provides a comprehensive review of literature of perceptions of older people. Research is reviewed in each of the following areas: society-level studies of general attitudes toward the elderly; individual-level studies of attitudes toward older people; studies of the consequences of attitudes toward older people; and studies which offer conceptual explanations for variation in perceptions of and attitudes toward older people. The literature review looks at studies from the 1940s to the early 1970s. The author discusses the methodologies used in different studies, as well as research findings. For example, McTavish points out that studies differ by source of data, instruments used, cultural areas investigated, and extent of analysis of attitudes in terms of other variables. Society-level studies employ several different approaches: one-site participant observation, cross-cultural interviews, and analysis of ethnographic records. According to McTavish, most investigators report findings which support the view that "attitudes toward the elderly are most favorable in primitive societies and decrease with increasing modernization to the point of generally negative views in industrialized Western nations." However, McTavish reviewed numerous studies which did not support the relationship between level of modernization and status of the aged. Individual-level studies also employ a variety of different methods including: Likert-type scales of attitudes toward older people or older workers; the semantic differential; content analysis; Q-sort; and generation rating scales. These methodologies are reviewed in some detail. As McTavish points out, the variety of methodologies used, the variety of different settings and populations surveyed, and differences in sampling and reporting practices make it difficult to draw any generalizable conclusions from existing research findings. Overall, however, findings suggest a high level of negative attitudes about old people. Stereotyped views of the elderly uncovered in a variety of studies include views that old people are generally ill, tired, not sexually interested, mentally slower, forgetful and less able to learn new things, grouchy, withdrawn, feeling sorry for themselves, less likely to participate in activities, isolated, in the least happy or fortunate time of life, unproductive, and defensive. Studies have correlated different variables with attitude. Age differences have been found fewer stereotypes and negative views about older people are held by older individuals. Race is another correlated of attitudes, with black Americans holding more negative views than other groups. The number of stereotypes held also increases with the age of the person to whom the attitudes are directed. Literature reviewed suggests that negative attitudes may negatively affect an older person's feelings of adequacy, usefulness, security, or depression. Self-hatred may result from the stereotyping. Negative attitudes held by employers may affect how they view and treat older workers. The explanations for negative stereotyping of elders, which exist in the literature, include: Ageism, lack of contact or closeness with older people, and the type of kinship system in place. This article concludes with suggestions for multi-level theorizing and research on a broad spectrum of social settings at several points through time in which valid and reliable instruments are applied to good samples.

036   **Mooradian, Arshag D., & Greiff, Vicki. (May, 1990). Sexuality in older women.** *Archives of Internal Medicine, 150*(5), 1033-1038.

This literature review focuses on the biology and epidemiology of female sexuality emphasizing the psychosocial aspects of sexuality in older women and the effects on sexual function of common coexisting diseases. The authors report that significant changes in the breast and genitalia occur with age and may contribute to the decline in sexual activity. Reduced vaginal size, thinning of the walls, poor lubrication, along with other factors can cause dyspareunia. Other biological factors such as age related changes in sex steroids and the abrupt decline in estrogen levels at menopause are discussed. The authors discuss cultural factors that they say are important determinants of attitudes toward geriatric sexuality. They identify marital status, past sexual experience, and age as determinants of sexual behavior in older women noting the most important factor being the availability of a secure relationship with a partner. They report that sexual activity declines with age but a remarkable proportion of elderly women retain sexual desire and remain active. They describe the effects of illness on sexuality citing cardiovascular disease and chronic obstructive pulmonary disease, cancer, diabetes, arthritis, urinary disorders, ostomies, and dementia. They also discuss the effects of psychosocial aspects on sexual behavior citing anxiety and depression, changes in physical appearance. The authors suggest ways of managing sexual dysfunction. They discuss specific recommendations including marital counseling and hormonal therapy.

037 SIECUS. (July, 1976). Sexuality and the aging: A selective bibliography. *SIECUS Report*, 4(6), 5-8.
      This bibliography prepared by the SIECUS includes books, chapters from books, pamphlets, and journal articles primarily published in the 1970s on the topic of sexuality and aging. Each publication is briefly annotated.

038 Teitelman, Jodi L. (August, 1987). *Sexuality and aging: Bibliography*. Richmond, VA: Gerontology Department: Virginia Commonwealth University.
      This bibliography lists reference data for approximately 100 journal articles and books related to sexuality and aging was prepared by the author at the Gerontology Department, Virginia Commonwealth University, MCV Station, Box 228, Richmond, VA 23298-0228.

039 Wharton, George F., III. (June, 1978). *A bibliography on sexuality and aging*. New Brunswick, NJ: Rutgers University.
      The author compiled a comprehensive bibliography on sexuality and aging. The work is divided into several sections including: Sexual Behavior in the Aged-General; Sexual Counseling and the Aged; Fertility and Reproduction; and Sex and Health. This work includes publications through 1978.

3

Texts and Chapters in Texts

Most textbooks written for nurses, physicians, and other health care workers include a chapter or two about gerontology and about sexuality. Gerontology texts usually include a chapter on elderly sexuality. The most widely cited of these books are those written or edited by Irene Mortenson Burnside, Ruth B. Weg, Nancy Fugate Woods, and Bernita Steffl. Each of these people has written texts for nurses and each has developed an interest in the problems associated with elderly sexuality. Other often cited texts are included here.

Also listed in Chapter 3 are professional books about aging which are often cited by people writing about elderly sexuality issues and other books on aging or sexuality which although written for the lay population are often cited by writers whose work appears in the professional, scientific literature.

The points of view expressed by the overwhelming majority of these writers is that sexuality in elderly populations is healthy, that elderly people want to express their sexuality, and that staff should permit sexual behavior and even encourage it.

040 **Atchley, Robert C. (1994).** *Social forces and aging: An introduction to social gerontology, 7th ed.* **Belmont, CA: Wadsworth Publishing Company.**

This text on social gerontology includes minor references to sexuality in older people. The author points out, however, that age changes in sexual behavior are not merely a reflection of changes in sex drives. Whatever instinctive drives we have to seek sexual gratification are shaped by culture so fundamentally that drives can be the effect as much as the cause of sexual behavior. He points out that the culture contains many images that contain sexual suggestions that can heighten sensitivity to and desire for sexual pleasure. He says that what we know about age patterns in sex drives comes mainly from Masters and Johnson's study of sexual response. Atchley reports that physical aspects of aging have a significant effect on sexuality of older women due to changes in the female sex organs after menopause that made intercourse and orgasm painful. He also summarizes findings related to older men, saying that sexual interest declines much less than the frequency of intercourse. He says that older men tend to "panic" when it requires longer than usual to achieve an erection. Atchley also cites the studies of married couples by Brecher (1984), Starr and Weiner (1981), and Ade-Ridder (1990). He concludes that older people maintain an interest in sex and that it means much the same to them as it does to younger people. The author focuses on the social aspects of sexuality in his discussion of these studies.

041   Bullough, Vern L. (1994). *Science in the bedroom: A history of sex research.* New York, NY: Basic Books, a division of Harper Collins Publishers.

Bullough chronicles the history of research on human sexuality from the early to mid-19th century through the present time. She explains the role that physicians have played and continue to play in this field. Beginning in the mid-20th century, social scientists such as Kinsey and his group became influential and made significant contributions. Political events also have played a role in human sexuality.

042   Burnside, Irene Mortenson. (1976). Sexuality and the aged. In Irene Mortenson Burnside (Ed.), *Nursing and the aged, 1st ed.* (pp. 452-464). New York: McGraw-Hill Book Company.

This chapter is part of a text for nurses about aging. The author begins by saying that the many myths about aging and sexuality are believed by the young, the middle-aged, and the aged themselves. She points out the lack of information available about elderly sexuality and discusses the negative cultural attitudes toward elderly sexuality. She uses the term sexuality broadly to include tenderness, touch, and all affectional needs. Burnside discusses sexual changes in the aging male and female citing data from the Duke University Studies and others. She discusses sexual needs and behaviors among older people living in institutions and provides personal observations about staff attitudes toward elderly sexual behavior. She says that it is not unusual for staff to discourage displays of affection between residents, especially if the people are the same sex. Other topics are love, romance, and marriage, peer and family relations, and implications for nursing. She suggests that nurses need to become better educated about sexuality, to discuss sexuality openly, to examine their approaches, and consider the positive aspects of sexuality in the aged.

043   Burnside, Irene Mortenson (Ed.). (1981). *Nursing and the aged,*
      2nd ed. New York: McGraw-Hill Book Company.
            This comprehensive text for nurses discusses aging and nursing, aging changes, mental health of the elderly, organic brain syndrome, cardiopulmonary abnormalities, renal abnormalities, musculoskeletal problem, foot problems, gastrointestinal problems, nutrition, drugs, reproductive system changes, and assessing sexual health. Several chapters relate directed to sexuality and the elderly. Thirty-three chapters are written by nurses. Burnside includes an appendix of recommended reading and films. She also includes a list of professional journals of interest to health care professionals. and a list of referral organizations, gerontology centers, and government programs.

044   Ebersole, Priscilla, & Hess, Patricia. (1981). Touch, intimacy, and
      sexuality. In Priscilla Ebersole, & Patricia Hess (Eds.), *Toward*
      healthy aging: Human needs and nursing response (pp. 325-341).
      St. Louis: The C. V. Mosby Company.
            This chapter presents sexuality as an expansive concept incorporating sensuality as a personal perception and intimacy as interpersonal experience. The authors view sexuality as one's expression of total being. The authors provide a comprehensive discussion of touch including information about the need for touch, patterns of touching, response to touching, touch zones. They explain touch deprivation, fear of touching, adaptations to touch deprivation, and therapeutic touch. Ebersole and Hess then provide a through discussion of sexuality, its importance, and its lack of support by staff in nursing homes. They explain how sexuality is validating and provides feelings of acceptance and companionship. They discuss feminine and masculine behavior traits and how they differ. The World Health Organization

definition of sexual health is presented and the authors comment that sexual health must be individually defined. They discuss age variables in terms of expectations, redefinitions, activity levels, cohort attitudes, biological changes, psychological factors, environmental factors. This chapter also includes information about physical changes in sexual responses in old age for females and males, alternative sexual life styles, sexual dysfunction, drugs that suppress sexual behavior. The authors include a section providing advice on helping people regain sexual function and the nurses' role in helping older people maintain sexual health.

045   Eliopoulos, Charlotte. (1979). Sexuality. In Charlotte Eliopoulos (Ed.), *Gerontological nursing* (pp. 318-326). New York: Harper & Row, Publishers.

This chapter provides information about elderly sexuality for nurses. The author says that attitudes toward sexuality have changed over the years and that sexuality has been accepted as natural and pleasurable. The author provides clinical and biological information on sexual intercourse and how it changes for aged males and females, sexual problems such as impotence and physical and mental barriers, and nursing considerations. She discusses the need for privacy in institutional settings, especially privacy for couples. She says that masturbation is often beneficial in releasing sexual tensions and maintaining continued function of the genitalia. She stresses that nurses be aware of, respect, and encourage the aged's sexuality.

046   Hayflick, Leonard. (1994). *How and why we age.* New York: Ballantine Books.

This book is about the biology of aging and addresses definitions of aging, influences on life span, how people age, changes with age, theories of aging, and how people can control aging. The author summarizes data from the Baltimore Longitudinal Study of Aging related to changes in sexual activity. He also discusses effects of aging on the cardiovascular system, immune, endocrine, female reproductive, male reproductive, skeletal, and nervous systems and the brain. He describes the effect of aging on height, weight, chest size, arm span, face, skull, skeleton, body composition, body water, and skin. Hayflick states that sexual activity for both men and women at any age fulfills deeply felt personal needs, reinforces pair-bonding, and is helpful in maintaining the stability of the family and our social structure. Because of its importance, any loss of sexual drive and functionality is reason for concern. He says that there is some evidence that intercourse maintains the prostate in good condition. Hayflick discusses changes in the postmenopausal women and discusses risk and benefits of estrogen therapy. This book includes a lengthy list of materials for further reading.

047   Hogan, Jean, & Sorrentino, Sheila A. (1988). Sexuality. In Jean Hogan & Sheila A. Sorrentino, *Long-term care assistants* (pp. 436-444). St. Louis: The C.V. Mosby Company.

This chapter in a text prepared for long-term care staff defines key terms related to sexuality. The authors describe the differences between sex and sexuality; explain the importance of sexuality throughout life; describe five types of sexual relationships; explain how injury and illness can affect a person's sexuality; identify the illnesses, injuries, and surgeries which affect sexuality; explain how aging affects sexuality in the elderly; explain how the nursing team can promote a resident's sexuality; and list reasons why residents may become sexually aggressive; identify the ways in which you can deal with a sexually aggressive resident; explain how sexually transmitted diseases (STDs) are spread; and describe the common sexually transmitted diseases. The authors refer to homosexuality and heterosexuality as sexual preferences. They state that sexual relationships are psychologically and physically important to the elderly and that love, affection, and intimacy are needed throughout life. The authors say that most elderly women experience decreased frequency of sexual activity due to weakness, fatigue, pain, and reduced mobility. They say that elderly people may have sexual intercourse but their sexual needs may also be expressed through hand holding, touching, caressing, and embracing. The authors suggest ways that the long-term care assistant can help meet the resident's sexual needs. Suggestions include grooming, providing privacy, accepting the resident's sexual relationships, allowing couples to share a room, allowing single elderly to develop new relationships. The authors include a detailed list of STDs, signs and symptoms, and treatment. Each chapter in this book ends with a set of multiple choice questions. The article includes photographs.

048   Kelly, James J., & Rice, Susan. (1986). The aged. In H. L. Gochros, J. S. Gochros, & J. Fischer (Eds.), *Helping the sexually oppressed* (pp. 98-116). Englewood Cliffs, New Jersey: Prentice-Hall.

The purpose of this chapter is to discuss the aged as a sexually oppressed population and to suggest a variety of interventions to deal with and change this situation. The authors provide demographic data about the elderly and substantiate their claims that the elderly are oppressed through a review of the literature. They suggest intervention by creating policies and at the direct service level. They suggest educating staff in the facts about elderly sexuality and provide a list of ten questions that can be used in staff training. They also list guidelines provided by the Grey Panthers for nonagist portrayals of sexuality. They recommend developing specify programs for the elderly to help them become more comfortable with sexuality. They also discuss direct intervention such as medical treatment for specific problems, understanding drug that cause sexual dysfunction, and providing therapy and counseling. The authors discuss special populations: single older women, elderly people living in institutions, older lesbians and gay men. The authors encourage human service practitioners to seek out advocacy roles. They offer a short list of questions to add to health history and a longer list of questions developed by Irene Burnside. Also included are guidelines for professionals intervening in the area of sexuality by Bernita Steffl. The authors also include suggestions by Robert Butler and Myrna Lewis. The chapter includes a comprehensive reference list.

049   Masters, William H., Johnson, Virginia E., & Kolodny, R. C. (1986). *Sex and human loving.* Boston: Little, Brown.
      This book is the most recent study published by these authors.

050   Peña, Chris. (1996). Sexuality and the older adult. In Ann Schmidt Luggen (Ed.), *Core curriculum for gerontological nursing* (pp. 667-686). St. Louis: Mosby.
      This chapter is in a text for gerontological nurses. Topics include recognizing changes that affect sexuality in older adults; defining sexual dysfunction; identifying potential causes of sexual dysfunction in older adults; treating sexual dysfunction; and identifying appropriate nursing interventions. Peña states that older adults in good health are able to maintain a satisfying sexual relationship. Although there are changes in the older adult that can affect sexual expression, the impact can be minimized. Health disorder in females that affect sexuality are: osteoporosis, carcinoma of the cervix, uterus, fallopian tubes, or ovaries, and

Alzheimer's disease or Parkinson's dementia. Health disorders in older males that affect sexuality are: benign prostatic hypertrophy, prostatic cancer, Alzheimer's disease, or Parkinson's dementia. Other problems that could lead to sexual dysfunction are described. A large table listing drugs that may affect sexual function is also included. The text includes a discussion and illustrations of an external vacuum therapy system. Other age related physical phenomena affecting sexuality are vision, hearing, and smell. Other topics discussed in the chapter are: common physical causes of anorgasm in women, causes of impotence in men, and organic causes of sexual dysfunction in males and females. Several pages of interventions are provided. The chapter ends with multiple choice questions and answers.

051 **Renshaw, Domeena C. (1996). Sexuality and aging. In Joel Sadavoy, Lawrence W. Lazarus, Lissy F. Jarvik, & George T. Grossberg (Eds.), *Comprehensive review of geriatric psychiatry— II, 2nd ed.* (pp. 713-729). Washington, DC: American Psychiatric Press, Inc.**

This chapter begins with an overview of societal attitudes toward aging which may relate to sexual problems that can be considered to be psychiatric disorders. The author describes and discusses sexual dysfunctions after age 50, brief sex therapy, and impotence or erectile disorder. Renshaw also discusses chemical, surgical treatment, mechanical devices, and premature ejaculation. This chapter also describes inhibited male orgasm (delayed or absent ejaculation), female sexual dysfunction, hypoactive sexual drive, libido differences, and special circumstances which may be associated with sexual problems. Renshaw says that most older people will seek sex counseling from their physicians. In most cases physicians can help. Brief sex therapy may be needed. In some cases patients should be referred to a sexual dysfunction clinic.

052 **Starr, Bernard D. (1987). Sexuality. In George L. Maddox (Ed.), *The encyclopedia of aging* (pp. 606-608). New York: Springer Publishing Company.**

Starr's entry on sexuality provides a good basis for understanding the problems associated with and the concerns of elderly on the subject of sexuality. Starr discusses myths about sex and the elderly, new findings on the topic of elderly sex, and the differences of sexual behavior and activity between males and females. Starr says that masturbation has become an increasing acceptable form of sexual release and is widely practiced. Starr discusses the wide spread problem of impotence and other problems that occur as the body ages, physical and mental, that effect sexual activity. Starr examines some possible treatments for age related problems. Starr concludes the entry with a discussion of the concept of sexual intercourse versus pleasuring. He points out that with problems of aging, intercourse may no longer be possible for some but other avenues of sexual pleasure are still open. Starr recommends that sexual pleasuring should be adopted as a possible outlet for sexual gratification.

053   **Steffl, Bernita M. (1984). Sexuality and aging. In Bernita M. Steffl (Ed.),** *Handbook of gerontological nursing* **(pp. 450-464). New York: Van Nostrand Reinhold Company.**

Steffl begins her chapter on sexuality with a quote from L. E. Lamb (1973), "The most important sex organ is the brain." She devotes the chapter to issues and problems that confront health professionals who work with older adults in a variety of settings. She begins with a list of stereotyped ideas about sex in old age as well as a list of fears and myths common among older adults. She summarizes current research findings and concludes that most research supports the idea that healthy older males and females are interested in and capable of continuing sexual activity. She describes sexual changes in the aging male and female. She states that menopause causes no decrease in sexual ability. She says that there is a loss of sexual responsiveness among older men for several reasons which can be corrected with the proper actions on the couple's part. She describes physical changes in the male: a flaccid penis and testes, fewer sperm, smaller openings in the testicular tubules, a loss of fatty tissue in the genital area, larger prostate gland, and a decline in sex hormones. Physical problems which affect sexual activity are arthritis, hysterectomy, common gynecological problems (vaginitis, uterine prolapse, cystocele, rectocele), male problems (prostatectomy, impotence), cardio-vascular conditions, and Parkinson's disease. Steffl suggests ways to resume sexual activity after an illness. Other topics are organic brain syndrome, aphrodisiacs, drugs and sexuality, and sexercise. She makes suggestions as to what to teach older people and addresses the specific problems of older people in institutions. Steffl includes a list of questions that can serve as guidelines for improving sexuality problems for patients in nursing homes. She concludes with counseling guidelines for professionals.

054 **Weg, Ruth B. (Ed.). (1983).** *Sexuality in the later years: Roles and behaviors.* **New York: Academic Press.**

This widely cited textbook on the subject of sexuality among the elderly contains chapters by many well-known writers in the field of sexuality and aging.

055 **Weisbord, Merrily. (1991).** *Our future selves: Love, life, sex and aging.* **Toronto: Random House of Canada.**

The author explores the experience of aging, based on interviews with such people as sociologist Betty Friedan, biochemist Linus Pauling, gerontologist James Birren, Grey Panther Maggie Kuhn, writers Morley Callaghan and M. F. K. Fisher, and her personal friends and acquaintances. Research from the sciences and humanities is examined in terms of the knowledge it offers of the aging experience. Myths about aging are contradicted by both the research and the personal experiences of the interviewees. Themes addressed include beauty, memory, identity, and sexuality, among others. Biographies of the contributors are provided.

056 **Whitley, Marilyn, & Berke, Patricia. (1984). Sexuality and diabetes. In Nancy Fugate Woods (Ed.),** *Human sexuality in health and illness, 3rd ed.* **(pp. 328-340). St. Louis: C. V. Mosby Company.**

This chapter discusses sexual dysfunction in diabetic men and women. The author describes the incidence, etiology, and treatment of impotence and the effect of diabetes on sterility and fertility. The author also discusses orgasmic dysfunction in diabetic women and reports the results of a study of this population. Assessed variables were duration of diabetes, age, frequency of intercourse, masturbation, interest in sexual activity, experiences with orgasm, evidence of retinopathy and neuropathy, and nephropathy. They also investigated experiences with pain and dryness during sexual activity. The author concludes that while diabetes may be associated with sexual dysfunction does not necessarily exist in all people with diabetes. The incidence of dysfunction increases with the duration of the disease. Diabetic men may experience transient episodes with erection dysfunction when their diabetes is controlled. Difficulty with arousal and vaginal lubrication contributes to sexual problems in diabetic women. In women, problems may be complicated by vaginitis.

057   Woods, Nancy Fugate. (1984). Sexuality through the life cycle: Young adulthood through aging. In Nancy Fugate Woods (Ed.), *Human sexuality in health and illness, 3rd ed.* (pp. 63-81). St. Louis: The C. V. Mosby Company.

   The purpose of this chapter is to examine the changes in sexuality as people age and to explore the similarities and differences in women's and men's experiences. Woods considers biologic, psychological, and sociologic aspects of the aging process and sexuality from young adulthood through the later years. Factors likely to interfere with sexual function were explored. She concludes that there is a decline in both reported sexual interest and activity with age but there is no point at which it must cease. Psychosocial demands placed on individuals influence sexual interest, activity and function. Aging is accompanied by changes in sexual anatomy and physiology for both men and women. Sexual activity and interest persist well into old age if the person is in relatively good health and has an interested and interesting partner.

4

Research Methodology and Measurement Issues

Conducting research in the area of elderly sexuality raises numerous issues related to methodology. Kinsey's studies of male and female sexuality (see Chapter 1) include lengthy chapters explaining methodological issues and Kinsey's approaches. These chapters are essential reading for anyone conducting research in this field.

This chapter includes articles in which writers have sought to address issues specifically related to sexuality research with elderly populations. Some of the issues addressed in these articles are reliability, validity, reliability of self-report measures, design, protection of human subjects, interview techniques, cross validation, measurement error, sampling bias, and response bias. These writers offer valuable assistance to anyone who intends to develop an instrument related to sexual knowledge, attitudes, or behaviors of the elderly or their caregivers.

Several researchers have endeavored to develop instruments to reliability assess attitudes of caregivers and others toward elderly and elderly sexuality. The most widely used instruments are Tuckman and Lorge's *Attitudes Toward Old People* (1953), Kogan's *Old People Scales* (1961), *Sex Knowledge and Attitude Test* (Lief & Payne, 1975), *Aging Sexual Knowledge and Attitudes Scale* (White, 1982), and *Facts on Aging Quiz* (Palmore, 1977; 1988). All of these instruments include questions about sexuality.

Articles describing the development of other instruments are also included here. A recently developed instrument is *The Sexual*

Beliefs and Information Questionnaire (Adams et al., 1996). Also included here are articles about the development of the *Aging Semantic Differential* (Rosencranz & McNevin, 1969), *Sexual Knowledge Inventory for Elderly Persons* (Friedeman, 1979), the *Adult Sexuality Knowledge and Attitude Test* (Walz & Blum, 1986), and the *Sexual Experience Scale* (Andersen & Broffitt, 1988).

Other assessment instruments used for cross-validation or used to measure variables which might be related to or affected by sexuality issues are also included in this chapter. They are *Behavioral Intentions in Relation to the Elderly* (Robb, 1979), *The Geriatric Depression Scale* (Brink et al., 1982), the *Lubben Social Network Scale* (Lubben, 1988). Many other instruments are referenced within the abstracts of these and other items listed in this volume.

058   **Adams, Serrhel G., Jr., Dubbert, Patricia M., Chupurdia, Kimberly M., Jones, Adolph, Jr., Lofland, Kenneth R., & Leermakers, Elizabeth. (June, 1996). Assessment of sexual beliefs and information in aging couples with sexual dysfunction. *Archives of Sexual Behavior*, 25(3), 249-260.**

The purpose of this study was to evaluate the psychometric properties of a brief instrument designed to assess information and beliefs regarding sexual functioning in the elderly population. *The Sexual Beliefs and Information Questionnaire* (SBIQ) was developed for use in the psychology sexual dysfunction consultation clinic. The SBIQ is a criterion-referenced test that includes 25 items derived from current literature on sexual myths and behavioral and medical etiological factors in erectile dysfunction. Items were written in simple terms and required a true, false, or don't know response. Items were designed such that incorrect responses would indicate endorsement of sexual myths or lack of information about normal sexual function and change often experienced with aging. The reading level of the SBIQ is 8th to 9th grade. The test was administered to three groups. Average age of the first group was 41.5. The subjects were 271 men and 116 female partners. The average age for the men was 56.6 and for women 52.9. Participants in study three were 63 older male veterans drawn from the same clinic as in study 2. Their average age was 60.05. Subjects included males and females as well as single, married, divorced widowed, separated people. African Americans were represented in one group. One group of subjects also completed the *Beck Depression Inventory* (BDI) and the *Dyadic Adjustment Scale* (DAS). Results indicate that the SBIQ had adequate test/retest reliability and is an internally consistent measure of sexual knowledge and beliefs. A copy of the instrument is included as an appendix to the article.

059   Andersen, Barbara L, & Broffitt, Barbara. (December, 1988). Is there a reliable and valid self-report measure of sexual behavior? *Archives of Sexual Behavior, 17*(6), 509-525.

This study was designed to provide a psychometric analysis of the reliability and validity of the *Sexual Experience Scale* (SES) derived from the *Derogatis Sexual Functioning Inventory*. The SES assesses frequency of sexual intercourse, partner kissing, and orgasm. It also includes a global sexual evaluation of present sexual life and a diagnosis of sexual dysfunction. The authors administered the SES to a sample of normal, heterosexual, sexually active women ages 22 to 65 (mean = 41.5) and a comparable sample who had undergone gynecological treatment that resulted in a predictable and clinical level of sexual dysfunction ages 24 to 61 (mean = 41.0). All of the subjects were women who were ob-gyn outpatients at a large university hospital. Reliability, stability, validity, and a content analysis of the test results are reported.

060   Axelrod, Seymour, & Eisdorfer, Carl. (1961). Attitudes toward old people: An empirical analysis of the stimulus-group validity of the Tuckman-Lorge questionnaire. *Journal of Gerontology, 16*(1), 75-80.

This study was designed to provide a direct test of the stimulus-group validity of the *Tuckman-Lorge Attitudes Toward Old People* questionnaire. Subjects were 280 students (170 male, 107 female) in three sections of the introductory psychology course at Duke University. The instructions on the questionnaires were identical except that for random fifths of each section, the groups of people to whom the subjects were instructed to apply the statements were 35-year-olds, 45-year-olds, 55-year-olds, 65-year-olds, or 75-year-olds. The authors found the number of stereotypic traits referred to as a group increased monotonically with the age of the group. They found that 96 of the 136 items were valid and suggest that investigators using any scale meant to measure attitudes toward old people consider the stimulus group validity of its item. One trait significantly assigned to people to the two oldest age groups by the students was the statement "They have no interest in the opposite sex." A copy of Tuckman-Lorge's questionnaire is included with this paper.

061   Bentler, P. M., & Abramson, Paul R. (June, 1981). The science of sex research: Some methodological considerations. *Archives of Sexual Behavior, 10*(3), 225-251.

The purpose of this paper was to make suggestions aimed at improving the quality of research on human sexual behavior. The authors evaluated substantive theoretical, methodological, and statistical issues relevant to conducting research on human sexual behavior. Guidelines for maintaining rigor and precision in future investigations are proposed. The authors address issues that pervade all research on human sexual behavior. They discuss six topic areas: theory-related issues, issues involving research design, issues involving subject selection, measurement issues, data-analytic issues, and issues concerned with human subjects protection. The authors conclude with a list of suggestions.

062   Blair, Ed, Sudman, Seymour, Bradburn, Norman M., & Stocking, Carol. (August, 1977). How to ask questions about drinking and sex: Response effects in measuring consumer behavior. *Journal of Marketing Research, 14*, 316-321.

The authors investigated the impact of asking threatening interview questions about drinking and sex. They studied response effects based on answers from 1,172 respondents to threatening behavioral questions presented in various formats. Respondents consisted of men and women over the age of 18 from the National Opinion Research Center's national master sample list. The results indicate that threatening questions requiring yes or no answers can be asked in any format without complications. Results indicate that threatening questions requiring quantified answers are best asked in open-ended, long questions with wording familiar to the respondent.

063   Brink, Thomas L., Yesavage, J. A., Lum, O., Heersema, P., Adey, M., & Rose, T. L. (Fall, 1982). Screening tests for geriatric depression. *Clinical Gerontologist, 1*(1), 37-43.

This article explains the construction of the *Geriatric Depression Scale* (GDS), an instrument that was standardized and developed specifically for the elderly. The GDS is a 30-item self-report scale with a simple yes/no format. Responses to individual items are summed, thus total scores can range from 0 to 30. Brink suggests that 0 to 10 indicates the range for normal nondepressed elderly, 11 to 20 indicates mild depression, and 20 to 30 indicates moderate to major depression. The GDS sensitivity is reported as 84% and specificity as 95%. A copy of this instrument and permission to use in research may be obtained from the first author by email: tlbrink@sbccd.cc.ca.us. Translations of the GDS are available in Spanish, French, Polish, Danish, Korean, Hebrew, Yiddish, Chinese, and Japanese. The authors recommend oral presentation. If written format is used, the answer sheet must have printed "yes and no" after each question.

064 Catania, Joseph A., Gibson, David R., Chitwood, Dale D., & Coates, Thomas J. (November, 1990). **Methodological problems in AIDS behavioral research: Influences on measurement error and participation bias in studies of sexual behavior.** *Psychological Bulletin, 108*(3), 339-362.

This comprehensive article is a review of the existing literature on measurement error and participation bias in research on sexual behavior. The authors believe that despite the unprecedented number of human sexuality studies which have been initiated in response to the acquired immune deficiency syndrome (AIDS) epidemic, findings are of limited generalizability to the varied populations at risk for HIV infection such as elderly transfusees. In their review of 20 studies, they cite measurement error, over and underreporting, refusal rates, and test/retest reliability. The authors also discuss respondent influences on measurement error, memory problems, self-presentation bias, motivation, instrument variables, order effects, terminology, and question structure. They also discuss in detail mode effects, interview variables, and participation bias. The authors discuss the relevance of their findings for AIDS-related sex research and make recommendations to guide future investigations. This article includes a lengthy reference list of articles related to conducting research related to sexuality issues.

065 Catania, Joseph A., McDermott, Lois J., & Pollack, Lance M. (February, 1986). **Questionnaire response bias and face-to-face interview sample bias in sexuality research.** *Journal of Sex Research, 22*(1), 52-72.

In this study the authors investigated response bias in self-administered questionnaires (SAQs) and sample bias associated with face-to-face (FTF) interviews. They examined the untested assumption that threat associated with disclosing sexual information elicits bias (threat operationalized as the self-reported ease or difficulty with disclosing sexual information). They examined the characteristics of subjects who fail to respond to particular SAQ items (partial responders). Also they investigated item order effects in SAQs assessing sexuality variables. Finally, they also investigated characteristics of volunteers and non-volunteers for FTF interviews. Subjects were 193 university students ages 18 to 52 years, mean age 24.6, 66 males and 127 females all of whom were Caucasian heterosexuals. Of these, 89% of the subjects had prior coital experience and 65% having had coitus with their current partner. Data were gathered via a questionnaire with follow-up interviews administered to volunteers. The items about masturbation were the most frequently unanswered. They concluded that people who partially respond fail to answer sexuality questions because they are uneasy making personal disclosures of sexual information. They also found the threat to partial responders varies inversely with sexual knowledge and experience indices. No significant order effects were found within SAQs. The FTF interview study showed that volunteers, relative to nonvolunteers, are more willing to disclose sexual information independent of overall self-disclosure tendencies. Completing SAQs with sexuality items did not affect volunteering. Results from FTF interviews overestimate the breathe of sexual behaviors and knowledge. The FTF interview method may be less advantageous to use than SAQs. The authors also present data which support the reliability and construct and discriminative validity of a self-disclosure measure specific to the sexual content.

066   Darrow, William W., Jaffe, Harold W., Thomas, Pauline A., Haverkos, Harry W., Rogers, Martha F., Guinan, Mary E., Auerbach, David M., Spira, Thomas J., & Curran, James W. (February, 1986). Sex of interviewer, place of interview, and responses of homosexual men to sensitive questions. *Archives of Sexual Behavior*, 15(1), 79-88.

The authors investigated effects of sex of interviewer and place of interview to see if they had an impact on answers given by homosexual men. The subjects included 57 AIDS patients and 145 other homosexual men living in New York City, San Francisco, Los Angeles, and Atlanta. Data on sensitive topics were collected by five male and three female medical officers at convenient places to subjects. Most of the AIDS patients were interviewed in hospitals and doctors' offices. Some were interviewed in hotel rooms. The authors concluded that sex of interviewer and place of interview had little influence on the answers obtained.

067   Eisdorfer, Carl. (1966). Attitudes toward old people: A re-
analysis of the item-validity of the stereotype scale. *Journal of
Gerontology, 16*(1), 455-457.
    This article reports on three studies conducted (original and
two replications) to test the item validity of the age stereotype
scale developed by Tuckman and Lorge (1953). In all studies the
scale was administered to college students. Of the 96 items on the
scale, only 88 were valid at the .01 level of confidence. The first
replication administered only the 87 items significant at the .01
level (one item was dropped). When only the 87 items were used,
Eisdorfer found that 37 of the 87 formerly valid items were no
longer valid. The second replication used 137 items from the
original scale. In this trial, 24 statements of the valid 87 from the
first trial again differentiated significantly between reference
groups. The author concludes: "Thus, in using the Tuckman-
Lorge questionnaire any attempt to make it 'more efficient' by
eliminating nonvalid items would seem to result in a lowered
effectiveness of individual items of the instrument."

068   Friedeman, Joyce Sutkamp. (November-December, 1979).
Development of a sexual knowledge inventory for elderly
persons. *Nursing Research, 28*(6), 372-374.
    The author investigated the development of an instrument
which could be used to test sexual knowledge in older persons,
the *Sexual Knowledge Inventory for Elderly Persons* (SKE). The test
includes demographic questions and 25 sexual knowledge items,
followed by open-ended questions. SKE items pertain to illnesses,
surgical procedures, age changes that affect sexual expression,
masturbation, homosexuality, sexual satisfaction and drive,
hormones, and general issues. Subjects consisted of three study
groups: (1) 40 faculty members from a college of nursing; (2) 86
students from the same college; and (3) 100 older women from 10
independent housing units situated around Cincinnati. The first
two groups tested the questionnaire to determine the validity and
reliability of the instrument. The third group of women completed the questionnaire in a personal interview setting. The
interview setting was chosen to help determine the effects of each
individual's reaction. The researchers concluded that the older
women test group may have been biased because they volunteered to complete the study and the interview approach did not
work as well as expected. They also concluded that the test is
adaptable as an assessment tool as well as a teaching device in sex
education classes. The authors finished by discussing that this test

measures sexual knowledge as only a presumption, it has not been found valid or reliable at this time. A copy of the test instrument is included in the report. The item testing knowledge of homosexuality reads, "Homosexuals are not born that way, they develop that way as they grow up." The author indicates that the correct response to the item is "agree."

069   Golde, Peggy, & Kogan, Nathan. (July, 1959). A sentence completion procedure for assessing attitudes toward old people. *Journal of Gerontology, 14*(3), 355-363.

The purpose of this study was to test the hypothesis that attitudes toward old people are qualitatively different from those concerning the broader class of people in general. The authors designed a sentence completion test with 25 matched experimental control sentence stems in the left hand column. These items were intended to reflect the emotions, physical attributes, interpersonal qualities, and values attributed to old people and people in general. The experimental form read, "Most old people tend to resent ... " The control form read, "Most people tend to resent ..." Subjects were one hundred students ages 17 to 23. Fifty subjects completed the experimental form of the instrument; fifty others completed the control form. Data analysis revealed statistically significant differences in the beliefs and attitudes toward old people as compared to people in general. The article includes a copy of the instrument and a table showing the results of the study per item.

070   Hillman, Jennifer L., & Stricker, George. (April, 1994). A linkage of knowledge and attitudes toward elderly sexuality: Not necessarily a uniform relationship. *The Gerontologist, 34*(2), 256-260.

The purpose of this article was to critically review the literature about elderly sexuality reveals the existence of a positive relationship between the various cohorts, depth of knowledge and permissive attitudes. Some health care providers possess a negative linkage between attitudes and knowledge. The authors concluded that there is a need to use a moderator methodology, rather than aim for a consistent relationship, appears essential in order to understand discrepant findings.

071   Kogan, Nathan. (1961). Attitudes toward old people: The development of a scale and an examination of correlates. *Journal of Abnormal and Social Psychology, 62*(1), 44-54.

This paper reports research aimed at developing a Likert scale to facilitate study of attitudes toward old people with respect to both norms and individual differences. Subjects were two male samples (N = 128 and 186) from Northwestern University and a sample (N = 168, 87 males and 81 females) from Boston University. A set of 17 items expressing negative sentiments about old people was constructed. A second set of 17 items was then divided with items stated in the reverse of the first set. A table showing the mean responses and item sum correlations for each group of subjects is reported by item. Kogan found a high degree of consistency among the sample means. In all three groups, the negatively worded statements elicit more favorable sentiments. The author provided a detailed data analysis. The individual score is interpreted in relation to the distribution of scores made by the other persons in the group of persons taking the test. He found that unfavorable attitudes toward old people correlated with feelings of anomie and with negative dispositions toward ethnic minorities and physically disabled groups as measured on other scales developed by attitude researchers for the measurement of anti-minority attitudes, anomie, attitudes toward mental illness, and an attitude-to-blindness. He concluded that attitudes toward old people are scaleable. Kogan does not suggest it as a measure of an individual's attitude but as an indicator of a group attitude. Kogan's *Old People Scale* is widely used in research to measure attitudes toward old people.

072 Lief, Harold I., & Payne, Tyana. (November, 1975). Sexuality-knowledge and attitudes. *American Journal of Nursing*, 75(11), 2026-2029.

This article examined the usefulness of the *Sex Knowledge and Attitude Test* (SKAT) which was designed to be both a teaching tool and a research instrument. They describe the different parts of the test, methods of scoring of the test, and how it should be used to help expand peoples' minds on sexuality. The authors also included some of their interpretations of test administered over time. Some testing results showed nursing students to be more knowledgeable about sexuality and more liberal in their attitudes than graduate nurses, but both groups were less knowledgeable and more conservative than college graduates. The authors recommend including more information about sexuality in all medical fields, not just reproductive biology. A copy of the SKAT does not appear with this article.

073   Lubben, James E. (November, 1988). Assessing social networks among elderly populations. *Family & Community Health, 11*(3), 42-52.

    The Lubben Social Network Scale (LSNS) is a 10-item composite scale that was developed for measuring social networks and social support among elderly populations. It is a refinement of the *Berkman-Syme Social Network Index* which was developed for the general adult population. Three questions assess family networks, three questions assess friends networks, two questions assess confidant relationships, and two questions assess mutual support resources (i.e., helping others and cohabitation.) The questions yield total scores ranging from no social networks (0) to full social networks (50). Lubben recommends using a cut-off point of 20 to identify persons who are likely to have low social networks. Scores for the friend support subscale and the family support subscale were obtained by summing the three items. The internal consistency reliability coefficient (Cronbach's alpha) for the friend support scale was .84 and for the family support scale was .82. This article does not include a copy of the LSNS.

074   Matthews, Anne Martin, Tindale, Joseph A., & Norris, Joan E. (Winter, 1984). The Facts on Aging Quiz: A Canadian validation and cross-cultural comparison. *The Canadian Journal on Aging, 3*(4), 165-174.

    This paper describes the applicability of Erdman Palmore's *Facts on Aging Quiz* with Canadian subjects. It provides documentation for the quiz items. The authors note potential problems of misinterpretation of items relating to the rate of institutionalization and income levels. The paper also compares levels of knowledge and areas of misinformation among a sample (n = 585) of undergraduates, university faculty, and health care professionals. The usefulness of the quiz in identifying differences in knowledge levels is confirmed. A copy of the *Quiz* with results by subject groups is presented.

075   Moos, Rudolf H., Gauvian, Mary, Lemke, Sonne, Max, Wendy, & Mehren, Barbara. (February, 1979). Assessing the social environments of sheltered care settings. *The Gerontologist, 19*(1), 74-82.

    In this article Moos and colleagues describe one part of the *Multiphasic Environmental Assessment Procedure* (MEAP), the *Sheltered Care Environment Scale* (SCES). The SCES can be used to measure staff and resident perceptions of the social climate of a sheltered care setting for older adults. The social climate is the organizational equivalent of an individual's personality. The social environment is composed of "press," a term related to the amount of independence and control people have in an organization. The "press" can potentially satisfy or frustrate the needs of the person. This concept guided the development of the SCES. This article discusses how the instrument was developed. Observations were made of 40 sheltered care settings and residents and staff members were interviewed at each location. A pool of 300 items was reduced to 140. Data were collected from 388 residents and 322 staff in 20 skilled nursing facilities, from 535 residents and 122 staff in residential care facilities, and 720 residents and 49 staff in 10 federally-assisted apartment housing facilities. Three criteria were used to select final items: (1) each item had to be meaningfully related to its own subscale; (2) each item had to discriminate among facilities; and (3) the item had to have a reasonable distribution. These criteria resulted in a 63-item SCES composed of seven subscales: cohesion, conflict, independence, self-exploration, organization, resident influence, and physical comfort. Each subscale is defined in detail. The last part of this article presents some sample SCES profiles. The article concludes by citing from practical applications of the SCES: (1) the SCES can be used to describe how residents and staff perceive their environment; (2) such efforts may be further aided by asking staff and residents to complete the "ideal" form of the SCES; (3) the SCES may be used to keep ease the adjustment of residents to a new facility; and (4) the SCES can be administered at several points in time to monitor changes in the social climate.

076   Orb, Susanne S. (January-February, 1979). **Attitudes and intentions of baccalaureate nursing students toward the elderly.** *Nursing Research, 28*(1), 43-50.

The author conducted a quasi-experimental study to develop instruments that would reliably measure belief and behavioral intentions toward the elderly with controls for social desirability set within the belief measure. The study also examined the impact of a gerontologic nursing course on beliefs and behavioral intentions of nursing students toward the elderly. Data were collected from 153 female volunteers in a baccalaureate nursing program divided into several groups. One group was tested before and immediately after a gerontologic nursing course. Three other groups tested immediately, one, and two years after the course. The researcher's instrument, *Behavioral*

Intentions in Relation to the Elderly, was an index based on 45 behaviors a nurse could reasonably be expected to demonstrate or not, depending on attitude, in the course of interacting with the elderly. The instrument consisted of multiple choice items, 26 unfavorable, 30 favorable. Items were eliminated based on their item-total correlations to shorten the instrument. The researcher used the Kogan's *Old People Scale* and Marlowe–Crowne's *Social Desirability Scales*, both found to be highly reliable, as outside criteria. The author found a significant difference from pretest to posttest for students' behavioral intentions. Beliefs changed also but differences were not significant. The author concluded that the data indicates a limited support for the prediction of a positive course impact on behavioral intentions. She provided a full discussion of her findings. The article does not include a copy of Robb's instrument.

077   **Palmore, Erdman. (August, 1977). Facts on aging: A short quiz.** *The Gerontologist, 17*(4), 315-320.

Palmore's *Facts on Aging Quiz* (FAQ) consists of 25 true or false items covering some of the physical, mental, and social aspects of aging and addresses common misconceptions about aging. Half of the items are about the aging process and the elderly and the other half are false items constructed from frequent stereotypes. For each subject a total number of incorrect responses is calculated.

078   **Palmore, Erdman B. (1988).** *The facts on aging quiz: A handbook of uses and results.* **New York, NY: Springer Publishing Company.**

The first three chapters of this book present revised versions of the *Facts on Aging Quiz*, Palmore's 25-item quiz on aging. Each version is followed by updated documentation that provides the evidence supporting each item. Chapter 4 provides instructions on how to use the various quizzes, depending on the purpose at hand. This chapter explains how to use the quizzes as educational tools, to measure the effects of instruction, and to identify misconceptions of a group of people. The *Quiz* can also be used to measure attitudes on aging by computing a score. The results of more than 90 known studies using the quizzes are summarized. Comprehensive abstracts of all known studies are also provided. *Facts on Aging* includes one item on elderly sexuality.

079 Reid, David W., & Ziegler, Michael. (1980). Validity and stability of a new desired control measure pertaining to psychological adjustment of the elderly. *Journal of Gerontology, 35*(3), 395-402.

The four studies reported here were designed to test the reliabilities and predictive validities of a 70-item *Desired Control Measure*. This measure is based on the findings of a survey to establish what everyday reinforcements contributed to the happiness of senior citizens. Within the new measure, there were 35 "Expectancy" items indexing the extent to which senior citizens expected to realize these reinforcements and 35 were "Desire" items indexing the value older adults held for these reinforcements. The "Desire" items were used to weight the "Expectancy: items so as to derive a Desired Control score. Fifteen of the 17 correlations between Desired Control and a variety of measures of psychological adjustment reported across the four studies were significant and sizable (mean r = .4). Social Desirability responding had negligible effects on correlations. Furthermore, five of seven correlations between Desired Control measured at one time and Psychological Adjustment measured 12 months later were significant (mean correlation = .46). Consistent with theoretical expectations, expectancy scores were stronger predictors of well-being than were Desire scores. The results of these studies gave support for the supposition that personal control is and important variable in psychological adjustment among the elderly.

080 Rosencranz, H., & McNevin, T. (1969). A factor analysis of attitudes toward the aged. *The Gerontologist, 9*, 55-59.

The *Aging Semantic Differential* (ASD) is a questionnaire used to measure subjects' perceptions and attitudes about older adults. It consists of a 32-bipolar adjective checklist each with a 7-point scale. Subjects are asked to mark the scale at the point which they think best describes the average older person. The 32 adjectives can be broken down into three dimensions shown to be differentially attributed to young, middle-aged, and older adults. The three dimensions are Instrumental/Ineffective, Autonomous/Dependent, and Personal Acceptability/Unacceptability.

081 Rubinstein, Robert L., Lubben, James E., & Mintzer, Jacobo E. (March, 1994). Social isolation and social support: An applied perspective. *Journal of Applied Gerontology, 13*(1), 58-72.

In this article the authors discuss social support and isolation from an applied perspective. They discuss the parameters of social relations and mental health. Negative consequences of a lack of social interaction are major depression, suicide, poor nutrition, decrease in immunological function, and abuse and neglect. Critical variables in defining a desirable network are gender, marital status, age, and culture. The authors discuss context and social relationships including cultural and familial rules, co-residence, shared experience, normative life course events and institutions, and special circumstances. A major purpose of senior centers is providing a setting in which people can create supportive relationships. Fundamental principals concerning social support are discussed. The authors also discuss validation information regarding the 10-item *Lubben Social Network Scale* which they say is a promising tool for screening the elderly. Using this scale elderly can be grouped into four types: isolated, high risk, moderate risk, and low risk. A large majority of the test sample (66%) were found to be at low risk for social isolation. Another 16% were rated at moderate risk, 10% a high risk and 8% were rated as isolated. They identify several future areas of concern regarding social isolation among the elderly. Some of those future concerns are older people experiencing economic changes, individuals whose family members use drugs, suburban isolates, and the changing ethnic makeup of America.

082   **Silverman, Irwin. (1966). Response-set bias and predictive validity associated with Kogan's "Attitudes toward old people scale."** *Journal of Gerontology,* 21(1), 86-88.

This study investigates two aspects of Kogan's *Attitudes Toward Old Person Scales* (OP). The first aspect is the possible contamination of social desirability response. The second is the validity of the scale in terms of the degree to which it relates to the subjects' preference for associating with the aged in an actual behavioral situation. The subjects were 67 males and 22 females in an Introductory Psychology course who completed the *OP* and the Ford *Social Desirability Scale* (SD). The *OP* was administered again 3 months later during regular class sessions. The author found that males had a more unfavorable attitude toward the aged. Based on the data analysis, Silverman concluded that a relationship between the *OP* and *SD* did exist but that the relationship may be true only for males. He concluded that the *OP* was capable of predicting the preference for associating with the aged in an actual behavioral situation.

083 Stukenberg, Karl W., Dura, Jason R., & Kiecolt-Glaser, Janice K. (1990). Depression screening scale validation in an elderly, community-dwelling population. *Psychological Assessment: A journal of consulting and clinical psychology*, 2(2), 134-138.

In this study, the authors assessed the relative abilities of two pencil-and-paper depression rating scales: the *Beck Depression Inventory Short Form* and the *Brief Symptom Inventory* (BSI) depression scale. They contrasted those with an interviewer-based depression rating scale, the *Hamilton Depression Rating Scale* (HDRS). They hypothesized that the HDRS would be more sensitive without increasing the false positives. Subjects were 59 men and 118 women ages 56 to 88 (mean = 67.40). All three instruments identified major depression and depressive disorder not otherwise specified. None was consistently sensitive to cases of dysthymia. The interview-based instrument was not significantly better suggesting that the increased expense may not be justified.

084 **Tuckman, Jacob, & Lorge, Irving. (May, 1953). Attitudes toward old people.** *The Journal of Social Psychology*, **37(5), 249-260.**

The Tuckman-Lorge *Attitudes Toward Old People* questionnaire contains 137 items measuring thirteen dimensions of stereotyping of the aged: physical, financial, conservatism, family relationship, attitudes toward the future, insecurity, mental deterioration, activities, interests, personality traits, best time of life, sex, cleanliness, and interference. Respondents are required to supply "yes" and "no" answers to the items. The questions are so worded that a high score indicates an unfavorable attitude toward the aged. Shaw and Wright report a test/retest correlation was .96 for the yes or no responses made and .83 for the percentage in their book titled *Scales for the Measurement of Attitudes* published by McGraw-Hill in 1967, p. 462.

085 **Walz, Thomas H., & Blum, Nancee S. (1986).** *Adult sexuality knowledge and attitude test.* **Iowa City, IA: University of Iowa.**

The *Adult Sexuality Knowledge and Attitude Test* (ASKAT) was developed by the authors and appears in their book, *Sexual Health in Later Life*. The test consists of 49 true or false items designed to test sexual knowledge and 17 items designed to assess attitude toward sexuality. Items include attitudes and knowledge about sexuality in general and about older people in particular.

086   White, Charles B. (December, 1982). A scale for the assessment of attitudes and knowledge regarding sexuality in the aged. *Archives of Sexual Behavior, 11*(6), 491-502.

This study reported the development of an instrument for assessing the attitudinal aspects of sexuality in the aged and the individual's knowledge about age-related changes in sexual functioning. White's *Aging Sexual Knowledge and Attitudes Scale* (ASKAS) was used in the small group sex education/intervention approach. This scale consists of 61 items related to knowledge and attitudes toward sexuality in the elderly person. The instrument may be administered individually or in groups via personal interview or by pencil/paper format and is recorded on 7-point Likert scale as to degree of agreement or disagreement. His findings supported the validity and reliability of the scale in assessing sexual attitudes and sexual knowledge with specific reference to the aged. Significant changes in scale scores following intervention and significant relationships of sexual behavior to scale follow predicted directions. He concluded that a factor analysis supported the two dimensions of attitudes and knowledge in the instrument.

5

Societal Attitudes Toward Elderly Sexuality

Although very little empirical research has been conducted to support the premise that society has a negative view of elderly sexuality, a rather large number of people have written about societal attitudes toward elderly sexuality from an historical and present day perspective. These articles describe a variety of viewpoints and provide a starting point for most current day research efforts. The current scientific literature strongly supports the finding that many of societal attitudes toward the elderly and sexuality are based on stereotypes. Throughout history society in general has had a negative viewpoint toward elderly sexuality. The major goal of the most of the writers in this chapter is to convince other health care professionals that the elderly are interested in sexuality, have a capacity for sexual behavior as long as they are in good health, and have a right to express that sexuality, even in long-term care.

One of the most important books on this subject is Robert N. Butler's Pulitzer Prize winning book, *Why Survive? Being Old in America* (1975). Many well-known researchers have taken the time to write articles arguing against current societal stereotypes such as Irene M. Burnside, Myrna I. Lewis, Nathan Kogan, William Masters and Virginia E. Johnson, Domeena C. Renshaw, and Bernard D. Starr. Their articles are listed in this chapter.

Among the titles in this chapter are some literature reviews that focus almost exclusively on mythology associated with elderly sexuality. Also included here are any studies of societal attitudes that do not involve health care professionals, the elderly themselves, or other caregivers. Studies involving health care professionals or elderly populations are grouped together in Chapters 6 and 7 respectively.

087   Abramson, Paul R., & Mechanic, Mindy B. (June, 1983). Sex and the media: Three decades of best selling books and major motion pictures. *Archives of Sexual Behavior, 12*(3), 185-206.

    The purpose of the present study was to examine the expression of sexuality in best-selling books and major motion pictures. There are two reasons that such stimuli merit systematic analysis. First is the finding that best-selling novels and major motion pictures exist as a primary source of sexual information. There is also the need to examine such stimuli for myths and facades. Novels and films analyzed in this study are selected from the last years of three consecutive decades: 1959, 1969, and 1979. Books and movies used in this study came from the best-seller list and the rental-receipts list. The use of such materials enabled the researchers to examine stimuli that are accessible to large masses of people and allow for examination of sexually relevant stimuli. The author arranged the results in terms of historical changes (over three decades) and manifest themes. The authors read each book in its entirety, noting sexual passages as well as background information. Changes related to several aspects of sexual expression are described. Manifest themes for books and films are reported.

088   Arluke, Arnold, Levin, Jack, & Suchwalko, John. (August, 1984). Sexuality and romance in advice books for the elderly. *The Gerontologist, 24*(4), 415-419.

    The authors analyzed 65 advice books for the elderly to assess their romantic and sexual content from before 1970 and 1970 to 1984. *Books In Print* furnished the list of advice books. Samples consisted of books on wide varieties of subjects but not specific topics such as health. The authors found that sexual activity for the elderly is encouraged more frequently now than in the past and sexual advice is directed more to them. They concluded that a greater encouragement of sexuality seems to be part of a larger change in advice books which stress activity rather than disengagement. However, data also indicate little support for remarriage and dating.

089 Auerbach, Doris N., & Levenson, Richard L., Jr. (August, 1977). Second impressions: Attitude change in college students toward the elderly. *The Gerontologist, 17*(4), 362-366.

This exploratory investigation tests the applicability of constructs developed in ethnic contact studies to intergenerational contact. The attitudes of young subjects deteriorated significantly after one semester of classroom interaction with elderly fellow students. Factors operant in the deterioration of attitudes as well as limitations in the research are explored. Implications for program policy and further research are discussed. The researchers investigated the applicability to develop an ethnic contact study into a intergenerational contact study. Subjects were 30 males and 30 females between the ages of 18 to 22 in a class that contained adults over the age of 60. The control group consisted of 30 males and 30 females between the ages of 18 to 22 in a class without anyone over 60. At the beginning of the fall semester both groups completed a questionnaire. At the end of the semester the experimental group completed the same questionnaire but with a different order of the questions. The authors report that attitudes of young subjects deteriorated significantly after one semester of classroom interaction with elderly fellow students. The authors discuss the use of such integration to teach younger people about concerns, ideas, problems, and other areas that are important to the elderly.

090 Berman, Ellen M., & Lief, Harold I. (1976). Sex and the aging process. In Wilbur W. Oaks, Gerald A. Melchiode, & Ilda Filcher (Eds.), *Sex and the life cycle* (pp. 125-134). New York: Grune and Stratton.

This comprehensive paper discusses various aspects of human sexuality and aging within a variety of life styles. The authors, both medical doctors, review available studies of marital and sexual functioning in the elderly and discuss the Marriage Council's experience in treating sexual dysfunction in this age group. It is written from the point of view that sexual functioning, in addition to being a matter of physiology, is inextricably entwined with one's life situation and place in the life cycle. The authors point out that many myths reinforce society's belief that older people are sexless, that sexual activity for older persons is immoral, abnormal, and dirty, that sexual desires and physical capacity for sex automatically decline with age, that impotence is part of aging, and that sex is only for the young. In their discussion of physiology of sex and aging, they say that in the aging female that lubrication is slower and more direct stimulation is needed, the orgasmic phase may be shorter, and with low levels of estrogen there may be irritability of vaginal tissues, pain on clitoral stimulation, or painful uterine spasms during orgasm. These symptoms are easily treated with estrogen replacement. The female capacity to have an orgasm, including multiple orgasms, is unimpaired. They report that the majority of older men in good health continue to be sexually interested although the proportion of men engaging in sexual intercourse decreases with advancing age. Only one in five is active in their 80s. In men factors contributing to sexual functioning were age, drugs, and physical dysfunction. In women the principal factor was an available and interested partner. The authors also discuss sex and the older marriage. They found that couples with a previously good sex life often retain a high desire for and interest in sexual activity. Other topics discussed in this chapter are: (1) sex and the older single; (2) sex, the aging, and the doctor; and (3) the treatment of sexual dysfunction. They conclude that sexual dysfunction in older couples who remain healthy stems from lack of knowledge of changing physiology and a dysfunctional marital relationship. Counseling should be provided to those older couples who request it.

091   **Bishop, James M., & Krause, Daniel R. (February, 1984). Depictions of aging and old age on Saturday morning television.** *The Gerontologist, 24*(1), 91-94.

The authors investigated the nature and extent of material on aging and old age in children's television programming. They obtained a sample of 106 cartoons broadcast on commercial networks during a 6-week period. The researchers watched the three large commercial networks from 7:00 a.m. to 11:00 a.m. They recorded the cartoons each week by age of characters (young, adult, and old), type of characters (human or nonhuman), and themes. The data analysis indicated that, although old age is not a dominant theme in these programs, the topic does emerge and is typically framed in negative terms. The argument is made that these negative images, despite their relative infrequency, have the potential to reinforce dominant cultural stereotypes about aging and old age in American society.

092   **Brubaker, Timothy H., & Powers, Edward A. (1976). The stereotype of "old": A review and alternative approach.** *Journal of Gerontology, 31*(4), 441-447.

The authors contend that within the professional literature a negative stereotype of "old" has been emphasized. The authors analyzed 47 research reports on stereotypes of old age. They found that 21 studies used older persons in the sample, and half of these are based on institutionalized or indigent aged. The authors noted that several studies reported a positive stereotype of old age. They concluded that the aged may not accept a negative stereotype of old age. The authors' alternative model introduced an argument that the acceptance of a negative or positive stereotype by the aged is related to objective indicators of old age, the subjective definition of self, and self-concept.

093 Burnside, Irene Mortenson. (1973). Sexuality and aging. *Medical Arts and Sciences, 27*(3), 13-27.
    This article is the 1973 Mary Monteith Lecture presented at the Ethel Percy Andrews Gerontology Center School of Nursing at the University of Southern California. Burnside summarizes the current literature concluding that there was a paucity of data about sexuality and sex attitudes and habits of elderly people at a time when sex has become an obsession of American society. She describes cultural attitudes about sex life in aged people. She defines sexuality as "affectional needs—tenderness, stroking, flirting, flirting techniques used by both sexes—and also the sexuality involved in touching." She examines ways in which "professionals can help create an atmosphere that allows sex its proper role in the later years." Burnside describes current knowledge of sex and aging men and women. For women sexual activities were primarily confined to the marriage relationship. She points out that there was a general lack of interest in the sexual life of older women. For men the most common problem was impotency. She describes the sex life of the institutionalized elderly as mostly celibate and presents several case studies involving older people and older couples. She concludes that elderly people need affection, tenderness, and touch up until they die. Nurses can provide that affection. She points out that peer and family criticism can erect barriers to the sexual expression of others and that professionals may need to play a role in overcoming that problem. Burnside discusses attitudes and behaviors of professionals regarding sexuality in the aged including avoidance behaviors, anxiety about sexuality, and interventions. She lists a number of suggestions for interventions and concludes with a plea that professionals "increase their

knowledge about sexuality and strive for a more open, sensible, and sensitive approach in matters of sexuality in the elderly."

094   **Butler, Robert N. (Winter, 1969). Age-ism: Another form of bigotry.** *The Gerontologist, 9*(1), 243-246.

An incident in Chevy Chase, Maryland during which locals objected to the creation of a high-rise public housing for the elderly poor led Butler to write this article about ageism. He describes ageism as the subjective experience implied in the popular notion of the generation gap. Ageism reflects a deep seated uneasiness on the part of the young and middle-aged toward growing old, disease, disability, and fear of powerlessness, uselessness, and death. Cultural attitudes in society reinforce these feelings. For example, less than 1% of the budget of the National Institute of Mental Health is spent on the study of aging. Ageism, says Butler, is a serious national problem which is deeply embedded in the culture. He discusses problems associated with locating several public housing projects in the same area and creating areas where old or poor people live. He says that older people make up a large percentage of the electorate but at that time were not voting as a block. If that changed, the concept of "Senior Power" would become common. He closes by saying, "We don't all grow white or black, but we all grow old."

095   **Butler, Robert N. (1975).** *Why survive? Being old in America.* **New York: Harper and Row.**

The author discusses the problems of the elderly in American society. Discussion topics include ageism, the state of nursing homes, problems with the law, housing, and government. He discusses medical care for the elderly, the political power of the elderly as the size of the over 65 population increases. Butler was awarded the Pulitzer Prize in 1976 for this book.

096   **Butler, Robert N., & Lewis, Myrna I. (October, 1987). Myths and realities of sex in the later years.** *Provider, 13*(10), 11-13.

Based on their clinical and research work, the authors have concluded that sexual ability, desire, and satisfaction can continue up to the end of life. Despite these findings, mythology fed by misinformation surrounds late-life sexuality. In this article, the authors discuss these common myths: sexual desire automatically ebbs with age and hits bottom between ages 60 to 65; physical capacity for sex deteriorates with age; sex is a matter of physical conditioning and production and is therefore more suited to younger people; and sex ends in the nursing home. They point out that nursing home staff often regard sexual interest as a behavioral problem rather than a natural occurrence. In their experience staff often feel very uncomfortable about residents' sexual behavior and that lack of privacy in these places makes sexual behavior more public than it normally would be. The authors acknowledge the difficulty in changing negative attitudes toward love and sex between older people but suggest several steps to follow: watch educational films, hold discussion groups where staff can discuss their feelings, set up discussion groups and sex education classes for residents.

097 **Covey, Herbert C. (February, 1989). Perceptions and attitudes toward sexuality of the elderly during the Middle Ages.** *The Gerontologist, 29*(1), 93-100.

This article presents a historical overview of attitudes toward sexuality and aging during the Middle Ages. The author draws upon historical observations, art, and literature to identify and develop sexual themes involving older men and women in Western Europe during the Middle Ages. In the first section Covey reviews early religious positions of St. Augustine and others. Overall, the religious view of the period was that celibacy is best, and sexual intercourse should only be for procreation. Sex among elderly people was a "sin against nature." Old age has been viewed as one stage in the life span. Old age was associated with decay and decline. Sexual behavior was not viewed as appropriate for the later stage of life. Medieval scholars writing on romantic love viewed the old idea of romantic love. The aged were viewed and impotent; and sex between older married couples was depicted as unnatural and an "affront to dignity." In literature sexual activity of old men was portrayed as either disgusting, humorous, or impossible due to impotence. Sexual behavior of post-menopausal women was seen as inappropriate, if not evil, by artists, writers, and moralists. Sexual decline has been perceived as occurring much earlier in life for women than men. Older women, unlike older men, have had stronger proscriptions and limitations imposed on them, and strong negative cultural meanings attached to menopause. Historical themes common to elderly men include sex as humor, sex as self deception, sex as temptation, and younger sex partners as prolonging life and enhancing social status. Historical themes involving elderly women portray sex for older women as evil, sex with younger partners as a way to control men and as evil, and the view of older women as sexual predators.

098   **Demos, Vasilikie, & Jache, Ann. (April, 1981). When you care enough: An analysis of attitudes toward aging in humorous birthday cards.** *The Gerontologist, 21*(2), 209-215.

The present study represents a continuation of research on attitudes toward age and the aging process as expressed through humor. This specific study focused upon humorous birthday cards. One hundred and ninety-five birthday cards were analyzed. Coding of cards separated them into positive, negative, and neutral image as conveyed. The authors explained that this process of coding the cards portrayed more cards as negative toward aging. This is true for cards which focused upon physical and mental characteristics, age boundaries, and aging as an experience of others. The authors suggested that birthday card messages appear to be reflective of nonhumorous popular stereotypes about aging and consequently may reinforce ageist ideas.

099   **Downey, Gregg W. (June, 1974). The next patient right: Sex in nursing homes.** *Modern Health Care, 1*(3), 56-59.

In this article the author reports on presentations by Alex Comfort, author of *The Joy of Sex*, Eric Pfeiffer, a psychiatrist, and William Masters and Virginia Johnson who served on a panel at the 31st annual meeting of the American Geriatrics Society. Dr. Comfort predicted that "sex in the nursing home" would be the next major patient rights issue. Comfort also stated that changes in old age related to orgasm were functionally minimal and that even when actual sexual intercourse failed due to infirmity, the need for closeness and sensuality continued. Eric Pfeiffer, citing research at Duke's Center for the Study of Aging and Human Development, reported a high degree of sexual activity among elderly people in his studies. Both Comfort and Pfeiffer felt strongly that physicians need to abandon their outdated and scientifically incorrect stereotypes and biases related to elderly sexuality. Masters and Johnson presented a review of what needed to be understood by anyone who is elderly or will be. In their views only two conditions needed to be met to have effective sexual function regardless of age—reasonably good health and an interested and willing partner.

100   Falk, Gerhard, & Falk, Ursula A. (January, 1980). **Sexuality and the aged.** *Nursing Outlook, 28*(1), 51-55.

The authors discuss the often negative attitudes of society toward sexuality among older people. Perhaps the most important reason for this taboo is that the United States is a youth-oriented society which scorns those who exhibits the physical signs of aging and focuses on the elderly as sick and poor rather than healthy and active. The traditional age difference in spouses may contribute to women having their sexual activity reduced at a younger age than most men. Both young and older people tend to view the elderly as sexless. Children often view inhibition of sex among their elderly parents as protecting their financial inheritance and making them easier to manage, especially once they are placed in a nursing facility environment. The homosexual community is especially focused on youth, which leaves older homosexuals with decreasing ability to attract partners as their need for more permanent relationships increases with age. The authors conclude that caregivers should become knowledgeable about elderly sexuality and find ways to encourage sexual expression and freedom of choice among the elderly in their care.

101   Fox, Nancy L. (October, 1980). **Sex in the nursing home? For Lord's sake, why not?** *RN, 43*(10), 95-100.

The author discusses the reasons why mature married couples should not be denied their conjugal rights just because they live in a nursing home. She cites the case of Milton, an 80-year-old man who finds the nurses attractive. They respond to his sexual behavior by giving him sedatives. She points out that nurses are aware of the need for personal closeness and physical love in the aged. She asks why nursing homes stamp an expiration date on the need for loving relationships. She says that in other countries people have a much healthier attitude. In other countries, studies have found people in their 100s who are still sexually active. In United States nursing homes there is sometimes an across the board ban on romance. Nurses separate older people who express any sort of affection toward each other. She points out that sexuality is not just sex. In addition to sexual expression there is confidentiality, trust, empathy, mutuality of motivation, affectional expression, and emotional investment. She cites other case studies where older people, including married couples, are deprived of basic human rights for the convenience of the staff. She says, "There is really no excuse for American

nursing homes to be sexless, emotional mortuaries for the living."
She also calls for nurses to bring about a change and to be patient
advocates for allowing sexual expression among their patients.

102   **Hodson, Diane S., & Skeen, Patsy. (September, 1994). Sexuality
and aging: The hammerlock of myths.** *The Journal of Applied
Gerontology, 13*(3), 219-235.

      The purpose of this article is to present relevant information
on elder sexuality including historical myths and current societal
attitudes, sexual attitudes and behavior, benefits of sexual
expression, problems presenting by nursing home care, and the
need for education. Societal attitudes toward sex in the United
States are considered repressive. Today's elderly grew up in a
time when discussion of sexuality was highly inhibited and
sexual practices were limited to male-superior marital intercourse.
Young people have stereotypic views of elder people regarding
their sexuality. In recent years, Americans have become more
tolerant of other groups but these changes have not included the
elderly. Physicians also vary in their understanding and acceptance of elderly sexual needs. They are often uncomfortable in
dealing with sexual matters. Research studies on elderly attitudes
toward sexuality have found that the elderly are more open that
expected. Since there are fewer men available for marriage than
women and some older people prefer not to marry, Hodson and
Skeen believe that masturbation can be a useful sexual outlet. Sex
in older couples is estimated to occur at an average frequency
twice that practiced by similar couples a generation ago. Benefits
of sexual expression, both physical and psychological, have been
offered by many researchers and are summarized by these
authors. Hodson and Skeen also discuss particular problems
related to elderly sexuality in nursing homes—the lack of sensory
stimulation, sexual deprivation, loss of contact with family and
especially spouse, refusal of nursing homes to acknowledge their
patients' need for loving relationships, taboos surrounding sex,
lack of accurate knowledge of elderly sexuality among staff, use of
sedatives with "troublesome patients," and lack of privacy. The
authors offer suggestions for improving the education of the
elderly and the nonelderly. They offer a list of specific
suggestions some of which are: provide privacy for sexual
encounters; provide access to erotic literature in a private setting;
organize discussion groups; offer AIDS and safe-sex seminars;
provide frequent visits to beauticians, barbers, and clothing
consultants; and educate staff and family members. Hodson and

Skeen concluded that sexuality is an important force into old age and that medical professionals and health care professionals should become better informed in this area.

103 **Kogan, Nathan. (1975). Judgments of chronological age: Adult age and sex differences.** *Developmental Psychology, 11*(1), 107.

This one page article presents a brief summary of findings in a study of chronological age estimates of younger and older males and females. The mean age of younger subjects was 21.8 for the 62 males and 20.3 for the 137 females. The mean age of the 76 older male subjects was 71.3 and the mean age of the older females was 71.6. Subjects were randomly assigned to either an all-male or all-female photo sets. Each subject was shown photos of white individuals representing a broad range of ages from preadolescence to the aged. Each subject was asked to give their best estimate of the age of each person seen in the photos. For the male photo set, a significant main effect for subject age was obtained, reflecting somewhat higher overall age estimates on the part of older subjects. A significant sex by photo interaction was found for the male photo set and the female photo set. In both cases, males' age judgment exceeded those of females for younger stimulus persons (photos); and females' age judgments exceeded those of males for older stimulus persons.

104 **Kogan, Nathan. (1979). A study of age categorization.** *Journal of Gerontology, 34*(3), 358-367.

This study explores age categorization in a sample of 150 subjects ages 18 to 76. All of the subjects examined two sets of 33 photographs each (a male and female set). Subjects estimated the age of people in the photographs and assigned them to categories (adolescent, young, middle-aged, elderly, and aged adult). Finally they chose photos of three males and three females they would most like to meet. The author found a major bias related to sex and perceived age of the person in photos. The perceived age of females selected by females was much older than those chosen by males. The perceived age of males selected by both males and females was similar. Sex bias effects were less among older respondents.

105 **Kogan, Nathan, & Mills, Montie. (1992). Gender influences on age cognitions and preferences: Sociocultural or sociobiological?** *Psychology and Aging, 7*(1), 98-106.

This article is a review of research related to gender effects on cognition and evaluation of people varying in age. The authors offer evidence in support of the view that the double standard of aging derives from men's evaluations and cognitions. Men consistently view middle age beginning earlier for women than for men. The authors argue that this evidence cannot be adequately explained on the basis of sociocultural norms. The evidence from the literature indicates that women on the other hand tend to be relatively insensitive to age.

106   **Kuhn, Margaret E. (1976). Sexual myths surrounding the aging. In Wilbur W. Oaks, Gerald A. Melchiode, & Ilda Filcher, (Eds.), *Sex and the life cycle* (pp. 117-124). New York: Grune and Stratton.**

The author examined the origin, meaning, and current description of five prevalent myths about sex and old age. The author points out that these myths reinforce society's belief about older people. Kuhn discusses ageism that permeates our culture and institutions and the wasteful stereotyping of persons and groups on the bases of age and the arbitrary discrimination that robs some 21 million people of selfhood, status, and deprives society as a whole of the experience, skills, and wisdom of its elder. Myths condition people to reject themselves and their experiences, to lie about age, to despise gray hair, wrinkled skin, and stiffened joints, to accept society's view that old age is a disease and a disaster and that older people have nothing to contribute to society. These myths are reinforced by the media. Myth 1 is that sex does not matter in old age—the later years are supposed to be sexless. Myth 2 is that interest in sex is abnormal for old people. Myth 3 is that remarriage after loss of spouse should be discouraged. Myth 4 is that it is all right for old men to seek younger women as sex partners, but it is ridiculous for old women to be sexually involved with younger men. Myth 5 is that old people should be separated by sex in institutions to avoid problems for staff and criticism by families and the community. The author concludes each section with suggestions of ways to change people's minds about these myths.

107   **Limentani, Adam. (August, 1995). Creativity and the third age. *International Journal of Psycho-Analysis, 76*(4), 825-833.**

The author explores the possibility of a relationship between creativity and the third age, in so far as they are capable of influencing each other. After a definition of the third age, the author goes on to discuss the nature and aims of creativity.

Particular attention is paid to the roles of sexuality, regression in the service of the ego, narcissism, sublimation, the depressive position, and reparation. A discussion of therapeutic work with creative elderly individuals complements the author's points in the article. Limentani concludes that to overcome our ideals we must examine our own values about getting older think about how we would feel in an older person's situation.

108 **Masters, William H., & Johnson, Virginia E. (September, 1981). Sex and the aging process.** *Journal of the American Geriatrics Society, 29(9), 385-390.*

The purpose of this article is to enlighten those in the health care sciences who need to better understand sexual function and dysfunction in the elderly. The authors suggest that views of geriatric sexuality have undergone profoundly meaningful changes over the past 50 years. Earlier views related sexuality so thoroughly to reproductive function that sexual activity of older adults was viewed as either unimportant or as aberrant. Stereotypes views of the elderly as "dirty old men" or as "old witches" not only pervaded folklore but also made their way into purportedly scientific literature in the health sciences. They suggest that a minimum of sexual education would do a great deal in neutralizing sexual frustration and social barriers. They suggest that proper management of sexual problems will have great bearing upon elderly mental and physical health. The authors conclude that the inevitable process of aging requires adjustments, but these can be accomplished satisfactorily by enlightened understanding between sexual partners.

109 **Palmore, Erdman B. (Autumn, 1971). Attitudes toward aging as shown by humor.** *The Gerontologist, 11(4), 181-187.*

The basic premise of this study is that items of popular culture, such as the content of jokes, can be analyzed to determine the direction and intensity of attitudes toward a given subject or group, such as aging. Palmore examined 264 jokes about aging from several joke books to investigate the idea that jokes about aging affect attitudes. The author found that the majority of jokes about aging reflected a negative view of aging, especially those dealing with physical ability or appearance, age concealment, old maids, and mental abilities. Jokes implying an activity theory of aging are more positive than those implying a disengagement theory. He found that those jokes dealing with aged women are more negative than those dealing with aged men. He concluded that our society may have a "double standard" in which aging among women is viewed more negatively than aging among men.

110   Sedgwick, Rae. (September, 1975). Myths in human sexuality: A social-psychological perspective. *Nursing Clinics of North America, 10*(3), 539-550.

The author discusses several myths surrounding issues of human sexuality such as sex education, planning, relationships, deviance, sexual needs and gratification, aging, and age or sex stereotypes. Because nurses are in a position to correct these myths among the people in their care, the author emphasizes the importance of students and clinicians evaluating their myths and attitudes about sexuality in addition to gaining clinical knowledge on the subject.

111   Starr, Bernard D. (1985). Sexuality and aging. In Carl Eisdorfer (Ed.), *Annual review of gerontology and geriatrics: Volume 5* (pp. 97-125). New York: Springer.

This chapter examined sexuality and aging literature by highlighting the more positive aspects of sexuality in the later years. The author explored the key historical factors that led to a narrow quantitative conceptualization of sexuality. Then he discussed the value of a phenomenological approach to sexuality in revealing important aspects of sexuality that are masked by quantitative measures. He discussed recent findings on sex and aging from the phenomenological perspective and their methodological problems explored. He then discussed factors that limit the sexuality of older people is reexamined in the context of a new definition of sexuality that emphasizes pleasuring. He concluded with conjectures about sexual and social relationships among the elderly in the future, in the light of cohort differences, and changing mores and social factors.

112   Thomas, L. Eugene. (June, 1982). Sexuality and aging: Essential vitamin or popcorn? *The Gerontologist, 22*(3), 240-243.

The writer points out the general trend in the literature to promote sexuality among the elderly as essential. The author provides the "popcorn" theory as a means of pointing out the overzealousness of many writers. While sexuality and sexual activity in the later years adds zest, the author maintains that there are many other ways to find enjoyment of the sensualities of life than in genital sex. He warns that there is a danger of projecting middle class values and agendas on the elderly. He says the general problem faced by all social scientists is the challenge to learn from those they are studying and not just use them to confirm their preconceived assumptions. He suggests that researchers turn to the elderly to find out what sexuality means to them, rather than projecting the sexual agendas of youth and adulthood onto them.

113   **Ward, Russell A. (1977). The impact of subjective age and stigma on older persons.** *Journal of Gerontology, 32*(2), 227-232.

This article reports results from a study of 323 people 60 years and older drawn from Senior Citizen's Clubs in Madison, Wisconsin. The purpose of the study was to investigate the impact of shifts in age identification from "middle-aged" to "elderly" on attitudes toward old people and self-esteem. Age identification was determined from responses to the question of whether or not they thought of themselves as young, middle-aged, elderly, or old. To determine attitudes toward old people, respondents were asked to indicate extent of agreement with 19 statements such as "old people are cranky." A global measure of self-esteem was used. Health, activity, and age-related deprivation were also measure. Findings revealed that the label of "elderly" was not related to attitudes toward old people or self-esteem. Attachment of negative stereotypes or stigma to growing old, however, did have a negative effect on self-esteem.

114   **Whiskin, Frederick E. (April, 1970). The geriatric sex offender.** *Medical Aspects of Human Sexuality, 4*(4), 125-129.

In this article the author discusses attitudes toward the elderly sex offender. He says that elderly sex offenders are among the "most maligned individuals" in society today although he tends to be the "most benign and impotent individual." The reasons are that he is old, he has committed an act related to sex, and he has committed and abnormal act which relates to sex. A major problem, Whiskin believes, is the public's biases and incorrect beliefs about elderly people and their sexuality. The author discusses reasons why women are less frequently involved in committing sexual offenses. He discusses the relationship of chronic brain syndrome, brain changes, and sexual offenses. He cites two case studies involving elderly men who had been accused of molesting very young girls. He offers advice in managing the elderly offender and warns that there have been cases in which children have made up stories of seduction by older males which upon investigation were not based on fact.

6

Caregiver Attitudes Toward Elderly Sexuality

(O)ne of the most widely studied topics is the attitude of caregivers toward elderly sexuality. Nursing students, medical students, and staff of long-term care facilities are among the groups studied. Influences of different cultures have also been investigated. The most common finding is that caregivers in general hold stereotypical attitudes toward the elderly, especially regarding their sexuality. These negative attitudes are only mildly changed as the result of improved knowledge. Experiences on the job also affect attitudes and these experiences can have negative as well as positive influence. Most writers see a need for a more realistic view of the elderly regarding sexuality by doctors, nurses, and long-term care staff.

Variables assessed in these articles include job, levels of nursing education (e.g., registered nurses, licensed practical nurses, and others), sex of respondent, shift, salaries, level of education, and time spent caring for the elderly. Instruments frequently used to assess attitudes in these studies are White's *Aging Sexual Knowledge and Attitude Scale (1982)*, Palmore's *Facts on Aging Quiz (1977; 1988)*, Tuckman and Lorge's *Attitudes Toward Old People (1953)*, and Kogan's *Old People Scales (1961)*.

Also included in this chapter are articles and literature reviews related to the attitudes toward the elderly or toward elderly sexuality of medical professionals, primarily physicians, nurses, and staff of long-term care facilities. Research studies of the effect of training on caregiver attitudes are grouped together in Chapter 16.

115   Abu-Saad, Huda, Kayser-Jones, Jeanie, & Tien, Juliet. (September, 1982). Asian nursing students in the United States. *Journal of Nursing Education, 21*(7), 11-15.

The authors discuss the problems faced by Asian nursing students entering American schools. Traditional values in the Asian culture, such as gentleness, good manners, and willingness to acquiesce, can often been seen as overdependence, incompetence, and nonassertiveness in American nursing programs. The authors studied Asian nursing students to determine the sources of these difficulties. There were four major sources: the students themselves, the faculty, student peers, and the host culture. To minimize the difficulties of Asian students, the authors recommend that schools organize cross-cultural classes to familiarize students with different cultures, sensitize faculty and counselors to the problems associated with international students in current nursing programs, and help international students adjust to American society by providing programs in English tutoring and socialization with American families.

116   Aletky, Patricia J. (1980). Sexuality of the nursing home resident. *Topics in Clinical Nursing, 1*(4), 53-60.

The purpose of this article was to develop a frame of reference for the issue of sexual health care in a nursing home. First it is important to examine the stereotypes about sexuality of the aged. The article reviewed theories on why younger people do not think the elderly should be sexually active. The largest problem is when the sexless stereotype is held by physicians and other practitioners. When that happens the elderly are directly, and often physically affected. Second, there is a need for objective information about elderly sexuality. The article discussed the various studies on elderly sexuality to teach the reader about the facts. If sexual health care is to become an integral part of total care in the nursing home, the starting point must be the staff. Their attitudes and values will determine the quality of care in this area. The author concluded that to refuse to address sexual issues of nursing home residents is to ignore a basic part of their existence.

117   Allen, Mary E. (1987). A holistic view of sexuality and the aged. *Holistic Nursing Practice, 1*(4), 76-83.

This article discusses attitudes toward elderly sexuality, summarizing several studies which have assessed the sexual knowledge, attitudes, and practices of the elderly, caregivers, and knowledge, attitudes, and practices of the elderly, caregivers, and students. The author recommends a holistic approach to sexuality which includes more than just the physical aspects of sexuality. Having this broader context can help nursing students and staff be more accepting and tolerant of the sexual rights and behavior of the people in their care. The author recommends that a broader definition of sexuality should be encouraged by nurses in clinical settings, that elderly sexuality should be included in the curricula of nursing programs, and that consumer education programs about sexuality should be developed and marketed to institutions serving the elderly.

118   Brown, Lil. (1989). Is there sexual freedom for our aging populations in long-term care institutions? *Journal of Gerontological Social Work, 13(3/4),* 75-90.
       Despite the fact that research has shown that elderly people continue to have sexual needs, society continues to preserve myths about the elderly as sexless. These attitudes are often seen in nursing facilities, where sexual behavior is frowned upon, seen as problematic or abnormal, and often restricted or nearly impossible. The author explores the current regulations concerning the rights of the elderly in Canadian nursing facilities and recommends changes in policies to ensure the sexual rights of elderly residents.

119   Campbell, Margaret Eleanor. (March-April, 1971). Study of the attitudes of nursing personnel toward the geriatric patient. *Nursing Research, 20(2),* 147-151.
       The study investigated the relationship between acceptance by nursing-care personnel of stereotypes about old people and several demographic variables, the relationship between acceptance of stereotypes concerning old people and the age group with which nurses prefer to work, and the relationship between the incentives of shift preference or salary differential and increased willingness to work with geriatric patients. The subjects were 147 registered nurses, licensed practical nurses, and nursing assistants at two teaching institutions in central North Carolina. Subjects completed the Tuckman and Lorge questionnaire with 88 valid items. The results indicated that (1) every nurse had stereotypical attitudes toward the elderly; (2) registered nurses were least likely to accept the stereotyped statements; (3) licensed practical nurses and nursing assistants preferred working with the elderly more than registered nurses; (4) salary increase or shift

with older patients; and (5) the level of education and time spent caring for the elderly seemed to be important influences on the willingness of the nurses to accept stereotypes about the elderly. The author concluded that work with the elderly along with better teaching techniques would modify or change the stereotyped attitudes held toward older people.

120   Damrosch, Shirley Petchel. (July-August, 1982). Nursing students' attitudes toward sexually active older persons. *Nursing Research, 31*(4), 252-255.

This article reports on two experiments with nursing students. The research question investigated was "how does information that an older person is sexually active affect evaluations of that person?" This study investigated the attitudes of senior baccalaureate nursing students toward geriatric sexuality. Two separate experiments used vignettes as an unobtrusive measure of attitudes toward sexual activity in an older man or woman who was depicted as either married or widowed. All subjects read a vignette concerning a 68-year-old person who was temporarily living in a nursing home. Half read that the person was sexually active; there was not mention of sexual activity for the remaining subjects. Subjects evaluated the person on a 10-item questionnaire, employing 0 to 9 bipolar rating scales for such traits as well-adjustedness, cheerfulness, and mental alertness. Regardless of the stimulus person's gender or marital status, subjects showed a significant bias favoring the sexually active older person in both experiments. Implications for nursing practice are discussed.

121   Damrosch, Shirley Petchel. (June, 1984). Graduate nursing students' attitudes toward sexually active older persons. *The Gerontologist, 24*(3), 299-302.

The author investigated the attitudes of 114 registered nurses enrolled in a master's degree nursing program at a large eastern university toward sexually active older women. Each student read a 200 word account of a 68-year-old woman temporarily living in a nursing home. By random assignment, half the students read about a sexually active woman and the other half read about a nonsexually active woman. Each student rated the woman from 0 to 9 on such characteristics as cooperativeness and cheerfulness. The nursing students showed a significant bias in favor of the sexually active 68-year-old woman.

122   Damrosch, Shirley Petchel, & Fischman, Susan H. (December, 1985). Medical students' attitudes toward sexually active older persons. *Journal of the American Geriatrics Society, 33*(12), 852-855.

The authors investigated the attitudes of 140 first year medical students at a large eastern university toward sexually active older people. Each student read a 200 word account of a 68-year old man or woman temporarily living in a nursing home. By random assignment, half the students read about a sexually active person and the other half read about a non-sexually active person. Each student was asked to rate the person on 0 to 9 scale on such characteristics as mental alertness and cheerfulness. The medical students showed a significant bias in favor of the sexually active 68-year-old regardless of the gender. The authors concluded that evidence of a bias favoring the sexually active older person, regardless of gender, existed among their subjects.

123   Elliott, Bonita, & Hybertson, Diane. (October, 1982). What is it about the elderly that elicits a negative response? *Journal of Gerontological Nursing, 8*(10), 568-571.

This study examines the relationship between the expressed attitudes of nursing personnel toward individual geriatric patients and the objectively assessed characteristics of these patients. Fifty geriatric patients were randomly selected from a population of 100 skilled-care nursing home residents. The final sample consisted of 4 men and 29 women ages 66 to 102. The objective assessment was conducted using an 55 item instrument derived from Brody and Lawton's *Physical Self-Maintenance Scale*. The authors found that positive attitudes about providing care for geriatric patients appears to be related most significantly to the elders' level of social and interpersonal functioning. Bladder incontinence was the only physical condition related to nursing assistants' attitudes. Mental disorientation and confusion were not related.

124   Gillis, Sr. Marion. (November-December, 1973). Attitudes of nursing personnel toward the aged. *Nursing Research, 22*(6), 517-520.

The author investigated the differences in nurses' attitudes toward the aged based on four selected variables: age, education, length of employment, and type of nurse. Subjects were 86 nurses selected at random from five nursing homes and one general hospital. Each subject completed a questionnaire on caring for older patients. The hypothesis that a nurse 45 years and over, who had earned a B.S. degree in nursing, who had cared for the aged for more than 9 years, and who were employed in a hospital would be positive in their attitude toward the aged was rejected. The author concluded that nurses who are going to be working with the elderly need more training to prepare them for the task.

125   Glass, J. Conrad, Jr., Mustian, R. David, & Carter, Lois R. (1986). Knowledge and attitudes of health care providers toward sexuality in the institutionalized elderly. *Educational Gerontology, 12*(5), 465-475.

This study examined the relationship between the knowledge and attitudes of nursing home staff toward elderly sexuality. Fifty-seven nurses from five different nursing homes in North Carolina nursing homes completed White's *Aging Sexual Knowledge and Attitude Scale* (ASKAS). The authors found that education, religiosity, position, nursing education, time in current position, and continuing education were significantly related to knowledge and/or attitudes. The authors' analysis revealed that the more knowledge a nurse possessed, the more restrictive his or her attitudes were toward sexuality in the elderly.

126   Glasspoole, Leslie A., & Aman, Michael G. (1990). Knowledge, attitudes, and happiness of nurses working with gerontological patients. *Journal of Gerontological Nursing, 16*(2), 11-14.

This article reports findings as they relate to the nurses' knowledge of aging, attitudes toward and conceptualization of old age, degree of happiness in their work, and their reasons for working with the elderly. The subjects were 378 nurses in Auckland, New Zealand who completed a questionnaire. Most (58%) worked on the geriatric wards of general hospitals, another group (31%) worked in nursing homes, and the rest (10%) worked in psychiatric facilities. The 12-page questionnaire included 25 questions from Palmore's *Facts on Aging Quiz* (FAQ). The authors found that most of the nurses worked with the elderly by choice and expressed a high degree of satisfaction in their work. Aspects of care least enjoyed related to behavioral problems. Most nurses felt the need for higher staffing levels and more interaction with patients. Most thought the government should provide more funds for home-based services. The subjects made a number of errors on the FAQ items.

127 Holmes, Douglas, Reingold, Jacob, & Teresi, Jeanne. Sexual expression and dementia: Views of caregivers: A Pilot study. (1996). *International Journal of Geriatric Psychiatry, 11,* 1-7.

The purpose of this study was to measure the attitudes of health professionals in nursing homes toward sexuality and sexual expression in cognitively impaired and cognitively intact residents. Subjects were the staff of 300 randomly selected nursing facilities located in three states. Of these, 114 representatives responded by completing a questionnaire developed by the authors and pretested by staff of one facility for internal consistency. The data suggested that administrators of those facilities were more conservative than were the respondents who engaged in direct service delivery; however, none of the differences were statistically significant. A large majority of respondents (92 to 100%) agreed that sexual expression among cognitively intact nursing home residents is healthy and can contribute to quality of life. A majority (74 to 84%) also thought the same was true for people with dementia. Only a small percent (0 to 5%) thought that masturbation should be prohibited. A majority (60 to 63%) also thought that sexual expression should be encouraged. Respondents also reported that about 13 to 20% of residents engage in sexual behavior. Respondents almost all agreed that additional staff training should focus specifically on dealing with resident sexual expression.

128 Ingham, Roger, & Fielding, Pauline. (1985). A review of the nursing literature on attitudes toward old people. *International Journal of Nursing Studies, 22*(3), 171-181.

This review article examined recent research on nurse's attitudes toward aging. Each of the studies reviewed attempted to relate attitudes toward old people to one or more of the following variables: (1) characteristics of the nurses studied; (2) characteristics of the patients; (3) the effects of intervention in the form of special educational programs; and (4) related attitudes of nurses and the link between behavioral intention and behavior. Based on their review of existing literature, the authors drew the following conclusions. First, research on attitudes of nurses is inconclusive. Second, greater dependency of the patient evokes more negative evaluations from nurses. Third, studies which attempt to measure change in attitudes related to educational institutions do not employ appropriate methodological designs so no conclusions can be drawn. Finally, the largest omission from the reviewed work has been any systematic attempt to relate attitudes to actual behavior in the job.

129   **LaTorre, Ronald A., & Kear, Karen. (June, 1977). Attitudes toward sex in the aged.** *Archives of Sexual Behavior, 6*(3), 203-213.

The authors assessed the attitudes of 80 university students and 40 nursing home employees toward sexual behavior in the aged. Each subject was given three different stories of a decision-making process, sexual intercourse, and masturbation. Each subject had an assigned main character presented as old or young, male or female. After each, the subject then rated the story in eight different categories. Nursing home employees had more negative attitudes toward sexual stories than the university students in general. Gender of the raters had little effect on the results. The authors found that the story on sexual intercourse had a higher overall rating for the male character than the female character and the opposite occurred in the masturbation story with the female scoring higher.

130   **Lewis, Myrna. (1984). Sexual activity in later life: A challenging issue for nurses.** *Imprint, 31*(4), 48-49.

The author offers reasons why nurses sometimes have difficulty in accepting the sexuality and sexual needs of older patients. One major problem, she states, is that nurses often view older people in parent or grandparent roles instead of as "fellow adults." She also discusses physical changes and other problems associated with aging that affect sexuality such as a slower response, estrogen loss, impotence, medication effects, excess alcohol, and surgeries, illness and disability, emotional problems, lack of available partners. Lewis points out that approximately 10% of older adults are homosexual. Lewis provides guidance to nurses regarding their responses to the sexual needs of older adults such as taking the initiative in conversation and bringing up the subject of sexual problems, seeking information and sharing it with patients, recognizing a wide diversity of sexual needs and desires, and helping patients receive medical help when needed.

131   **Luketich, Gail Furman. (1991). Sex and the elderly: What do nurses know?** *Educational Gerontology, 17*(6), 573-580.

The author investigated the knowledge and attitudes toward geriatric sexuality of graduate nursing students. All of the subjects (N = 42) worked in a hospital, had received their B.S. in nursing (B.S.N), and were enrolled in the first required course for graduate students at a private midwestern school of nursing. Subjects completed White's *Aging Sexual Knowledge and Attitudes Scale* (ASKAS), a questionnaire on elderly sexuality knowledge and attitudes. The author found that these students presented high levels of knowledge regarding elderly sexuality and had a positive attitude toward elderly sexuality. The author concluded that the onset of a more liberal attitude among nurses and an exposure to courses that deal with sexual activities, not only in the elderly, had contributed to this finding.

132 **McCartney, James R., Izeman, Henry, Rogers, Donna, & Cohen, Norma. (April, 1987). Sexuality and institutionalized elderly.** *Journal of the American Geriatrics Society, 35***(4), 331-333.**

Staff reaction to two cases is used to illustrate the need for programmatic interventions with staff, residents, and families. Case one is a 79-year-old widowed man who was flirtatious with staff and visitors. Case two is a 72-year-old man who entered the facility with his wife. While there she died, and he developed a relationship with another female resident, a widow. The couple were married. The authors suggest that staff attitudes and beliefs often lead to discomfort in dealing with the continued sexual interests of patients. In their view it is clear if sexuality has been an important part of self-image and contending with difficulties, then it remains important in later life. The authors conclude that nursing homes need to be more supportive of sexual activities and take steps to improve and support residents in reaching out to others.

133 **Meyer, Mary M., Hassanein, Ruth Stephenson, & Bahr, Sr. Rose Therese. (October, 1980). A comparison of attitudes toward the aged held by professional nurses.** *Image, 12***(3), 62-66.**

This study investigated differences in attitude toward the elderly of professional nurses giving direct nursing care to the elderly and professional nurses who do not give direct nursing care to the elderly. Subjects were 25 full-time and 11 part-time nurses from nine facilities providing nursing care for the elderly and 24 full-time and four part-time nurses in two pediatric settings. Subjects were given a two-part questionnaire consisting of the Tuckman-Lorge *Attitudes Toward Old People* (ATOP) instrument and a structured demographic questionnaire designed to obtain information regarding the subjects' age, ethnicity, past experiences with the elderly, education, and salary. The ATOP contains 137 items measuring thirteen dimensions of stereotyping of the aged. The authors found that nurses who did not work with the elderly had significantly lower scores in stereotyping (i.e., more positive attitudes) as compared to those who did.

134   Penner, Louis A., Ludenia, Krista, & Mead, Gayle. (1984). Staff attitudes: Image or reality. *Journal of Gerontological Nursing, 10*(3), 110-117.

The purpose of this study was to investigate the nursing staff's general attitudes toward the elderly. Subjects were 58 members ages 25 to 66 of the nursing staff at a large nursing home for veterans. Subjects completed Palmore's *Facts on Aging Quiz*, Kogan's *Attitudes Toward Old People Scale*, and the *Semantic Differential*. From the data analysis, the authors concluded that nursing staff's experiences with elderly patients, rather than the staff's general feelings about the elderly, are the primary determinant of their attitudes toward elderly patients. Subjects held the most negative attitudes toward those elderly with whom they were most familiar, an older patient who is a veteran. They found no relationship between general stereotypes about and attitudes toward the elderly and their attitudes toward their own patients. None of the demographic variables were found to correlate significantly with general feelings about the elderly were significantly related to the staff's attitudes toward their patients.

135   Pratt, Clara C., & Schmall, Vicki L. (April, 1989). College students' attitudes toward elderly sexual behavior: Implications for family life education. *Family Relations, 38*(2), 137-141.

The authors examined attitudes toward elderly sexual behavior in college students (N = 290, 39% males, 61% females, mean age = 19.6). The authors developed a sexual attitude inventory using a semantic differential technique. Ten 7-point rating scales were used in which the extreme ends were defined by opposing evaluative adjectives such as "good-bad," "healthy-unhealthy," "desirable-undesirable." and "nice-awful." Six versions of the questionnaire were used. The sexual behaviors described were the same in each version but the actor's age, sex, and hypothetical family relationship were varied. Behaviors examined were married sexual intercourse, unmarried sexual intercourse, living together, sexual activity among institutionalized elders, masturbation, disinterest in sexual activity, refusal of lifesaving surgery, and homosexuality. Attitudes toward sexual activity of nursing home residents were positive. Attitudes toward masturbation were neutral. Attitudes toward homosexuality were negative. Their results indicated that the most salient factor related to attitudes was the specific behavior being evaluated and not the age, gender, or relationship to the subject. The authors discussed the implications of this research for family life and sex education programs.

136   Quinn-Krach, Peg, & Van Hoozer, Helen. (October, 1988). Sexuality of the aged and the attitudes and knowledge of nursing students. *Journal of Nursing Education, 27*(8), 359-363.

This study examined the relationship of attitude and knowledge to ethnicity, age, experience in health care, family income, religious affiliation, religiosity, living arrangements, and level of education. The subjects were 158 female nursing students who completed White's *Aging Sexuality Attitude and Knowledge Scale*. Data analysis showed that higher knowledge was related to more positive attitude scores. Age was also significantly related to both positive attitude and higher knowledge. Older students in this sample had a more positive attitude toward the elderly and were more knowledgeable about aged sexuality than younger students. Asian students in this study had a significantly more negative attitude and were less knowledgeable about aged sexuality than Caucasian students. The study suggests that nurse educators should pay special attention to the age and ethnicity of students when planning gerontological learning experiences.

137   Sachs, Bernice C. (March, 1983). Aging well. *Psychosomatics, 24*(3), 225-230.

The author addresses several myths of aging and the attitudes and roles of physicians in dispelling myths and promoting healthy aging. Common myths about the elderly promote stereotypes of illness, senility, sexlessness, and uselessness. The author suggests that physicians overcome their own myths and fears about their own aging and retirement in order to help their patients do the same.

138   Smith, Gregory C., Tobin, Sheldon S., & Gustafson, Joseph D. (Spring, 1987). Perceptions of geriatric practice: The role of theoretical orientation, age, and gender. *Clinical Gerontologist, 6*(3), 29-46.

The purpose of this research study was to understand perceptions of four dimensions of geriatric practice: the evocation of age-related countertransference issues, touch as particularly important, increased activity by practitioners, and the special value of reminiscence. Subjects were 541 subscribers to the *Journal of Gerontological Social Work*. Subjects completed a 20-item Likert-Type *Perceptions of Practice Questionnaire*. The perception of the evocation of more age-related countertransference issues in geriatric practice was associated with having a psychodynamic orientation, and with fewer years of practice with the elderly. The perception of touch as therapeutically important was associated with being female, not having a psychodynamic orientation, and with working in long-term care settings. The perception that increased activity is required with the elderly was associated with being female and with younger ages of practitioners. The perception of the special value of reminiscence was positively related to years of practice with the elderly, amount of formal education, and being female. The authors concluded that these modest associations should be substantiated, possibly through behavioral observations.

139   Smith, Shirley P., Jepson, Virginia, & Perloff, Evelyn. (February, 1982). Attitudes of nursing care providers toward elderly patients. *Nursing and Health Care, 3*(2), 93-98.

This study investigated attitudes of three groups of nursing care providers—registered nurses (RN), licensed practical nurses (LPN), and nurses aides—toward elderly patients in a large long-term care facility. A stratified, random sample of nursing care providers (N = 55) was selected from a total working group of 154. Of these 40 participants completed Kogan's *Old People Scale*. Data analysis showed that the registered nurses appeared slightly more positive in their attitudes toward elderly patients than either the LPNs or nurses aides. The RNs were also less negative toward elderly patients. The older providers (over 50) and the younger providers (under 30) had more positive attitudes toward the elderly than the middle group (30 to 49).

140   Spennrath, Susan. (1983). Understanding the sexual needs of the older patient. *American Urological Association Allied Journal, 3*(4), 14-18.

In this article the author discusses the reluctance of young caregivers to discuss sexuality with their older patients or family members. She also discusses the difficulty that older people have in initiating such a discussion themselves. Reasons for these problems include culturally derived sexual stereotyping, ageism, pride, dread of growing old, lack of information. She lists common medical myths held by nurses and other health professionals about the elderly such as that sexual desire ceases with menopause, sex is only for the young, older widows and spinsters are sexless, menopausal women need to take hormones to stay sexually active, menopause makes women crabby, after a prostatectomy a man is impotent, nothing can be done to treat impotence in old men. The author discusses the facts related to each myth. She concludes by stating that sexuality is a basic human feeling and human right that persists from cradle to grace. She recommends that since the elderly rarely raise the topic themselves, people who care for the elderly should open the discussion and provide information as needed.

141 Taylor, Kathleen Heitzeg, & Harned, Thomas Lee. (September-October, 1978). Attitudes toward old people: A study of nurses who care for the elderly. *Journal of Gerontological Nursing,* 4(5), 43-47.

The purpose of this study was to evaluate the attitudes toward old people of professional nurses who care for the elderly. Attitudes were measured using Kogan's *Old People Scale.* Data were gathered during the spring of 1974 during six 2-day conferences in Oklahoma. All participants in the conferences were offered the voluntary opportunity to complete the scale before the conference began and again before the conference adjourned the following day. Subjects were participants who were registered nurses, had completed one pretest of the scale, identified themselves by name, and returned a subsequent questionnaire. Of the 579 completed tests, 71 nurses participated in this study. Data analysis found that all of their scores were in the positive to neutral range. Younger nurses and nurses with fewer years of experience both with nursing and with the elderly scored the most positive attitudes.

142 Thorson, James A. (August, 1975). Attitudes toward the aged as a function of race and social class. *The Gerontologist,* 15(4), 343-344.

The objective of this study was to investigate the effect of race and social class on attitude toward older people. Subjects were 98 people who were approximately the same age and had the same years of education. This group consisted of 48 blacks and 50 whites of whom 46 were categorized as lower income and 52 were middle income. Subjects completed Kogan's *Attitudes Toward*

Old People Scale (OP). Data from a previous study with 59 practitioners, 61 university undergraduate and graduate students who had not been classified by race or social class. Of the 218 subjects who completed the OP, the only significant difference in attitude was related to years of education. Positive attitude toward the elderly increased with the number of years of education of the test subjects. No difference was found related to race or social class.

143   Wolk, Robert L., & Wolk, Rochelle B. (July, 1971). **Professional workers' attitudes toward the aged.** *Journal of the American Geriatrics Society, 19*(7), 624-639.

The purpose of this study was to investigate the nature of prejudices about the aged held by professional workers and to determine if there were differences between younger and older workers and between those engaged in work with the aged and those not so employed. Subjects were 220 professional staff members from several agencies, schools, and institutions who returned complete questionnaires soliciting their ideas about what old people are like, stereotypes about old people, and feelings about working with old people. Responses were categorized into seven groups by occupation and subdivided according to age of respondent and whether or not the respondent chose to work with the aged. Only 24 of the subjects were over 45 years of age. No significant differences were found between the number of positive or negative attitudes of the older and younger groups who chose not to work with the aged, between the number of positive or negative attitudes of the older and younger respondents who chose to work with the aged, and between the number of negative attitudes of the young group who chose to work with the aged and the older group who did not, and between the number of negative statements elicited from the older group who chose to work with the aged and the number of negative statements elicited from any other group. A significant difference was found between the number of positive attitudes of the younger group who chose to work with the aged and the younger group who chose not to work with the aged and when comparing the number of positive statements elicited from the older professional group who chose to work with the aged and the number of positive statements elicited from any other group. Differences among groups of subjects (social worker students, psychology students, nursing students, social work practitioners, psychologists, registered nurses, practical nurses were analyzed and discussed. The authors found that only 44 of their subjects chose to work with the aged rather than other age groups. Of those 44, 15 were registered nurses with considerable exposure to the aged. Of the 24 subjects older than 45, 11 chose to work with the aged, a significantly greater proportion than other age groups. Their data suggest that the most obvious differences between the attitudes of professional workers was related to their ages. Older professionals accepted positive attitudes and emphasized the older person's maintenance of physical independence. Younger people were more likely to accept the stereotype of the older person as physically deteriorated. The authors concluded that older professionals tend to over-idealize the older person and so become disenchanted when working with gerontological patients. Older workers do not or cannot meet the challenge of the older person's dependency. Younger professionals do not identify with the aged patient as easily as the older professional. They see them as a parent-like figure. They see an opportunity to capitalize on the role reversal, i.e., they are parent, the older person is child, and may encourage dependency. Neither group, therefore, views the older person appropriately.

7

Attitudes of the Elderly
Toward Sexuality

Attitudes toward elderly sexuality by the elderly have been investigated in several settings using questionnaires and face-to-face interviews. Settings for studies have been nursing homes, congregate housing units, retirement homes, and senior centers. Populations studied have been residents, elderly men whose wives have Alzheimer's, and widows. Among the many aspects of sexuality investigated were types of sexual expression and sexual interest, sexual identity, and sexual fantasies. Researchers have investigated feelings about physical attractiveness, problems with partners with Alzheimer's disease, reluctance to express sexual concerns, importance of age-related changes, feelings about loss of sexual activity due to being widowed, and ideas about homosexuality and masturbation. Variables in these studies have included education level, age, marital status, parenthood, religiosity, income, heterosexual involvement, mental condition, gender, race, urban versus rural, geographic region, health disability, and cultural influences.

One study (Kaas, 1978) compared the attitudes of residents with staff at a nursing facility. Studies by Smith and Schmall (1983), Steinke (1994), and Story (1989) have investigated the knowledge of elderly people about sexuality. Studies indicate that change in knowledge can be achieved through education but attitude is not necessarily related to changes in knowledge. In general, researchers have concluded that the elderly could benefit from education regarding their sexuality.

Instruments used in these studies are the *Sexual Attitude Scale*, *Aging Sexual Knowledge and Attitudes Scale* and the *Sex Knowledge and Attitude Test* (SKAT) developed at the University of Pennsylvania.

There is some evidence that older people share the general views of society about elderly sexuality and accept the same set of myths; however, there has been little research interest in the ideas of the elderly about sexuality.

144   Bond, John B., Jr., & Tramer, Richard R. (Summer, 1983). Older adult perceptions of attitudes toward sex among the elderly. *Canadian Journal on Aging, 2* (2), 63-70.

This study investigated whether older adults perceive differences among various reference groups in attitudes toward sex among the elderly. The authors also investigated whether older adults perceive different attitudes among persons fulfilling various social roles toward sex among the elderly. The reference groups included the respondents, the respondents' children, clergy, doctor, friends, and spouse. Subjects were 273 married, independent living adults, ages 56 to 75. Respondents completed a 5-point Likert scale which questioned how they thought various groups felt toward sex among the elderly. The authors found that older adults believe that the younger the age of the person, the less favorable the perceived attitudes of that person toward sexual relations among the elderly. Elderly women and the young were equally seen as the least favorable. The respondents' physicians were seen as holding attitudes most similar to the respondents'. The self, doctor, and spouse were viewed as having more favorable attitudes toward sex among the elderly than friends, clergy, or children. Elderly males were perceived as having more favorable attitudes than all other groups combined.

145   Kaas, Merrie Jean. (August, 1978). Sexual expression of the elderly in nursing homes. *The Gerontologist, 18*(4), 372-378.

The author states that "The denial of sexuality can have a destructive effect not only upon one's sex life, but also on one's image and interpersonal relationships." The purpose of this study was to compare differences between elderly nursing home residents and nursing home nursing staff in attitudes toward sexual expression of the elderly. Subjects were residents and staff chosen from three different Detroit city nursing homes and two Detroit suburban nursing homes. Resident subjects were selected from the resident roster from each home. Subjects were 85 nursing home residents ages 65 and older, spoke English, and were oriented to time, place, and person and 207 staff ages 18 and older. Data were gathered by having subjects complete a questionnaire consisting of 32 statements related to attitudes toward sexual expression and perception of sexual needs developed by the investigator. Kaas presented a detailed analysis of the data including responses to each of the items. Most of the questions specifically related to sexual expression of older people. Kaas found differences in attitudes toward sexual expression of the elderly between residents and staff. Generally both groups accept sexual expression of the elderly. The major mode of sexual expression as seen by the residents is trying to remain physically attractive. Yet the majority of residents did not feel sexually attractive any more. The staff evidenced a high level of agreement with the statement "Would like to know more about sexuality and aging." The item Kaas concluded there was evidence of the breakdown in the sexuality of the elderly and urges staff to help the elderly maintain their physical attractiveness and their sexual identify.

146 Litz, Brett T., Zeiss, Antonette M., & Davies, Helen D. (February, 1990). Sexual concerns of male spouses of female Alzheimer's disease patients. *The Gerontologist, 30*(1), 113-116.

This article focuses on sexual concerns of males whose spouses have Alzheimer's disease (AD). The authors present a case description of a 72-year-old male caregiver and husband of a patient diagnosed with AD six years earlier. General themes emerged: many spouses of Alzheimer's patients are reluctant to report sexual difficulties and are reluctant to see help; caregivers may be reluctant to raise sexual concerns for fear that these concerns might indicate selfishness, taking advantage of their partner, or they feel they cannot meet the sexual needs of their partner and feel guilty about attending to their own sexual needs; and the disease process can lead to changes in the way in which sexual desires are manifested as well as changes in the arousal pattern. The authors discuss treatment of the problems. The authors conclude that more information about sexuality related to Alzheimer's patients is needed.

147 Malatesta, Victor J., Chambless, Dianne L., Pollack, Martha, & Cantor, Alan. (Spring, 1988). Widowhood, sexuality, and aging: A life span analysis. *Journal of Sex and Marital Therapy, 14*(1), 49-62.

This article reports results of a study of 100 widows ages 40 to 89. The study was designed "to examine the relationship between levels of sexual/affectional behaviors, perceived obstacles to sexual expression, and need perceptions among different age groups." Authors wanted to "understand how middle-aged and older women adapt to and cope with some of the affectional and sexual changes that accompany widowhood." Women were divided into five different age groups: 40 to 49 years; 50 to 59 years; 60 to 69 years; 70 to 79 years; and 80 to 89 years. There were 20 women in each age group. All women were asked to complete a 101-item, 5-point Likert-scaled questionnaire, designed to assess three major areas of affectional/sexual adaptation to widowhood. The three areas covered were: (1) degree of importance posed by age-related changes (e.g. body changes, environmental changes) in meeting sexual needs; (2) degree of unhappiness associated with loss of marriage related heterosexual activities; and (3) endorsement of activities that indirectly help to satisfy affectional and sexual needs (e.g. masturbation). Education, income, heterosexual involvement, and family contact were all statistically controlled. Questionnaire responses across the continuous age variable were analyzed with the Spearman Rho correlation technique. Partial correlations were used to control for years of widowhood and for women's age where appropriate. Results indicated differences with age. "Age correlations were uniformly negative, indicating that increasing age was associated with lower rating of sexual and affectional interference. In particular, younger widows, when compared with older counterparts, viewed changes in body image, the dearth of unattached men, and limited financial resources for social activities as representing significant sexual barriers." Compared to older women, younger widows consistently rated themselves as unhappier. With respect to activity endorsement, the two younger age groups were the only ones to highly endorse heterosocial activities. In contrast, older women endorsed having their hair done, wearing lingerie, and other such activities. The lowest rated activities in all age groups were: taking a tranquilizer; following the movie and TV stars; watching TV soap operas; babysitting; dreaming; giving yourself a massage; drinking alcohol; and touching your body to feel good. All five groups rated the following activities highly: Kissing or hugging your children or grandchildren; being with your children or grandchildren; wearing nice clothes; and praying. Analyses revealed that increasing age was significantly associated with systematic decrease in the rated effectiveness of more direct, heterosocial, and autoerotic activities (e.g., going on a date, dancing, lying naked, touching your body for sexual feelings) in meeting affectional and sexual needs.

148 **McIntosh, Diana. (1981). Sexual attitudes in a group of older women.** *Issues in Mental Health Nursing, 3*(1-2), 109-122.

This study investigated the sexual attitudes of older women with a focus on the relationship between educational level, age, marital status, parenthood, and the importance of religion to permissiveness in sexual attitudes. Subjects were 100 women ages 60 to 94 who lived in independent congregate housing units. The women were asked if they agreed with, disagreed with, or were uncertain about each of the items on the *Sexual Attitude Scale* (SAS). They found a substantial majority (81%) thought it was morally wrong for older persons to be homosexuals and most (72%) disagreed that it was all right to masturbate in private. A majority (72%) thought most older married couples were interested in having sexual relationships with each other. Most (62%) did not think it was permissible for older people to live together without marriage. McIntosh reports that the study could have been biased by some of the respondents' lack of knowledge or understanding of terminology. Specifically, several women said they did not know the meaning of the terms "homosexual" and "masturbation."

149 **Portonova, Marydonna, Young, Elaine, & Newman, Margaret A. (1984). Elderly women's attitudes toward sexual activity among their peers.** *Health Care for Women International, 5*(5/6), 289-298.

This study investigated the attitudes of elderly women ages 60 to 90 toward sexually active older adults. Sex, marital status, and living site is systematically varied in eight versions of a vignette depicting a sexually active older adult. Subjects (N = 120) assignment was systematic to one of eight versions of the vignette, yielding equal numbers (15) for each of the experimental cells. Subjects completed a short questionnaire interview. Their analysis of variance revealed no difference in relation to sex. Marital status of the person in the vignette did have an effect. Subjects' attitudes are more positive toward married sexually active older adults than those who widowed. In addition, subjects' attitudes are more positive toward married sexually active older adults and widowed sexually active older adults living in a nursing home. The authors concluded that in general, attitudes are positive toward sexual activity in older adults in all the social relationships identified.

150   Poulin, Nicole, & Mishara, Brian L. (Spring, 1994). A comparison of adult attitudes toward their parents' sexuality and their parents' attitudes. *Canadian Journal on Aging, 13*(1), 96-103.

This study compared the attitudes of adult children toward the sexuality of their older parents with their parent's own attitudes toward sexuality. Subjects were 41 pairs of French-speaking Montreal residents. All of the subjects were Catholic. Each pair included an adult child and his or her parent ages 65 or older. The ages of the adult children ranged from 29 to 64, mean age 43.9. The parent group consisted of 31 women and 10 men ages 65 to 90, mean = 73.6. Nineteen of the parents were married. Participants completed a 56-item questionnaire using a 6-point Likert scale which assessed attitudes toward sexuality of older parents. The authors found that in general parents and their adult children held positive attitudes toward sexuality. The adult children had significantly more positive attitudes than their parents. The differences were due to attitudes toward physical aspects of sexual behavior. A copy of the questionnaire was not included with the article.

151   Smith, Margaret M., & Schmall, Vicki L. (1983). Knowledge and attitudes toward sexuality and sex education of a select group of older people. *Gerontology and Geriatric Education, 3*(4), 259-269.

This study examined the sexual knowledge, education and attitudes of older men and women. Subjects were Caucasian males (N = 15) and females (N = 17) residing in the community who were members of a volunteer, nonpartisan organization of older people. Researchers collected data by personal interviews in homes and in a local senior center. The results suggest that there is an interest in sexual information by older individuals. The researchers observed that many of the subjects were ignorant of many types of sexual knowledge as a result of years of suppression by society and were eager to learn.

152   Steinke, Elaine E. (1994). Knowledge and attitudes of older adults about sexuality and ageing: A comparison of two studies. *Journal of Advanced Nursing, 19*, 477-485.

Two studies using separate samples sought to explore

differences among male and female elders on their knowledge, attitudes, and sexual behavior using a nonexperimental approach. Two different samples from separate health and wellness groups were surveyed using White's *Aging Sexual Knowledge and Attitude Scale*. Additional data were collected on sexual satisfaction, sexual activity, and demographic variables. In the first study, questionnaires were mailed to the homes of 759 members of the wellness group. The second study was conducted in a similar manner, but with random selection of 400 males and 400 females. Both groups showed a moderate amount of knowledge and permissive attitudes with no significant differences observed between males and females. Reported sexual satisfaction was variable. Subjects were sexually active with activity varying from 0 to 30 times per month, with a mean of four times per month. Findings suggest that males and females are comparable on their knowledge and attitudes about sexuality in aging and most are sexually active. Many are seeking further information on the impact of chronic illness and medications on sexuality.

153 Story, Marilyn D. (1989). Knowledge and attitudes about the sexuality of older adults among retirement home residents. *Educational Gerontology, 15*(5), 515-526.

The author investigated the knowledge and attitudes about the sexuality of older adults held by well elderly people living in an Iowa retirement home (N = 133). She compared their knowledge and attitude scores with test norms and with a comparison group of Iowa university students (N = 133). She also explored what demographic factors affected knowledge and attitude scores. General attitudes of both retirees and students toward the sexuality of the elderly were very positive, but their attitudes toward specific sexual behaviors were less positive. She found that retirement home residents had less knowledge and less positive attitudes about the sexuality of older adults than did university students. There was a correlation between greater knowledge and more positive attitudes. Story concluded that older adults need more in-depth education about their sexuality and sexual functioning.

154 Tucker, M. Belinda, Taylor, Robert Joseph, & Mitchell-Kernan, Claudia. (1993). Marriage and romantic involvement among aged African-Americans. *Journal of Gerontology, 48*(3), S123-S132.

This article reports on findings from the first nationally

representative cross-sectional survey of the adult (ages 18 and older) black population living in the continental United States. The present analyses was based on the 581 respondents ages 55 and older when interviewed. The study examined the extent and structural correlates of marriage, romantic, and preference for romantic involvement. The three dependent variables used in the analyses measure were the probability of being married, having a main romantic relationship, and desiring a main romantic relationship. Independent variables included gender, age, education, personal income, urban versus rural residence, geographic region of residence, health disability, and, for unmarried subjects, marital status (i.e., divorced, separated, widowed, never married). Data were analyzed using logistic regression analyses. Results revealed that 4 out of every 10 respondents were married. Among the unmarried 16.5%, reported having a main romantic relationship. Of those who had no main romantic relationship, 17.3% indicated that they would like one. Analyses revealed significant gender differences. Men were significantly more likely than women to be married, in a romantic relationship, or desirous of a romantic relationship. Age was also significantly related to all three dependent variables. Older respondents were less likely than their younger counterparts to be married, romantically involved, and desirous of a romantic involvement. Younger people and those living in urban areas were much more likely to be married than were older people or those living in rural areas. There was a significant interaction between gender and income. Among women, there was a significant negative association between personal income and the probability of being married; whereas, men with higher incomes were more likely to be married. Being romantically involved was associated with being younger and male. Unattached men and younger people were also more likely to desire a romantic relationship. Results also revealed a dramatic decline in the proportion of women who are married after age 74, which reflects male mortality. Older women were disinclined to get romantically involved, which could be due to lack of available partners or genuine disinterest. The authors point out that "the declining rates of marriage among future cohorts of older blacks in general, and older black women in particular, have financial implications." Married couples had a lower incidence of poverty and higher incomes than their non-married counterparts.

155   Turner, Barbara F. (December, 1979). The self-concepts of older women. *Research on Aging, 1*(4), 464-480.

In this article the author discusses the self-concepts of older women that are influenced by gender and age. The four most commonly studied dimensions of self-concepts are self-esteem, internal control, age identification, and the content of self-concepts, or identity. Cultural prescriptions for "femininity" have a significant effect upon the four dimensions throughout a woman's life. The author concludes that women in late middle age appear to derive benefits, in enhanced self-esteem, from shifts toward a more "masculine" and less "feminine" self-concept.

156   Wasow, Mona, & Loeb, Martin B. (February, 1979). Sexuality in nursing homes. *Journal of the American Geriatrics Society, 27*(2), 73-79.

The authors investigated sexuality among the elderly in nursing homes. Subjects were 27 men and 36 women ages 65 to 85 and older who were residents of Wisconsin nursing homes. A recently designed questionnaire-based interview was used in this study. When asked if a person their age should have sex, 39% of men and 53% of women said, "No." Asked if old people should be allowed sex, 81% of men and 75% of women said, "Yes." When asked if sex was different for men and women, more of the men (50%) than of the women (30%) agreed but almost 39% of women said they did not know. In response to the question, why women want sex, the most common responses were: viewed sex as love (17%), because it's natural (35%), and I don't know (35%). In response to the question, why men want sex, the most common responses were: it is natural (50%), and it is their marital duty (28%). The most common response of the men was: because it is natural (73%). The researchers asked residents what they thought about masturbation. Half of men thought it was natural or okay. Over 60% of women viewed it in a negative light. The authors concluded that most elderly adults lack the opportunity to have sex and this reality was reflected their answers to the interview questions. They also found that most of the subjects admitted having sexual thoughts and feelings on a semi-regular basis. Medical and behavioral personnel showed great reluctance to discuss the subject. The authors concluded that people living in nursing homes who desire appropriate sexual activity should be able to and that this opportunity would improve their quality of life.

157   Wiley, Diana, & Bortz, Walter M., II. (May, 1996). Sexuality and
       aging—Usual and successful. *Journal of Gerontology, 51A(3)*,
       M142-M146.
       This study investigated sexual expression of men and
       women attending an instructional program on aging and
       sexuality. Participants (N = 158) completed a survey questionnaire
       which asked them to report their frequency of sexual activity 10
       years ago, currently and desired. They also asked about their
       preferred form of sexual activity 10 years ago and currently.
       Subjects were asked about their feelings about decreased sexual
       frequency. The males were asked to identify their ease of erection
       as compared with 10 years previous and their comfort level.
       Researchers mailed a follow-up questionnaire 6 months following
       the initial lecture and received a response from 118 participants.
       The mean age of subjects was 68.3 for males and 64.0 for females.
       Researchers found a high current desire for sex for both men and
       women although they did not report having sexual activity as
       often as they desired. Males reported having more problems with
       erections than they had had 10 years previously. The authors
       recommend an increased attention to the potency issue if sexuality
       is to be maintained in robust form in older people. The follow-up
       questionnaire showed no real change in sexual behaviors but a
       substantial expression of increased knowledge, confidence, and
       sensitivity. Desire for intercourse and masturbation were also
       reported to be increased at the follow-up interval.

158   Winn, Rhonda L., & Newton, Niles. (August, 1982). Sexuality
       and aging: A study of 106 cultures. *Archives of Sexual Behavior,*
       11(4), 283-298.
       This article reports the results of one of the few cross-cultural
       studies of sexuality and aging. Winn and Newton researched the
       293 cultures available using the Human Relations Area Files,
       which codify information from cultural studies of primarily
       preindustrial and traditional societies all over the world. Infor-
       mation was found for 106 cultures of 36% of the cultures in the
       files. The files contained data on continued sexual activity in
       males; continued sexual activities in older females; reduction in
       inhibitory mechanisms in older individuals; and factors that
       appear to inhibit sexual behavior in older people. Results of this
       ethnographic study revealed continued sexual activity in older
       males and females in most (77%) of the cultures for which
       information was available. Half of the reports of sexual decline in
       females was found in the context of a discussion of a change in

aged females' role as procreants. Associated with continued sexual activity older people was a finding that in 22% of the societies older adults, especially women, tended to become less inhibited in regard to conversations related to sexuality, sexual humor, and sexually tinged gestures. Factors identified, which inhibited sexual activity in the aged were cultural ensure of activity in this age group, and tendencies by young people to view the old as sexually undesirable. Many reports of older men having sexual relations with and/or marrying much younger girls were found in the files.

8

Effects of Aging on Sexuality

The books and articles in this chapter discuss the effects of aging on sexuality. This topic encompasses characteristics and functions of sexual organs, sexual behavior, and sexual desire. Much of the most important work in this area is included with major studies, Chapter 1 of this book. This chapter does not include articles that focus on sexual dysfunction or sexual practices of the elderly.

Aging does cause physiological changes for both men and women that affect sexual behavior and sexual desire. Many of the articles in this chapter summarize what is known about the effects of aging on sexuality and were written by nurses, physicians, and researchers for other medical professionals.

The research articles included in this chapter have examined general effects of aging that relate to sexuality. In most cases the subjects underwent physical examinations but in some projects the researchers relied on self-reports. Much attention is given to changes in hormone levels. Changes in sexual performance and changes in sexual needs associated with aging are discussed or investigated.

The study populations are often patients in a clinic but some study groups are found in other places such as organizations whose members consist primarily of older people such as the Foster Grandparent Program.

159   Butler, Robert N. (February, 1963). The facade of chronological age: An interpretative summary. *American Journal of Psychiatry, 119*(8), 721-728.

The purpose of this article is to examine and interpret a large project on human aging. The research examined the physiological and physical parameters of older men and a control group of younger men. Subjects included 47 male volunteers ages 65 to 91 (mean = 71) who lived in a home they owned. The researchers split the sample into two groups by medical standards. The first group consisted of 27 men in optimal health without any evidence of diseases. The second group consisted of 20 men in good health but with evidence of disease. These subjects completed a 2-week stay at the Clinical Center in Bethesda, Maryland and completed a series of investigations following a routine schedule. Each subject went through 23 medical tests that included questionnaires and medical equipment such as an EKG. The researchers also conducted three psychological interviews per subject. The project obtained a massive amount of data that were compared to the control group to determine if any differences could be attributed to human aging. The results showed that in most subjects the data collected differed slightly from those of the control group. When data did differ it resulted from lower hormones or from a disease. The researcher concluded that many previous notions of aging affecting the health of a person as a sole exhibitor of aging is incorrect. He said that many factors control aging in humans from mental health to social-cultural effects and there is a need to discover how these aging effects of humans can be controlled.

160   Butler, Robert N., & Lewis, Myrna I. (1976). *Sex after sixty: A guide for men and women for their later years.* NY: Harper & Row.

This monograph addresses later-life sexuality. The writers report that older people can continue having orgasms well into their 80s. Postmenopausal changes can be treated by regular sexual activity, hormone replacement therapy, home remedies (lubricants such as K-Y jelly), cleanliness, hygiene, or douching. The authors state that older men take longer to obtain an erection, it may not be quite as large, straight or hard, and their orgasms are less explosive. They discuss all of the common medical problems that affect sexual expression including heart disease, strokes, diabetes, arthritis, anemia, backache, hernia or rupture, Parkinson's disease, chronic prostatitis (enlarged prostate gland), stress incontinence, excessively enlarged vagina, Peyronie's disease (bowing of the penis), and impotence based on physical causes. They discuss surgery that affects sexual activity such as hysterectomy, mastectomy, prostatectomy, orchidectomy (removal of the testes), colostomy and ileostomy (removal of sections of the intestine). They discuss side effects of drugs on sex. The authors comment that most people do not realize that alcohol is a drug and that it is a depressant, not a stimulant which in large amounts usually interferes with sexual performance by reducing potency in males and orgasmic ability in females and creating drowsiness. The excessive use of alcohol is a frequent and too little recognized factor in sexual problems of the old. The authors recommend that people remember that tolerance for alcohol increases with age because of changing kidney excretory power. They identify common emotional problems with sex such as: fear of sexual impotence, emotional and physical fatigue, effect of unresponsive sexual partner, and for women, lack of a partner. Of the 11 million women over 65, 6 million are widows, 1.2 million are divorced or single, and 7% have never married. The authors also discuss widowhood and grief, sexual guilt, and shame of older people who are still interested in sex. To maintain a sexual experience, the authors recommend keeping fit through exercise, brisk walking, and aerobic and flexibility exercise. They recommend exercise for trouble spots, such as sagging chin, potbelly, back muscles, flabby thighs, sagging breasts, weakened pelvic muscles. They also recommend good nutrition, following a healthy diet, going easy on salt, increasing fiber or bulk in the diet, avoiding laxatives, not eating fried foods, taking Vitamin E, and getting enough rest.

161 Campbell, Janis M., & Huff, Marlene S. (1995). Sexuality in the older woman. *Gerontology & Geriatrics Education, 16*(1), 71-81.

This article begins with a review of the concepts of gender identity, age, and sexuality, and how these concepts relate to the older woman. Several major concepts are identified. Gender norms and roles are superimposed on age role expectations. Society attributes different emotional states to males and females. Older women often receive stereotypical negative reactions from societal members. The second part of the article is an analysis of a sample of older women's perceptions of their gender identify. The data were collected in order to identify depression in older adults living in the community. Subjects were 80 women ages 64 to 82 living independently in the community who had self-expressed good physical health. Of those, 50 women worked part time in the Foster Grandparent Program (FGP). These women expressed gender identity by being concerned about personal appearance, physical fitness, energy level, and having a nutritionally sound diet. They were interested in make-up, clothes, wigs, and physical appearance. The authors analyzed their attitudes toward their sex roles and the effects of jobs and other variables on their attitudes. They also discussed the relationship between gender issues and sexual expression. They concluded that many women adapt to new role expectations as they age and fulfill gender feelings through sexual expression in addition to other venues. Health care professionals need to consider gender issues in their work. Copies of this article are available from the Haworth Document Delivery Service 1-800-342-9678.

162   Comfort, Alex. (October, 1974). Sexuality in old age. *Journal of the American Geriatrics Society, 22*(10), 440-442.

The author expresses the viewpoint that while aging brings about some changes in human sexual performance, these changes are functionally minimal. In the absence of disease, sexual requirement and capacity continue throughout the life span. He says that the elderly have been "hocused out of continuing sexual activity" by society and their well-meaning relatives. Comfort believes that geriatricians need to support and encourage the sexuality of the old to the extent possible and to the extent patients are willing.

163   Griggs, Winona. (August, 1978). Sex and the elderly. *American Journal of Nursing, 78*(8), 1352-1354.

Sexual needs and interests continue into the later years of an individual's life and deserve respect and accommodation if nurses are to provide "total care" for the older person. Nurses need to be open to sexual behavior and activity to help understand their sexual needs. The article first discussed the affects of aging on an individual including loss or lack of hormones and cellular disability and slower replacement and how these factors affect sexual organs. The author also discussed the impact of illness on sex. Illnesses can cause the partners to discontinue all sexual activity or they may only cause problems with sexual activities. Both problems can be alleviated to some degree. The author provides suggested ways that nurses can learn to overcome these difficulties and provide "total care" for the elderly. The main suggestion is for nursing programs to include more sexuality courses and elderly sexuality courses.

164   Hobson, Karen Green. (1984). The effects of aging on sexuality. *Health and Social Work, 9*(1), 25-35.

     The author discusses the effects of aging on elderly sexuality and the social worker's role in providing sex education and support for their older clients. Because aging does cause physiological changes for both men and women which affect sexual performance, the professionals can provide education about adjustments in sexual behavior to improve the performance of their clients. Other problems, such as illness, lack of a partner, and living in a nursing facility can impede sexuality among elderly people. The author suggests that sexual adjustment in aging is related to a change of focus from the traditional emphasis on physical ability and pleasure to an emphasis on the emotional gratification of sexual behavior.

165   Horn, Jack C., & Meer, Jeff. (May, 1987). The vintage years. *Psychology Today, 21*(5), 76-90.

     This article points out the changing activities and attitudes of elderly people. The authors cite three major changes in the way people view the years after 65. First, the financial, physical, and mental health of older people have improved so they no longer fear old age. Second, the population of older people has risen from 18 million in 1965 to 28 million in 1987. Third, researchers understand aging better and have found that aging itself does not erode physical and mental abilities to the extent formerly thought. Better medical care, improved diet, and increased interest in physical fitness have allowed more people to reach 75 in good health. The authors point out the increasing political power of older people, a higher percentage of whom register and vote than any other group. They cite the growing number of studies on aging supported by the National Institute on Aging (NIA), the federal support exhibited by the White House Conferences on Aging, the benefits of Medicare and the Older Americans Act. Knowledge on aging has surged between 1971 and 1985. The authors refute the popular misconception that aging is associated with physical and sexual failure. They point out that changing times affect sexual activity and that the level of sexual activity among older people may rise. They also point out the differences between primary aging effects (slower reflexes, hearing and eyesight loss, decreased stamina) and secondary aging effects (results of disease, abuse, and disuse). The authors discuss the key to life satisfaction in old age which depends as much on money as on time spent doing things that seem meaningful. This article includes the *Alzheimer's Quiz* developed by Neal B. Cutler of the Andrus Gerontology Center. The authors conclude with a discussion of ageism and age biases evidenced by lack of job security and mandatory retirement. No reference list is included.

166   Kaplan, Helen S., & Sager, Clifford J. (June, 1971). **Sexual patterns at different ages.** *Medical Aspects of Human Sexuality,* 5(6), 10, 14-16, 19, 23.

In this paper, the authors, both medical doctors, discuss age-related changes in sexual functioning of men and women and some of the clinical and theoretical implications of these data. Men are intensely sexual during youth, reach their peak at 18, and decline thereafter; while women are by comparison not as intensely sexually oriented during youth but slowly become so and reach their erotic peak in middle age, declining only slowly thereafter. The explanation for these differences is a complex set of physical, psychological, and ecological determinants. They speculate that in males, the physical determinants of sex are relatively more important than in females. The authors examine clinical implications of their findings.

167   Mulligan, Thomas, Retchin, Sheldon M., Chinchilli, Vernon M., & Bettinger, Cynthia B. (June, 1988). **The role of aging and chronic disease in sexual dysfunction.** *Journal of the American Geriatrics Society,* 36(6), 520-524.

The authors investigated the connection between sexual dysfunction and age or comorbid disease. The researchers surveyed two groups of elderly male veterans (N = 225) in a geriatric ambulatory care clinic: ages 65 to 75 years ("young-old") and ages 75 and over ("old-old"). The researchers compared the responses of the study group to another group from a general medical clinic for unstable medical patients ages 65 and under ("old-young") for comparison. The subjects completed a health and sexual function questionnaire. The researchers reported absent libido in 30% of old-young, 31% of young-old, and 47% of old-old. Erectile dysfunction was reported in 26% of old-young, 27% of young-old, and 50% of old-old. They used ordinal logistic regression and found overall sexual dysfunction to be significantly related to subjective poor health, diabetes mellitus, and incontinence while controlling for age. These data suggested that, although sexual dysfunction is more common in the aged, it is often related more to comorbid illness than aging alone.

168   Myers, Wayne A. (October, 1985). Sexuality in the older individual. *Journal of the American Academy of Psychoanalysis,* *13*(4), 511-520.

In this article, a psychiatrist explores the issue of elderly sexuality. In his view, society, especially younger people, prevents older people from being as happy as they could be. He makes reference to demographic and social factors affecting older people and presents his findings from a survey of the psychoanalytic literature on the subject of sexuality in the older patient. He also offers clinical material from his own work with older patients. This article discusses sexuality in the elderly from a psychoanalytic perspective. Case studies of older people in therapy who are dealing with sexual dysfunction are included.

169   National Institute on Aging. (1994). *Age Page: Sexuality in later life.* Author.

This publication from the National Institute on Aging states that most older people want and are able to enjoy an active, satisfying sex life. Over time, however, a slowing of sexual response is normal. Normal changes with aging in women and men are briefly listed. Illnesses or disabilities which may affect the ability to have a satisfying sex life are discussed including heart disease, diabetes, stroke, and arthritis. Types of surgery that may impact on sexual enjoyment are also described including hysterectomy, mastectomy, and prostatectomy. Other issues related to sexuality which are briefly discussed in this pamphlet are alcohol, medicines, masturbation, and AIDS. Emotional concerns are also addressed.

170   Neugarten, Bernice L. (December, 1973). Patterns of aging: Past, present, and future. *Social Service Review,* *47*(4), 571-580.

This article examined changes in people's awareness and imagery related to old age. In the past, negative stereotypes of old age were strongly entrenched in a society that prided itself on being youth-oriented, future-oriented, and oriented toward doing rather than being. The present brought images of diversity by age category. Many people are living longer so there is more time for being instead of doing. The author concluded that the future can bring many things and if scientists are right and man's life is being extended the political, economic, social, and ethical problems for the society at large will become enormous for both the young and the old.

171   **Pfeiffer, Eric. (November, 1974). Sexuality in the aging individual.** *Journal of the American Geriatrics Society,* **22(11), 481-484.**

This article was a paper presented by the author as part of the Symposium on Sexuality in the Aging Individual, at the 31st Annual Meeting of the American Geriatric Society in 1974. Among the key points in the article, Pfeiffer says that for too long aging people were thought not to have sexual feelings and certainly not to have an active sex life. He stresses that physicians need to understand that aging patients retain the right to sexual expression and to obtain counsel from doctors. He provides information related to physiology, psychology, and sociology that physicians need to know. (Pfeiffer mentions that William Masters is also on the panel and will be speaking on the physiology of sexual expression in the later years.) Pfeiffer concludes his speech by offering implications for practice. He believes that physicians should encourage and aid their patients in expressing sexuality. He points out that sexual expression requires privacy and that many older people do not have it, whether living with adult relatives or in institutions. He says that because many older people do not have partners that "there must be great acceptance by physicians of solitary sexual expression, and this acceptance should be conveyed to patients and to other caregivers as well as to family members." He also says that remarriage can be emotionally, socially and economically satisfying in addition to extending the likelihood of survival of both participants.

172   **Renshaw, Domeena C. (September, 1985). Sex, age, and values.** *Journal of the American Geriatrics Society, 33(9),* **635-643.**

This article discusses the relationship of sexuality to age and values among the elderly. The author describes sexual changes which are expected after age 50, many of which can be overcome by counseling or changes in sexual practices. Surgery such as hysterectomy or hemorrhoid removal can cause anxiety about sexual performance. Specific medical problems such as arthritis, alcoholism, cardiac disease and stroke, diabetes, malignancy, drug interactions, genital and bladder problems, and clinical depression also have an impact on the sexual behavior of the elderly. The author suggests that physicians take a routine sexual history of their patients, and recommends ways that they can provide basic sex therapy to encourage and improve their older patients' sexual functioning.

173   Schiavi, Raul C., & Rehman, Jamil. (November, 1995). Sexuality and aging. *Urology Clinics of North America*, 22(4), 711-726.

The objective of this investigation was to gather within a cross-sectional framework, behavioral, hormonal, and psycho-biological data in healthy men ages 45 to 74 living in stable sexual relationships. Seventy-seven couples underwent an extensive interview. Male subjects received a comprehensive medical and urological evaluation, completed a battery of medical and psychological tests, and were studied in a sleep laboratory for 4 nights. They found that age was significantly and negatively correlated with sexual desire, sexual arousal, and sexual activities but there were no age differences in degree of satisfaction with the men's own sexual functioning or enjoyment of marital sexuality. Aging was related to increased prevalence of erectile difficulty and retarded ejaculation. Sexual interest, responsive-ness, and activity continued to be observed even in some of the oldest subjects. All partners were interviewed to cross-validate sexual and relationship information. The authors also assessed nocturnal penile tumescence and found a high proportion of subjects above age 65 failed to show evidence of full sleep erections even though they and their partners reported having intercourse on a regular basis. Aging was negatively correlated with testosterone. Other hormone changes associated with aging were discussed. Relationships between age and sleep disorders were found. They also found the men continued to have satisfying sexual experiences. The authors state that any illness associated with weakness, a febrile state, or pain is likely to have an effect on sexual function. They discuss specific effects of cardiovascular disease, post-prostatectomy impotence, diabetes, cancer, and effects of medications on sexual functioning. Several detailed charts and a length reference list are included. The article begins with a comprehensive literature review in which the authors discuss the sexual responses in the aging male, the physiologic aspects of aging male sexuality, psychological aspects of aging and sexuality, studies on aging male sexuality asexuality, studies on aging male sexuality, a psychobiological investigation of healthy aging men, medical causes of erectile dysfunction in elderly men, and the effect of medications on the sexual functioning of aging men.

174   Schiavi, Raul C., Schreiner-Engel, Patricia, Mandeli, John, Schanzer, Harry, & Cohen, Elliot. (June, 1990). Healthy aging and male sexual function. *American Journal of Psychiatry, 147*(6), 766-771.

This study investigated age-related variations in sexual and nocturnal penile tumescence dimensions and assessed the associations between them in healthy older men in stable sexual relationships. The researchers used 65 couples, males ages 45 to 74, to collect data. Each couple was interviewed together then separately to provide psychosexual, psychiatric, and marital information. Both completed the *Locke-Wallace Test and Dyadic Adjustment Scale* to assess marital adjustment. The males also completed the *Michigan Alcoholism Screening Test* (MAST) and the *Mini-Mental State Examination*. Sleep patterns of the males were studied from four nights in a sleep laboratory. The data suggested a significant negative relation between age and sexual desire, arousal, and activity and an increasing prevalence of sexual dysfunction with age but no age difference in sexual enjoyment and satisfaction. They did find significant age-related decreases in frequency, duration, and degree of nocturnal penile tumescence found. Sexual desire, arousal, coital frequency, and prevalence of erectile problems correlated with nocturnal penile tumescence measures. The authors discussed the relevance of these findings in the understanding of sexual function in aging men.

175   Solnick, Robert L., & Birren, James E. (February, 1977). Age and male erectile responsiveness and sexual behavior. *Archives of Sexual Behavior, 6*(1), 1-9.

The purpose of the study was to determine the difference in the rate of penile circumference increase per unit time between a group of young and a group of old normal males when exposed to the same erotic movie, and the correlation coefficient between penile shaft temperature increase and penile circumference increase. The researchers attempted to replicate the erection response time findings of a 1966 Masters and Johnson study under conditions which would yield data representation of a broader male population. Subjects were 20 male volunteers who were divided into a young (ages 19 to 30) and an old (ages 48 to 65) group. There was no significant difference in the mean, flaccid penile circumference between young and old groups. Younger males responded at an erection rate 5.8 times faster than the older men.

176 Stanford, Dennyse. (April, 1977). All about sex . . . after middle age. *American Journal of Nursing,* 77(4), 608-611.

The purpose of this article was to provide information about elderly sexuality to health professionals whom the author believes are in an ideal position to counsel the elderly. She notes the lack of literature on sexuality of the aged on the prevailing negative attitudes of society. In her view, negative attitudes can be attributed to the idea that sexual activity was condoned for reproductive purposes only and that sexual enjoyment was considered selfish and sinful. The author summarizes major findings of Masters and Johnson regarding elderly sexuality. Key points are: (1) the female experiences little sexual impairment as she ages; (2) older men are usually able to continue some form of active sex life until their 70s and 80s; (3) men experience a slight, gradual decline in sexual desire as they age; (4) reasons for a loss of sexual responsiveness a number of common problems of the elderly such as: boredom, mental or physical fatigue, pre-occupation with business interests, overindulgence in food or drink, fear of failure, and physical illness such as diabetes and hypertension. The author suggests that health professionals include an assessment of present sexual function in the person's medical history, include both partners in counseling sessions, and explain aging differences to clients. The article includes a table listing changes with age in sexual response patterns between younger and older men and women.

177 Steinke, Elaine E., & Bergen, M. Betsy. (June, 1986). Sexuality and aging. *Journal of Gerontological Nursing,* 12(6), 6-10.

The purpose of this literature review was to provide a base for what is known about sexuality and aging today. Elderly people in our society are often stereotyped as being asexual. Research literature demonstrates that the aging individual is a sexual being. Nurses often hold the same stereotypes as the rest of society, and should therefore examine their own beliefs and attitudes about sexuality in the elderly. The topic of sexuality in the aging should include both physiologic and psychosocial per-spectives. Consideration of nutrition, fitness, rest, and personal appearance are important to maintaining a positive self-image. Encouraging these in the elderly can improve sexual attractiveness and desire.

178 Thienhaus, Ole J. (August, 1988). Practical overview of sexual function and advancing age. *Geriatrics,* 43(8), 63-67.

The purpose of this article is to explain sexual adaptations and changes associated with aging to physicians in order to help them relieve needless distress and dysfunction in their older patients. Thienhaus, a medical doctor, explains physiological changes associated with aging: vaginal atrophy, orgasm, erection, and ejaculation and recommends counseling couples. He also discusses psychosocial factors: lack of a partner, biases against masturbation and homosexuality, societal views of sex, and gender disparity. He describes organic causes of sexual dysfunction: physical illness, medications, effects of other illnesses, psychological complications associated with physical problems and recommends counseling. Emphasis throughout any counseling sessions must be placed on the potential for mutual sexual fulfillment that older partners can continue to provide. He recommends that primary care physicians play a role in helping to maintain that sexual fulfillment.

179   Traupmann, Jane. (1984). Does sexuality fade over time? A look at the question and the answer. *Journal of Geriatric Psychiatry, 17*(2), 149-159.

This article investigates the question "Does sexuality fade over time?" The author cites the conclusions drawn by Kinsey, the Duke University Aging Studies, and Brecher's analysis of the Consumer Union data as evidence that there is a declining sexuality in the later years. In this paper the author explores the bases for the popular view among both professionals and lay persons that sexuality declines in the later years. She draws upon the reports from the Duke University longitudinal study of aging and *Love, Sex, and Aging* by Brecher and the editors of Consumers Union. Her goal is to take a critical view at the arguments. Traupmann questions the conclusions drawn by Kinsey, the authors of the original Duke University Studies and Brecher. She points out that the studies compared subjects from generations in which people were more repressed sexually and lacked information available to present generation. She also points out that loss of partner through illness, death or divorce is ignored in these analyses. Masters and Johnson, she says, concluded that previous levels of sexual activity were the best predictors of late life sexual activity. Traupmann concludes that education of the elderly regarding sexuality could have a major effect on the scientific theory that predicts sexual decline is a normal part of aging.

180   Troll, Lillian E., & Parron, Eugenia M. (1981). Age changes in sex roles amid changing sex roles: The double shift. *Annual Review of Gerontology and Geriatrics, 2,* 118-143.

This essay is a review of existing literature on sex-role differences. It addresses the following questions: Do individuals really experience sex-role changes during their adult years? Are any sex-role behaviors lost or added at some point in aging? If there are sex-role transformations or reorganizations in midlife what causes them? What would be the consequences in coping or mental health for later life? This article includes a discussion of background issues involving economics, biology, and socialization. Economics issues affecting sex-roles are: the increased number of employed women; the decreased number of men continuing to work as they get older; and the financial abandonment of women, the displaced homemaker. Biology issues affecting sex-roles are: comparative longevity of women as compared to men, decreased vigor of men as they age and decreased attractiveness of women as they age. Socialization issues include: effect of early socialization, effect of socialization over time, and effect of changes in social theory on individuals as they age. In the light of those background issues, the authors address their four fundamental questions. They conclude that there are developmental sex-role changes during adulthood. They also conclude that sex-role behaviors change during various developmental stages and people may revert to early behaviors in later life. These changes are caused by biological factors, by life events such as marriage, parenting, divorce, widowhood, job and retirement, by societal expectations, by dialectic processes, and reciprocal socialization. The authors discuss the impact of sex role changes in later life which can be positive lead to problems if the other partner is not pleased with the changes.

181   Vermeulen, A. (1979). Decline in sexual activity in ageing men: Correlation with sex hormone levels and testicular changes. *Journal of Biosocial Science, 6*(Supplement), 5-18.

In this review of the literature the author presents evidence related to the decline of male sexuality with age including decline in sexual interest, arousal and activity, capacity for orgasm, slower sexual arousal, less forceful ejaculations, quicker detumescence, decreased vasocongestive increase in testicular size, and reduced psychosexual pleasure. He concludes that there is clear cut evidence that the decrease in sexual activity with age is paralleled by a decrease in androgen secretion both by the testes and by the adrenal cortex. He further concludes that there is no convincing evidence available that sex hormone therapy is useful for males with climacteric complaints.

182   Walbroehl, Gordon S. (March, 1990). Better sex for the older patient. *Medical Aspects of Human Sexuality, 24*(3), 15-16.
        This article is a guide for patients. The author, a medical doctor, contends that sexuality remains an important part of any person's well-being throughout life. He explains normal sexual changes of aging for women and men and as they apply to couples. He explains how various experiences associated with aging affect sexuality such as use of medications, illness, and diabetes. He also discusses dating among elderly who are widowed or divorced. An insert is included explaining the importance of healthy aging life style. He recommends eating right, giving up cigarettes, reducing alcohol intake, and exercising daily.

183   Weg, Ruth B. (1981). Normal aging changes in the reproductive system. In Irene Mortenson Burnside (Ed.), *Nursing and the aged, 2nd ed.* (pp. 362-373). New York: McGraw-Hill Book Company.
        In this chapter, the author discusses the role of sex and sexuality in old age. She points out that the need for intimacy and love continues all through life. She examines sexual changes in the male, both physical and psychological. She then identifies the four stages of intercourse and the progressive changes found in the elderly. The stages are the excitement phase, plateau phase, orgasmic phase, and resolution phase. She identifies in detail the six stages of the climatic period in a woman's life. The author identifies the four stages of intercourse in a woman's life. She also evaluates sexual dysfunction in the elderly. She concludes by discussing implications for the helping professions and gives suggestions on what they can do. She suggests establishing departments of geriatrics in nursing schools, medical schools and hospitals. She recommends evaluating and revising gynecological textbooks to delete myths related to aging men and women. She suggests that sex education be instituted for middle aged and older people. She says that the need for affect and sexual expression outside of intercourse be recognized as essential to being and feeling alive. She also recommends a greater acceptance of alternative life styles and masturbation as an acceptable and necessary means of sexual release and maintenance of genital tissue readiness. Finally she recommends consideration for

replacement-estrogen therapy for women as an alternative to psychotherapy and sedation in the prevention and treatment of emotional and physiological changes of middle and old age.

184 **Whitbourne, Susan Krauss. (Summer, 1990). Sexuality in the aging male.** *Generations, 14*(3), 28-30.

In this article the author examines the effect of aging on the sexuality of males. Men in their late 60s and 70s do not experience a distinct climacteric phase during which they lose reproductive capacity. Instead, they experience a gradual loss of the ability to father children as the quantity of viable sperm becomes reduced. More noticeable to the aging male are a variety of changes in the prostate gland and the rhythmic contractions of which contribute to the sensation of orgasm. Although some studies have reported a decrease in the amount of testosterone produced by the Leydig cells of the testes across age groups of men, these studies appeared to be flawed methodologically. Other studies show that lower testosterone is not an inevitable feature of the aging process. Research has found that older men experience a general slowing down of the progression through the phases of the human sexual response cycle, from excitement through resolution. Older men need to adapt to these normal changes and take a sanguine approach to a slower sexual response. The literature suggests that men's pattern of sexuality in earlier years is the best predictor of their sexuality in old age. Changes in the aging male's sexuality inevitably influence his heterosexual relationships; in a marital relationship spanning many decades, both partners face challenges of adapting to changes in their bodies that ultimately influence their sexual interactions with each other.

9

Sexual Behavior of the Elderly

Researchers investigating sexual behaviors among the elderly offer evidence that sexual behaviors vary among this population in the same way they vary among younger groups. There is sufficient evidence to conclude that while sexual expression may change as people age, the need for such expression, and the acting out of those needs continues among older people as long as the health of the partners permits. The frequency of sexual activity appears to decline with aging for a variety of reasons but primarily because of (for women) a lack of a partner and (for men) poor health. Some writers point out environment restraints on sexual expression, especially lack of privacy.

Recent investigations suggest changing expectations of older people regarding their right to express their sexuality including those older people in long-term care facilities. Research also suggests that definitions of "appropriate" sexual expression of families of the elderly and staff of long-term care facilities may not match those of the elderly themselves. In general staff of long-term care facilities find expression of sexuality among their residents to be unacceptable. Evidence also suggests an increase in sexual and romantic relationships among elderly residents of long-term care facilities. Researchers from Kinsey to the present time have expressed surprise by the extent to which older people continue to engage in sexual activity.

Sexual interest has been investigated by many researchers. While it also appears to decline with aging, elderly people in general maintain an interest in sex throughout their lives.

Most of the studies rely on self-report data. Most have concentrated their investigation on sexual intercourse but some have investigated other types of sexual expression. Variables included in these studies are sexual orientation, types of sexual activities, sexual interest, environmental restraints, and sexual satisfaction. Demographic variables in study designs include age, household income, race, education, gender and others. People have studied the relationships between medical, emotional and social factors and sexual function. They have investigated changes in arousal rates and frequency of sexual activity.

Many of the studies listed in Chapter 1 also include information about sexual behavior.

185   **Adams, Catherine G., & Turner, Barbara F. (May, 1985). Reported change in sexuality from young adulthood to old age. *The Journal of Sex Research*, 21(2), 126-141.**

In this comprehensive study the authors examined changes in qualitative and quantitative aspects of sexuality reported by people ages 60 and over from young adulthood to old age. Subjects (62 women and 40 men) completed a questionnaire. Five respondents were also interviewed. The majority of respondents (78% of men and 61% of women) were currently married. From a list of seven sexual activities, respondents were asked to check those in which they participated at the present time and between ages 20 to 30. Sexual activities listed were: daydream, dream, pet, masturbate, intercourse, homosexual, and other. Frequency of predominant activity was rated on a 5-point scale from always to never. With few exceptions self-reported occurrence of each of the seven types of sexual activity tended to decline from the respondents' 20s to the present. The reported declines were statistically significant only for nocturnal dreams among men and for heterosexual intercourse among women. None of the men in this sample reported homosexual activities. The reported occurrence of masturbation among women increased significantly over time. Reports of masturbation in old age were more common among the unmarried for both men and women. The authors report detailed results from their complex statistical analyses.

186   **Bachmann, Gloria A., & Leiblum, S. R. (1991). Sexuality in sexagenarian women. *Maturitas*, 13(1), 43-50.**

The authors examined sexual interest and behavior of 59 healthy sexagenarian women (ages 60 to 70, mean age = 63.9) not on estrogen replacement therapy or other medication known to affect sexual function. They studied coital activity and sexual desire in women with partners, the type and prevalence of sexual complaints in couples, the relationship between gonadal hormones and sexual expression, and the impact of coital activity on genital health. The women had an individual psychological interview to assess the presence and frequency of dyspareunia, anorgasmia, and arousal problems. They completed a *Locke-Wallace Test of Marital Adjustment* and a detailed questionnaire assessing medical, gynecological and sexual history. They also had a gynecological examination. Sexual desire was assessed by interviews. Partners of the subjects completed a mail-back questionnaire. Subjects were divided into two groups: coitally active women reported a mean frequency of five coital encounters monthly; the others were classified as inactive or abstinent. On almost all sexual parameters, the active group reported greater satisfaction than the inactive group. Hormone levels were not related to coital frequency, sexual arousal, dyspareunia, touch aversion, or genital health. Active women had less genital atrophy than inactive women. For the entire group, they reported 51% of their partners had decreased sexual interest, 49% had difficulty achieving an erection, and 44% had difficulty maintaining an erection. Males partners complained of lack of privacy (12%) and boredom with partner (3%). The authors concluded that there are widespread sexual problems in both men and women but that the majority of couples continue to be sexually interested and coitally active. They found a lessening of sexual interest for men and women after age 50. The women reported a reduction in sexual desire following menopause. The authors provide a lengthy discussion of the role hormones play in sexual interest for women. They recommend that physicians should encourage couples to communicate their sexual needs and problems to their partner and educating them regarding changes that occur with aging.

187   Barton, David. (February, 1972). **Sexually deprived individuals.** *Medical Aspects of Human Sexuality, 6*(2), 88, 92-97.

The author examined the impact of sexual deprivation on certain individuals. He examined case studies in several different fields that involve the loss or neglect of sexual activities. Denial of sexual expression through illness, injury, death of loved one, environmental restraint (such as a prison), and abstinence through choice are all included in this study. The author suggested that with the avoidance of medical personnel as well as patients this topic is not well understood. He discussed several reasons for avoiding the topic, but the key reason seems to be physicians imposing their own value system on patients. The author concluded that this puts the patients in a difficult position usually forcing them to not seek help; the deprivation of sexual activity continues.

188   Bell, Robert R., & Bell, Phyllis L. (December, 1972). **Sexual satisfaction among married women.** *Medical Aspects of Human Sexuality, 6*(12), 136, 141-144.

The authors investigated sexual satisfaction among married women by a self-report questionnaire. Respondents included 2,372 married women from various parts of the United States. Age ranges were 26 to 30, 31 to 40, 41 to 50, and 50 and older. The researchers chose 75 women from the rosters of the National Council of Family Relations and the Family Section of the American Sociological Society. These women distributed the questionnaire to other women. This population had a bias towards higher education. The authors reported that a large number of the women have a high level of satisfaction from sexual encounters. They also discussed that a lack or excess of sexual satisfaction in one area can affect other areas in the questionnaire. The authors concluded that a general sexual satisfaction or dissatisfaction is usually a result of various interrelated activities both sexually and socially.

189   Bretschneider, Judy G., & McCoy, Norma L. (April, 1988). **Sexual interest and behavior in healthy 80- to 102-year olds.** *Archives of Sexual Behavior, 17*(2), 109-129.

The study investigated the sexual interest and behavior to determine a complete picture of sexuality throughout a subject's life in mentally and physically healthy older men and women subjects over the age of 80. Included in this study were 100 white men and 102 white women subjects aged from 80 to 102 years old. Each subject filled out an anonymous questionnaire about their past and present sexuality experiences. The researchers' results showed that individuals that are healthy and above the age of 80 are just as interested as those under 80. The author discussed older individuals choose touching and caressing without sexual intercourse over personal masturbation over sexual intercourse when it comes to sexual activity. The author suggested that current sexual activity is related directly to past sexual activity for all subjects. A higher sexual activity in youth was also high at an older age. Based on the observed correlation between past and present frequency of sexual behavior, the authors suggested that current physical and social factors play an overriding role in sexual activity.

190   Bulcroft, Kris, & O'Conner-Roden, Margaret. (June, 1986). Never too late. *Psychology Today, 20*(6), 66-69.

This study investigated dating and sexual activity of single people over 65 who are widowed or divorced. The researchers interviewed 45 older people in a midwestern metropolitan area. Researchers interviewed subjects in their homes or a comfortable place. Subjects answered questions that dealt with how they met their partner, what was done on a date, how important sexuality was in their relationship, and how family and friends felt about the person dating. Many of the responses indicated that older people are very interested in being in relationships. They prefer the company of another individual and in some enjoy the romance involved. A typical date for some of the subjects included what most younger people do on dates; such as bowling, going to the movies, and so forth. The authors concluded that the dating relationship is a critical, central part of elders' lives and that it provides something that cannot be supplied by family or friends.

191   Cameron, Paul, & Biber, Henry. (Summer, 1973). Sexual thought throughout the life span. *The Gerontologist, 13*(2), 144-147.

This report presents normative data regarding the frequency of both ephemeral and focal sexual thought throughout the life span. Subjects were 4,420 people ages 8 to 99 who completed a questionnaire or participated in an interview designed to assess the frequency of sexual thoughts. The sample consisted of 82 males and 80 females ages 65 and older. Subjects were asked "What were you thinking about over the past 5 minutes? Did you think about sex or were your thoughts sexually colored—even for a moment (perhaps it crossed your mind)? What was the central focus of your thought over the past 5 minutes?" Cameron and Biber found no systematic variations in sexual thought as a function of marital status or race. Sexual thought varied by age and sex. They found the frequency of both in-passing and focal sexual thought was related to age, reaching a high point in the teenage and young adult years. Males reported significantly more sexual thought than females. Older men and women both reported significantly less sexual thought than young men and women. However 9% of older men and 6% of older women had had a sexual thought in the previous 5 minutes.

192   Catania, Joseph A., & White, Charles B. (April, 1982). Sexuality in an aged sample: Cognitive determinants of masturbation. *Archives of Sexual Behavior, 11*(3), 237-245.

The authors studied the relationship of masturbation to locus of control, sexual status, and sexual knowledge among elderly people. Results indicated that locus of control was the best predictor of masturbation frequency. Older people who perceived an internal locus of control, especially those with more sexual knowledge, masturbated more frequently than those who perceived external control. Older people without sexual partners tended to masturbate more frequently than those with partners. The authors suggest that other variables not included in this study, such as religious beliefs or physiological changes, may also be involved in the frequency of masturbation among this population.

193   Charatan, Fred B. (September, 1978). Sexual function in old age. *Medical Aspects of Human Sexuality, 12*(9), 151, 155, 159, 163-164.

This article discussed the medical, emotional, and social factors that sometimes interfere with sexual function in old age. The author stated that every recent medical study proves conclusively that there is no biological reason why older men and women should not have an active and rewarding sex life. Sex is a major psychological concern in the later years and is intimately linked to the older person's self-esteem. The author goes on to state that one of the advantages of the aging process with specific reference to sexual functioning is that control of ejaculatory demand in the ages 50 to 75 is far better than the ages 20 to 40. While sexual arousal occurs at a slower rate as a person ages, the older male is likely to engage in sexual foreplay for a longer time, giving a greater pleasure to himself and his partner. The author noted that common health problems are known to interfere with sexual functioning. In some cases patients with a heart disease fear dying or having a stroke during sexual activities and stay away from them. This is just one example of many possible concerns on a male's mind to stop him from sexual activities. The most important problem facing males with sexual function is psychological or emotional. An example is some older men are jealous of their partner's ability to perform while he is unable. So a man becomes cautious and watchful of his partner to see what she is up to and to make sure another man does not steal her away from him. The author concluded that as a man ages he should not think of the future as an asexual experience but as a sexual experience that with correct thinking and medical help, he will be able to enjoy some sexual activities.

194   Christenson, Cornelia V., & Gagnon, John H. (1965). Sexual behavior in a group of older women. *Journal of Gerontology, 20*(3), 351-356.

This article examined the impact of sexual behavior in elderly women. The authors also wanted to see if there is a difference between older men and women. The Institute for Sex Research files were used to obtain the subjects for this study. A nonrepresentative sample of 241 white females, ages 50 and older, who had been married comprised the data. Each subject completed an interview on a variety of subjects that involved sexual behavior, sexual anatomy, and sexual experiences. The authors found that elderly women who had living husbands had much more of a sex life than elderly unmarried women. They also found that both groups experienced a substantial decrease in sexual behaviors between ages 50 and 65. The authors concluded that women are different even at older ages than men when it comes to sexual behavior. They also concluded that data such as from this study should serve to aid in making more realistic appraisals of the role of sexuality among the aged.

195   Christenson, Cornelia V., & Johnson, Alan Blaine. (1973). Sexual behavior in a group of older, never-married women. *Journal of Geriatric Psychiatry, 6*(1), 80-98.

This report is based primarily on material collected by Kinsey and his associates during the 15 years prior to his death in 1956. A sample of 71 never-married white women ages 50 and over were interviewed as part of the large program of the Institute for Sex Research which included interviews with over 7,500 women. The majority of the women (85%) were Protestant; 84% had gone to college. Of the entire group of 71, only 10 said they had never wanted to marry. One third (23 of the sample) had never experienced sexual activity beyond simple petting. Of the remaining 48, 79% had masturbated, 62% had had intercourse, 52% had orgasmic sex dreams. Eight subjects had extensive homosexual contacts. None of these women, however, was exclusively homosexual in her orientation. All reported heterosexual experience as well. Data analysis reveals decreased sexual activity as the subjects ages from 45 to 60. As compared to a group of previously married women, they had less sexual activity but both groups showed a decline with age.

196   Clements, Mark. (March 17, 1996). Sex after 65. *The Washington Post, Parade Magazine,* 4-6.

This article reports the results of a survey of Americans ages 65 and older. Subjects were 1,604 men and women ages 65 to 97 (mean = 71). The survey was conducted in April 1995 by the independent firm of the author. The overall sample was selected to conform to the latest available United States. Census data for men and women in that age range representing nine geographic divisions by age, household income and household size and weighted for the latest Census data for age, race, and education. The re-searchers found that about 40% of the men and women surveyed were still sexually interested and active. The seniors had sex an average of 2.5 times a month compared to 7.1 times for the 18 to 65 year olds surveyed by *Parade* in 1994. Both younger and older respondents said they would like to have more sex, ideally 5.1 times a month. At all ages, more men than women said sex is important. Sex was not the priority for the subjects. When asked what mattered most in an intimate relationship, only 5% said "sex." The most common answer (87%) was companionship; 8% said romance. The happiest people in the survey were those who were sexually active. They were more likely to be physically active and to exercise regularly than those who are not sexually active. Almost half (45%) were satisfied with the quality of their sexual activity. Men were less satisfied than women. The subjects (60%) thought they were knowledgeable about sex. The subjects tended to have conservative values. A substantial majority thought extramarital sex, premarital sex, and homosexuality were wrong. About 62% were in a monogamous relationship. The average length of the partnership was 37.7 years. Married respondents were more satisfied with their sexual life than singles. Sexual behaviors included intercourse, hugging, touching their lovers' bodies, and orgasms. Many more women than men do not usually reach orgasm. If they could, older men and women would choose a younger sex partner. Sexual problems increase with age affecting 43% of the subjects. One of the most common causes of sexual problems is medications. A higher percentage of older men than women reported sexual difficulties. The most common male problem was inability to maintain an erection. Among women, problems are low sex drive, difficulty achieving orgasm, and self-consciousness during sex. Due to a fear of AIDS, a small number of older respondents had changed their sexual behavior. Of those who report changing behaviors, the most common behavior for women was to abstain from sex; for men the change was to reduce the number of sex partners.

197 **Cohen-Sachs, Bernice. (1993). Coping with the stress of aging — Creatively.** *Stress Medicine, 9,* **45-49.**

This article offers the author's suggestions on coping with the stress of aging. A medical doctor in her 70s, Cohen-Sachs emphasizes the importance of exercise which she says can be summed up in two words "Keep moving." She also encourages controlling eating and following a well-balanced, nutritious diet. She also believes in the importance of sex and says that regular sexual activity is beneficial to health as well as attitude. She says that impotence is not a natural consequence of aging and cites several examples of older men who had children in their later years. She also says that senility, depression, and loss of cognitive functioning are not inevitable consequences of aging. She advises combating ageism by trying to reduce stress creatively and by keeping cheerful.

198 **Conway-Turner, Katherine. (1992). Sex, intimacy and self-esteem: The case of the African American older women.** *Journal of Women & Aging,* **4(1), 91-104.**

The author studied the relationship between intimacy and self-esteem in older African-American women. Intimacy is viewed as a multifaceted construct consisting of both psychological indicators (such as degree of empathy, affection, and love) and behavioral manifestations (such as kissing, caressing, and sexual intercourse). Participants were 25 married, non-institutionalized black women ages 60 to 93 (mean age = 75.3), who were recruited from senior citizen centers. Two to three hour interviews were conducted with each participant to collect two types of information: structured information on intimacy and self-esteem, measured by the *Caring Relationship Inventory* and the *Culture Free Self-Esteem Scale,* and unstructured information on the women's sexual relations with their partner. The unstructured portions of the interviews were taped and transcribed. Results show that these African-American women were engaged in intimate and sexual relationships with their spouses, with kissing and mutual touching very much a part of this intimacy. Participants were generally open about the quality of their relationships. Intimacy variables denoting a sense of connection or relationship (such as affection, friendship, and empathy) were associated with positive self-esteem for these women. Interestingly, however, higher levels of sexual intercourse were associated with lower levels of self-esteem.

199   Crose, Royda, & Drake, Lisa K. (1993). Older women's sexuality. *Clinical Gerontologist, 12*(4), 51-56.

This article reports results of a study of practices and attitudes about the sexuality of older women. Subjects were ten women ages 61 to 82 recruited from an educational outreach program for healthy, active older people. Subjects were interviewed using a semi-structured interview consisting of open-ended questions in six areas: incidence of sexual activity, interest in sexual activity, frequency of orgasm, feelings of sexual desire, feeling of pleasure with sex, and satisfaction with sex life. The researchers asked them whether each aspect had increased, decreased, or stayed the same. The majority of women felt that their attitudes about sex had become more positive over time. When asked about changes in their sexuality over the years, many noted a decline in the frequency of sex due to the lack of a partner or their partner's failing health. Only one woman reported an increase in incidence of sexual activity; five reported a decrease; and four reported no change. Subjects described a satisfying sexual experience as "having love, not just another body, "displays of affection, a peck on the cheek," "tenderness and consideration, no bam, bam, thank-you ma'am." The authors concluded that older women are ready and eager to talk about their sexuality. They discussed the importance of initiating discussion of sexuality with older clients to probe for a history of sexual abuse, sexual harassment, and other sexual problems or concerns.

200   Davidson, Julian M., Chen, Jeanette J., Crapo, Larry, Gray, Gary D., Greenleaf, Walter J., & Catania, Joseph A. (1983). Hormonal changes and sexual function in aging men. *Journal of Clinical Endocrinology and Metabolism, 57*(1), 71-77.

The authors conducted this study to determine whether age-related changes in circulating pituitary and gonadal hormone levels are related to quantitatively assessed changes in sexuality over the age span. The subjects were 220 men, ages 41 to 93. Men who appeared to be in good health entering a medical center for a blood sample were approached and asked to participate in this study. Each subject completed a questionnaire describing their sexual activity, general medical status, alcohol and drug intake, simple demographic data, and sexual relationships. The data suggested that aging and hormonal changes are more strongly related to sexual activity than social activities. The authors concluded that hormones do not play a key role in age related sexual activity decline but are a factor.

201   de Nigola, Pietro, & Peruzza, Marino. (August, 1974). Sex in the aged. *Journal of the American Geriatrics Society, 22*(8), 380-382.

The authors investigated the connection between healthy aged individuals and good sexual activities and habits. This connection is analyzed by literature and personal observation of subjects. This project utilized 85 individuals (53 males, 32 females) ages 62 to 81. All members of the project had sexual intercourse at least once a month and no more than five times a week. The authors discussed the importance of diseases and of environmental, social, and psychological factors with the impairment of sexual activity in old people. The authors suggested sexual activity in the aged is not exceptional and may give serenity in old people. They concluded that medical, social, and psychological prophylactic counseling should be applied as early as possible by geriatricians in collaboration with sexologists.

202   Dean, Stanley R. (July, 1974). Geriatric sexuality: Normal, needed, and neglected. *Geriatrics, 29*, 134-137.

This article examined the problems elderly people have with sexuality. The author discusses elderly taboos, an elderly decline in sexuality, generational differences, and living arrangements, all of which need to be reexamined by society. The largest problem in dealing with geriatric sexuality is the many taboos against sex in older people. People believe that elderly sex is immoral and wrong but Dean states that "if it works—and harms no one—it is right and proper." Dean goes on to say as the body ages it is unable to do all activities it used to do, including sexual activity. He discusses ways the elderly can help alleviate sexual problems by using different sexual positions and by education on sexuality. Another misunderstood aspect of the elderly is their ability to have relationships. Dean stated that it should be of no surprise when elderly people become involved in romantic entanglements. The last topic in this article is "Living in sin—or dignity." He cites a report in the *Miami News* that thousands of elderly people were living together without marriage because getting married would mean losing pensions and Social Security benefits. The author concluded that aging is regarded as a demon that heralds approaching death, whereas sex is equated with life. This is why sexuality is significant for an older person's morale.

203   **Diokno, Ananias C., Brown, Morton B., & Herzog, A. Regula. (January, 1990). Sexual function in the elderly. *Archives of Internal Medicine, 150*(1), 197-200.**
         The authors studied the sexual behavior among the elderly living in the community. Individuals living in Washtenaw County, Michigan ages 60 and older and living in non-care households were included in this study. A total of 1,956 individuals volunteered to complete the survey. Each individual had a 40-minute interview in their home. Then a selection from the total completed a clinical evaluation consisting of a complete physical examination, a urine analysis, and another 40-minute interview. The researchers found that the estimated proportions of individuals who are sexually active were 73.8% for married men and 55.8% for married women; among unmarried men and women the proportions are 31.1% and 5.3%, respectively. The authors found that the levels of sexual activity decreased significantly with age in both genders. They found that impotency was highly prevalent in elderly men, 40% of their subjects. The researchers concluded that the prevalence of impotency was significantly associated with a history of heart attacks, urinary incontinence, and the use of sedatives. They found that urinary incontinence and interrupted urinary stream were highly correlated with impotency. This study was supported by a grant from the National Institute on Aging.

204   **Downey, Lois. (August, 1980). Intergenerational change in sex behavior: A belated look at Kinsey's males. *Archives of Sexual Behavior, 9*(4), 267-317.**
         This report is an analysis of the data collected for the original Kinsey investigation. The author compares five generations of male respondents in terms of total frequency of sexual activity, and frequency and incidence on nine specific categories of sexual behavior. Downey found that men of five birth decades differed significantly in their sexual behavior regarding masturbation (later generations masturbated more and

worried about it less), premarital petting and coitus (later generations did it more and regretted it more), and extramarital coitus experiences (later generations did it more). Later generations were less likely to have had sexual contact with animals. A generational effect was also evident for males having dreams to orgasm and homosexual activity. After age 15, there were generally more males in each succeeding generation actively engaging in homosexual activity. The author discusses the possible causes of these changes and other findings.

205　Drench, Meredith E., & Losee, Rita H. (May-June, 1996). Sexuality and sexual capacities of elderly people. *Rehabilitation Nursing, 21*(3), 118-122.

In this article, the authors explore sexuality, psychosocial issues, and sexual capabilities of elderly people, including issues of menopause and erectile dysfunction. The authors address the role of rehabilitation nursing in helping older adults understand and adjust to changes. They recommend that nurses provide sexual counseling routinely for elderly patients. They suggest that nurses need to learn how to identify sexual problems and to educate elderly rehabilitation patients about altered sexual needs and capacities. This article provides information and the physiology and sexual needs of older adults and myths about sexuality that can help rehabilitation nurses become more knowledgeable about elderly sexuality as well as to understand their own values and attitudes regarding sex and sexuality as well as the values and attitudes of individual patients better. People who read the article and return an application form can receive continuing education credit from *Rehabilitation Nursing*.

206　Fieldman, H. A., Goldstein, I., Hatzichriston, D. G., et al. (1994). Impotence and its medical and psychosocial correlates: Results of Massachusetts male aging study. *Journal of Urology, 151*, 54-61.

The authors conducted a longitudinal study with a random sample of 1,290 community-based males ages 40 to 70. They collected data using a self-administered sexual activity questionnaire. The evaluation included sexual behavior, aging, sexual function and 17 hormones. They found a decline of sexual activity with age. Sexual satisfaction did not change with age. Impotence does not inexorably accompany aging but is augmented by modifiable para-aging phenomenon.

207   Finkle, Alex L. (1973). Emotional quality and physical quantity of sexual activity in aging males. *Journal of Geriatric Psychiatry, 6*(1), 70-79.

In this article, the author points out that the male is generally the lifelong aggressor in sexual relations but "the wife usually regulates the frequency of intercourse by granting and denying coitus." He states that impotence in elderly men is usually independent of physical condition. He adds that some men feel that it is necessary to continue to behave in a sexual way reminiscent of earlier years. He points out that it is erroneous to believe that impotence invariably follows radical perineal prostatectomy and that with the cooperation of a willing partner sexual competence can be reinstated. He reports two detailed case studies in the paper.

208   Gershenfeld, Matti K., & Newman, Judith. (1991). *How to find love, sex & intimacy after 50: A woman's guide.* New York, NY: Ballantine Books

This guidebook offers advice to women, primarily those who are widowed or divorced, on finding love, sex, and intimacy after age 50. Major life issues—friendship, self-definition, loneliness, attractiveness, and relationships—are examined to assist women who seek a mature relationship in midlife. Personal accounts and self-directed exercises are sprinkled throughout this manual. Specific information is provided on identifying places to meet men, understanding "dating rules," dispelling myths and fears about sex, introducing a new man to friends and family, and deciding whether or not to marry. A problem-solving handbook for older newlyweds is included.

209   Greenblatt, Robert B., & Leng, Jean-Joël. (February, 1972). Factors influencing sexual behavior. *Journal of the American Geriatrics Society, 20*(2), 49-54.

This article discussed many factors that can shade and color the intensity and direction of human sexuality. Some of the possible causes for the loss of sexual behavior are male pseudo-hermaphroditism, congenital adrenal hyperplasia in a completely masculinized female, Sheehan's disease, and several other chromosomal conditions. The first three listed above are illustrated by case studies in the article. Neither gonads nor chromosomal sex decide the direction of overt sexual behavior, stated the authors. The authors observed that libido can be compared to a test-tube equation. They state that many of these sexual dysfunctions can be cured or relieved with testosterone to regain sexual behaviors. The authors conclude that age need not alter performance nor eliminate the satisfaction and pleasure that attend sexual gratification.

210 Hällström, Tore, & Samuelsson, Sverker. (June, 1990). Changes in women's sexual desire in middle life: The longitudinal study of women in Gothenburg. *Archives of Sexual Behavior, 19*(3), 259-268.

The purpose of this longitudinal study was to describe changes in sexual desire in women in later middle life and to examine the relationship of change to age, sociodemographic factors, the quality of the marital relationship, mental disorder, and life events. The subjects were 497 Swedish women ages 38 to 54 at the time of the first interview who were living with their spouses or other partners during interviews in 1968-1969 and six years later. Nearly two-thirds of the subjects reported the same degree of sexual desire at both interviews. The strongest predictor of decrease in sexual desire was the strength of desire at the first interview. Conversely an absent or weak desire predicted an increase in the period between interviews. A strained marital relationship as well as major depression predicted a decrease of sexual desire. The main conclusion of the study is that sexual desire shows considerable stability over time even though a substantial proportion of married middle-aged women experience major changes in sexual desire, mostly as a decrease.

211 Hays, Antoinette M. (1984). Intimacy and sexuality in the elderly: Discussion. *Journal of Geriatric Psychiatry, 17*(2), 161-165.

The author discusses several issues related to elderly sexuality. Some of the most profound sexual myths in society relate to sexuality among older people, and especially for older women. Studies have shown that there is no "strict" correlation between age and sexual activity. Opportunity, the availability of partners, and health problems have been shown to effect sexual activity among the elderly. Because health care providers have been affected by the myths and misconceptions about elderly sexuality, the needs of older people have often not been met adequately. The author suggests that health personnel educate themselves about the sexual needs and problems of older people so that they can dispel the myths and misconceptions among their patients.

212   Helgason, Asgeir R., Adolfsson, Jan, Dickman, Paul, Arver,
       Stefan, Fredrikson, Mats, Göthberg, Marianne, & Steineck,
       Gunnar. (July, 1996). Sexual desire, erection, orgasm, and
       ejaculatory functions and their importance to elderly Swedish
       men: A population-based study. *Age and Ageing*, 25(4), 285-291.
           The aim of the study was to obtain basic information on
       sexual desire, erection, orgasm, and ejaculatory functions and to
       assess to what extent a decline in function distresses elderly men.
       The subjects were 155 men ages 60 to 69 and 85 men ages 50 to 59
       randomly selected from Stockholm residents from the Swedish
       Population Registry who received a 140-item questionnaire.
       Radiumhemmer's Scale of Sexual Function was included. The
       questionnaire was returned by 319 men, median age = 68. Sexual
       dreams were reported by 65%, sexual desire by 88%, engagement
       in intercourse 71%, orgasm in intercourse or masturbation 83%,
       and orgasm during sleep 15%. A decline in function was noted in
       all assessed aspects of sexuality with increasing age. The
       researchers concluded that intact sexual function is common
       among elderly men, even those 70 to 80 years old. Only 17% of
       the men regarded sex as a trivial part of their life.

213   Johnson, Beverly K. (February, 1996). Older adults and
       sexuality: A multidimensional perspective. *Journal of
       Gerontological Nursing*, 22(2), 6-15.
           The purpose of this study was to describe a
       multidimensional perspective of older adults' sexuality and to
       differentiate dimensions of sexuality as experienced by men and
       women in a community-based sample. Subjects were 69 men, 92
       women, and three participants who did not specify gender/ages
       55 to over 80 who completed a survey distributed at senior
       centers, nutrition sites, AARP meetings, churches, senior housing
       sites, senior dances, and classes at the YMCA and YWCA. Partici-
       pants completed a 77-item questionnaire which included items
       regarding selected demographics, sexual activities, self-esteem,
       sexual knowledge, sexual attitudes, and intimacy. Items from the
       Weiss *Intimacy Ranking Scale*, Rosenberg's *Self-Esteem Scale*, and
       Alford's *Knowledge Regarding Sexuality in the Aged Scale* were
       included. The researchers found that men and women were found
       to be similar for demographic variables although more women
       than men lived alone and were widowed. They were significantly
       different in their sexual interest, participation, and satisfaction for
       a range of sexual activities. Women reported sexual activities of
       sitting and talking, making oneself more attractive, and saying

loving words as more important than did men. Men saw sexual activities such as erotic readings, erotic movies, sexual day-dreams, and physically intimate activities as body caressing, intercourse, masturbation, and oral sex as more important than did women. Men and women identified similar important sexual activities hearing loving words, kissing, and hugging and reported as less important similar activities sexual conversation, masturbation, and oral sex. In this study researchers found that older men and women were interested, active, and satisfied with a variety of sexual activities in the presence of different health concerns. Declines in sexual activity were more related to health than age. Gender differences in this study for sexual activities support our stereotypes of male and female sexual behavior. The authors recommend that clinicians use these findings to increase their understanding of older adults' sexuality from a holistic view.

214   Karlen, Arno. (April-May, 1992). Appreciating the sexual you. *Modern Maturity, 35*(2), 52-54, 56-57.
       This article offers information that counters many stereotypes about sexual desire in middle-aged and older adults. The myth is that age makes sexual pleasure fade and die. The truth is that middle and late life give a second chance at sexual pleasure and harmony, often a better experience than found in youth. Sexual pleasure is often easier in maturity, especially if the conflicts of youth are truly outgrown. The sexual system ages but still functions, often quite well. In fact, aging offers men and women a chance to understand each other as never before, and to find greater sensuality together. By age 50, many women are less inhibited and more assertive, both in and out of bed; at the same time, men find that desire, arousal, and orgasm are not always synonymous. Sometimes these shifts help solve old sexual problems. The right artificial lubricants and different foreplay and coital positions can all minimize physical aging. Honest talk between partners and a more positive sexual attitude can dramatically restore desire. Suggestions are offered for ways to respond to physical and emotional changes of sex in maturity, and an eight-item quiz assesses the reader's knowledge level about mature sex.

215   Keil, Julian E., Sutherland, Susan E., Knapp, Rebecca G., Waid, L. Randolph, & Gazes, Peter C. (February, 1992). Self-reported sexual functioning in elderly blacks and whites: The Charleston Heart Study experience. *Journal of Aging and Health,* 4(1), 112-125.

This article presents the findings from the Charleston Heart Study on self-reported sexual functioning in elderly blacks and whites. The study population included 123 white spouse pairs and 43 black spouse pairs. Nearly 50% of the respondents reported arousal problems. The percentage of people reporting problems ranged from 30% at ages 60 to 69 to over 60% at ages 80 and older. There was no significant difference attributable to race or sex. Significant predictors of arousal problems were: older age, lower pulmonary function, physical disability, increase usage of prescription drugs, and fair or poor perception of health. Arousal problems had a substantial effect on frequency of sexual activity, with frequency several times greater among individuals reporting no arousal problems regardless of age. After considering age and arousal problems, the most significant predictors of frequency of sexual activity across all race and sex groups were marital status and education or income. Among respondents with no problems with arousal, those reporting sexual activity three or more times a month were white men 36%, black men 29%, high socioeconomic black men 47%, and white and black women 14%.

216   Keller, James F., Eakes, Edward, Hinkle, Dennis, & Hughston, George A. (Winter, 1978). Sexual behavior and guilt among women: A cross-generational comparison. *Journal of Sex and Marital Therapy,* 4(4), 259-265.

This paper reported the results of a study of the relationship between guilt and sexual behavior among 45 married women, ages 65 and older, 40 to 50, and 20 to 30, with 15 women in each category. The subjects completed three questionnaires: (1) a background questionnaire; (2) the female form of the *Bentler Heterosexual Behavior Scale;* and (3) the female form of the *Mosher Forced-Choice Guilt Inventory.* The researchers found a negative relationship between the age of subjects and the extent of sexual behavior. A positive relationship was found between age and sexual guilt. The younger women's sexual behavior scores were higher than the other groups. The younger women's scores indicated less guilt associated with sexual behavior than for the other groups. The authors concluded that the kinds of sexual behavior acceptable in marriage seem to have changed over time as evident by the responses from the subjects.

217 **Krieger, Dolores. (May, 1975). Therapeutic touch: The imprimatur of nursing.** *American Journal of Nursing,* **75(5), 784-787.**

This article reviews early studies on the healing effects of touch or the laying-on of hands. This ancient therapeutic practice was recorded in the hieroglyphics, cuneiform writings, writings, and pictographs of earliest literature cultures. In the 1960s Bernard Grad demonstrated the healing effects of touch on mice and barley seeds. In Eastern cultures the explanation for the positive interaction that occurs during the laying-on of hands is that the healthy person or healer has an overabundance of life vigor or vitality, which (if the healer has the intent to do so) can be activated by will and transferred to the ill or diseased person. Based on the review of literature and the concepts of Eastern religions, Krieger designed several empirical studies of the effect of laying-on of hands on hemoglobin values. The four research studies reported on all found that the mean hemoglobin value of the experimental group after treatment by the laying-on of hands exceeded the before-treatment hemoglobin values; and the mean hemoglobin values of the control group at comparable times showed no significant difference. One study revealed that nurses can be taught the techniques with positive results. The author included an explanation of the laying-on of hands and provides pictures of the technique. This article offers support for the ancient practice of laying-on of hands as an important healing, technique in our modern technologically-sophisticated society.

218 **Martin, Clyde E. (October, 1981). Factors affecting sexual functioning in 60- to 79-year-old married males.** *Archives of Sexual Behavior,* **10(5), 399-420.**

This study examined a number of social, attitudinal, and behavioral variables derived from personal interviews with 69 to 79 year-old males. Married, upper-middle-class male members of the Baltimore Longitudinal Study of Aging volunteered for this study. Of those eligible, 3.6% declined to take part in the study. The data suggested that frequency of sexual expression proved to be independent of such factors as marital adjustment, sexual attractiveness of wives, sexual attitudes, and demographic features of the marital history. However, former levels of sexual functioning appeared as highly significant correlates of current functioning. The author discussed in the male, sexual frequency, erotic responsiveness to visual stimuli, and time comfortable without sex are closely interrelated phenomena, suggesting that all three variables are strongly commensurate with degree of motivation. He concluded that those subjects found to be less than fully potent are found to be virtually free of performance anxiety, feelings of sexual deprivation, and loss of self-esteem. He suggested that the lack of motivation being responsible for lower sexual functioning.

219   Masters, William H. (August, 1986). Sex and aging — Expectations and reality. *Hospital Practice, 21*(8), 175-198.

The author studied the effects of age and mental conditioning on sexual activities. He says that continued sexual activity in later years helps maintain normal function of sex organs. Since most older adults are kept from sexual activities, several mental and health problems may develop. Sexual activity may also help prevent the involutional changes caused by sex steroid deprivation. By making patients aware of this important fact and of the altered responses and altered needs for stimulation that accompany aging, Masters suggests that one can prevent the anxiety reactions that so often cause sexual dysfunction or abstinence.

220   McCarthy, Patricia. (February, 1979). Geriatric sexuality: Capacity, interest, and opportunity. *Journal of Gerontological Nursing, 5*(1), 20-24.

The author presents her views, supported by research findings, on geriatric sexuality. She points out that many elderly people have a capacity and interest in continuing to have a robust sexual relationship. For others, sexuality takes a different form with aging. The primary reason that women no longer have sexual relationships is a lack of a partner. For men the primary reason is personal inability to continue having sexual relationships.

221   McCracken, Ann L. (October, 1988). Sexual practice by elders: The forgotten aspect of functional health. *Journal of Gerontological Nursing, 14*(10), 13-18.

The purpose of this article is to provide nurses with information they need to take an active role in promoting active, healthy sexual functioning. Three areas are addressed: sexual education in respect to normal changes in the sexual system, sexual changes occasioned by chronic illness or treatment of chronic illness, and advocacy to dispel the myths associated with age and sex. The article includes instructions for taking a sexual history, a list of sexual facts frequently unknown by elderly people, and data from a study of elderly people (N = 65) listing the most common reasons given by a group of elderly nursing home residents for not being sexually active. They were (in order of most often cited): no partner, lost interest, poor health, inability to perform, no answer, celibacy, and not appropriate. McCracken concludes that sexual response is a complex reaction of physical, physiological, psychological, and societal factors at any age. Older persons are particularly at risk for unhealthy sexual functioning and so health professionals can make a major contribution in this area.

222 **Nay, Rhonda. (November-December, 1992). Sexuality and aged women in nursing homes. *Geriatric Nursing, 13*(6), 312-314.**

This article explored the centrality of sexuality to identity and its relationship to the depersonalized perception of old women that much of society holds, with a focus on elderly women in nursing homes. Despite all evidence that sexuality in all its forms is essential to health and identity, society continues to make the aged sexually invisible. Some aged people continue to suffer guilt for having sexual feelings or acting sexually, and many aged people internalize the misconception that they are asexual. Aged women have had their sexuality defined as being dependent on males and youthful beauty. Elderly women ache for closeness, touch, and intimacy, but may be afraid to reach out to other women in this way. They have often lost control over much of their lives, and the only pleasure available to them may be self-pleasuring and fantasy, but guilt, lack of privacy, and fear of being caught remove this option. Their self-image and self-esteem are diminished. Women reacting to a definition imposed on them forfeit the pleasures of wholeness. The author suggests that a solution will be found when women assert their rights as individuals and claim their bodies as their own. Before elderly women can feel and be treated as fully human, it must be recognized that to be fully human is to be fully sexual, whatever our age. The author concluded that gerontologic nurses who hold ageist views of elderly women's sexuality are not providing holistic care. It is not possible to provide care that aims at maximizing potential, independence, and control, while denying or ridiculing a "core" aspect of identity.

223   Persson, Göran M. (1980). Sexuality in a 70-year-old urban population. *Journal of Psychosomatic Research, 24*(6), 335-342.

The purpose of this investigation was to study the prevalence of sexual intercourse in a sample of 70-year-olds in a Swedish urban population and to analyze the relations between this prevalence and marital status, conditions in the marriage, somatic and mental health, personality dimensions and some previous events and social circumstances. The data were collected in 1971 to 1972 during interviews including a short life history with questions about sexual development and present sexual activity. Persson found that married subjects of both sexes were more often sexually active than unmarried subjects, especially for women. Among the married men, 52% were still active, whereas 36% of the women were active. Among women, frequency of sexual activity was related to the lower age of the husband, better physical health of the husband, and rating the marriage as happy. In men, sexual activity was associated with the rating of sexual drives during young adulthood. Other hypotheses tested were relationships between sexual activity and health, personality, mental health, and environmental variables. The author questioned the reliability of the information received since people did not usually expect questions about sexuality as part of a heath examination. This article provides a comprehensive discussion regarding the findings and interpretation of results.

224   Purdy, Matthew. (November 6, 1995). A kind of sexual revolution. *The New York Times*, B1; B6.

This article discusses sexuality and intimacy of older people in nursing homes. The writer cites the case of two elderly people who fell in love at the Hebrew Home for the Aged, a 1,200 bed nursing home and Alzheimer's research center in the Bronx. The man, age 76, has Parkinson's disease and is married to someone else. The woman is 85 and a widow. Caregivers, says Purdy, are beginning to recognize that sexual activity is normal and beneficial for patients—even those with Alzheimer's disease. Robert N. Butler, the director of the International Longevity Center at Mount Sinai Hospital, expressed the view that, "The importance of tenderness, touching, being together in bed is an expression that remains vital to the end of life." The policy at the Hebrew Home is that "residents have the right to seek out and engage in sexual expression" and the right to obtain "materials with sexually explicit content" including books, magazines, and videos. The home is training its staff to recognize and respect intimate relationships and officials there say they will try to assist budding romances by moving one member of a couple to a single room to provide privacy. This policy represents a change in viewpoint. Only a couple of years earlier, people who were sexually active were separated, according to a social worker at the home. Purdy reports that some homes around the country have set aside rooms that couples can use for privacy. Casual intimacy includes holding hands, and hugging; intercourse is rarely allowed for people with dementia.

225   Reiss, Ira L. (May, 1986). **A sociological journey into sexuality.** *Journal of Marriage and the Family, 48*(5), 233-242.

This article presents a brief overview of societal-level explanation of sexuality. The author, a sociologist, defines sexuality as a societal product whose importance lies more in its physical pleasure and self-disclosure aspects that in its reproductive potential. The major discussion topics are: a societal conception of sexuality and universal linkages to three elements of the social structure: marital jealousy, gender role power, and beliefs about normality. The author discusses sociological theories related to homosexuality. How society influences elderly sexuality is not included in this article. This paper is a revised version of the 1984 Burgess Award Address which was given at the annual meeting of the National Council on Family Relations in Dallas, Texas on November 7, 1985.

226   Renshaw, Domeena C. (Fall, 1978). **Sex and the senior citizen.** *NAPPH Journal, 10*(1), 56-61.

In this article, the author discusses problems associated with aging including dealing with stereotypes, retirement, physical illness, and death. She discusses general changes of aging including physical changes (e.g., connective tissues lose their elasticity), problems in dealing with physical changes, "second childhood responses," social and emotional changes (e.g., dependency, need for services). She also discusses sexual changes of aging for males, females, and both sexes and sexual misinformation. Renshaw discusses sexual tension for older people, the use of masturbation, and the need for education of nursing home staff. She points out the special problems of aging handicapped people who are thought to be asexual by their doctors and the problems related alcoholism and drug use. She concludes by recommending that physicians help senior citizens with their sexual questions by providing accurate medical information, being nonjudgmental, providing time for discussion, providing suggestions, and by continuing to study sexuality of aging patients. Physicians need to be aware that touching, caressing, closeness, companionship, caring, and helpfulness are lifelong needs.

227   **Renshaw, Domeena C. (February, 1976). Understanding masturbation.** *The Journal of School Health, 46*(2), 98-101.
    The author discusses views of masturbation from the medieval period to the present day. For centuries masturbation has been perceived as a mysterious and evil act blamed for insanity and numerous other harmful consequences. Renshaw points out that all domestic animals, birds, and all primates in the wild masturbate. Dire punishments and predicted bad consequences have not eradicated this behavior. Studies show a high incidence of this behavior throughout the life span. Current medical knowledge, she reports, has concluded that masturbation does not cause mental illness, physical weakness, or any type of disease or death and that it is a completely normal, natural aspect of human sexual development. In her view, sex is a natural need like the need for sleep, warmth, air or food and is completely enjoyable when fully expressed.

228   **Renshaw, Domeena C. (January, 1981). Sexuality in older women?** *Journal of Clinical Psychiatry, 42*(1), 3-4.
    Renshaw says that by 1999, half of the United States. population will be over 65. Of these, 120 million seniors, two thirds (80 million) will be women. Many will be widowed or divorced and large numbers will live alone. In this editorial, Renshaw questions whether physicians or psychiatrists will be adequately trained to accept the sexuality of older women and to ask explicitly about their sexual expression, desire, or questions. She points out that no one knows the sexual fantasies of average solitary elderly women because no one inquires. On the other hand the fantasies of older men are well known. She says that older women do have sexual dreams, hopes, fantasies, and satisfactions and that they are vulnerable to sexual exploitation as are needy older men. She says that doctors can help by giving permission to older women to accept their sexuality, enjoy their fantasies and accept normal coital alternatives: sexual self-expression, self-massage, use of a vibrator, romancing, caressing, mutual genital pleasuring with or without coitus. Physicians, she says, must teach about normal sexual feelings and heal needless sexual distress.

229 Renshaw, Domeena C. (Winter, 1983). Sex, intimacy, and the older woman. *Women and Health, 8*(4), 43-54.

The author studied normal romantic and sexual fantasies in elderly women. She comments that bodies age but dreams and feelings may not. The author suggests intimacy is a joy that has many levels, only one of which is sexual but all aspects are open to aware older women. She concluded that older women continue to care and to share with others. She suggested that they also recognize the barriers to, the benefits of, and the lasting ways to obtain closeness in later ages with others.

230 Richardson, James P., & Lazur, Ann. (January, 1995). Sexuality in the nursing home patient. *American Family Physician, 51*(1), 121-124.

This review of the psychological changes of aging that alter sexual response in the elderly is written to help family physicians deal more effectively with sexuality in the nursing home. The authors found few studies of elderly sexual behavior. They describe findings related to sexuality in elderly residents of nursing homes. They cite several barriers to sexuality there: lack of privacy, chronic illness, lack of a willing partner, attitudes of staff, loss of interest, feelings of unattractiveness, and lack of knowledge. Suggestions for improving the situation are: improving privacy, educating staff, allowing conjugal or home visits, assessing decision making capacity in cognitively impaired elderly, encouraging other forms of sexual expression, providing information and counseling, and evaluating patients' complains about sexual dysfunctioning. The authors conclude that a significant number of elderly want to be sexually active to some extent after admission to nursing homes and that health care professionals should be aware of those needs and facilitate expression of sexuality when possible.

231 Rose, Madeleine Kornfein, & Soares, Harriet Hailparn. (1993). Sexual adaptations of the frail elderly: A realistic approach. *Journal of Gerontological Social Work, 19*(3/4), 167-178.

The authors describe some realistic sexual adaptations adopted by the frail elderly. Information was drawn from reports from case managers who worked with Medicaid-eligible elderly clients (mean age = 82.5) at risk of institutionalization. Although the formal assessment tool did not gather data about sexuality, the case managers developed a typology of patterns of sexual adaptation with information shared during consultations with their clients. Five behaviors are present in this scheme: accommodation, alternative sexuality, voluntary sexual retirement, involuntary sexual retirement, and revitalization. In some cases, these adaptations were consistent with coping styles in other areas of life It is suggested that neither denial nor sexual "pep talks" are helpful when working with the frail elderly. Rather, social workers should help their frail elderly clients acknowledge their sexual losses as well as their sexual feelings, fantasies, and behaviors.

232 **Roughan, Penelope A., Kaiser, Fran E., & Morley, John E. (February, 1993). Sexuality and the older woman.** *Clinics in Geriatric Medicine, 9*(1), 87-106.

This comprehensive literature review of sexuality and older women begins with a discussion of cultural myths regarding sexual behavior including the idea that romantic love is a prerequisite for marriage and intimacy. The authors discuss the effects of the sexual revolution on that idea. They attempt to develop a definition of sexual health by using surveys of reported sexual behavior and function, physiologic studies, studies of physical and mental illness and their treatment, and sociologic studies of prevailing attitudes. They cite a long list of studies which have found that sexual interest and desire decline in older people. They note that the decline appears to be more severe in women than in men and offer reasons for these findings. They say that about half of the healthy older women over age 60 masturbate. They discuss the impact of menopause on hormone levels and list changes in sexual response reported by Masters and Johnson. Psychosocial aspects of aging relevant to sexuality are living arrangements, being single or married, and being in long-term care. Sexual difficulties are identified as loss of interest in sex, slow arousal, inability to be orgasmic, pain, and dissatisfaction with sexual experiences. They discuss the impact of individual psychological issues, relationship problems, and physical illness on sexuality. Illnesses include vaginal atrophy, urinary incontinence, hysterectomy, diabetes, arthritis, and medications, drugs, hemodialysis, and cerebrovascular accidents. They discuss the management of sexual issues by physicians. They point out the limitations on studies previously conducted and the need for better information. A lengthy reference list is included.

233 Savitz, Harry A. (February, 1967). Humanizing institutional care for the aged. *Journal of the American Geriatrics Society*, 15(2), 203-210.

This paper discusses ways in which an institutional setting can be made into a home-like setting. In Savitz's view, people who operate long-term care must change their attitudes toward old age. In terms of the physical setting, he recommends dining rooms be small, attractively decorated, with tables for two or four so that mealtime promotes congenial conversation. He says that institutions should provide single rooms so that people can maintain privacy and accommodations for married couples that would allow them to live together during this period of their lives. He recommends building entrance halls and corridors that accommodate wheelchairs and that every measure possible be taken to safeguard health and prevent accidents. He gives specific recommendations for sprinkler installation, bathroom safety, locks, safety rails, burn prevention, non-skid flooring, and others. Savitz also makes specific recommendations for providing medical care such as adequate day-time staff, resident physician on duty at night, a fully equipped infirmary, a modern physiotherapy department with a full-time therapist, a podiatrist, dental room, well-equipped occupational therapy department, and a psychiatrist on staff. He describes the four phases of the medical program: preventative, curative, rehabilitation, and environment. Savitz provides detailed instructions for a physical activity program which he considers a necessity. He also recommends encouraging mental activity as well. "Idleness," he says, "leads to apathy and eventually to depression." The author also provides recommendations for a nutrition program and describes the role of the social worker. Other services which Savitz feels are essential are a barber shop, a beauty parlor, a library, and a sound proof room for listening to music.

234 Sorg, David A., & Sorg, Margaret B. (February, 1975). Sexual satisfaction in maturing women. *Medical Aspects of Human Sexuality*, 9(2), 62.

This discussion of sexual satisfaction in older women includes case studies of a 34-year-old woman and a 66-year-old woman who become more sexually responsive in later life. The authors attribute these changes to decreased tension, increased familiarity, increased sense of security in the relationship, and reduced fear of pregnancy. The authors conclude that there is a lack of evidence to support the idea that older women derive increasing satisfaction in sexual intercourse and say that frequency of orgasms is not a good measure of sexual responsiveness or satisfaction. The article is followed by commentaries by Frederick Lemere, Victor Kassel, W. J. Jones, Jr., Leah Schaefer, and Eleanor Rodgerson. Lemere agrees with the Sorgs and says that generalizations about human sexual behavior are not particularly helpful to the individual patient. Kassel comments that he has found that most older women are sexually naive and know little about masturbation as well as simple facts related to pregnancy. He says that older women can enjoy sex with knowledge, skill and a competent partner. Jones says that orgasm is related to marital satisfaction by women. He discusses dysfunction in marriage and his ideas for treating couples with this problem. Schaefer says that the experience of orgasm has much more to do with desire and capacity than age. Although sex is a natural function, how to have an orgasm for women must be learned. She discusses factors in women's sexual responses which include lack of sex education, inhibition, low sex drive, and others. Rodgerson comments on changes in society which allow women to express themselves but that being liberated has led to the idea that orgasm is necessary or the sexual experience is a failure. She says that women do not always seek relationships to have orgasms.

235   Szasz, George. (July, 1983). Sexual incidents in an extended care unit for aged men. *Journal of the American Geriatrics Society, 31*(7), 407-411.

The author conducted a survey among the nursing staff of a 400-bed extended-care unit for aged men. Eighty-three nurses completed a questionnaire to find out which patient behaviors are identified as sexual by the staff and how they reacted to these behaviors. Three types of behavior are identified as sexual and as causing problems: sex talk (using foul language); sexual acts (touching or grabbing, exposing genitalia); and implied sexual behavior (openly reading pornographic magazines). Data suggested that as many as 25% of the residents are thought to create such incidents. He described acceptable sexual behavior identified by the staff is limited to hugging and kissing on the cheek, although their answers implied that residents could need more intimate touching and affection. This study raised several questions about the nature and causes of different types of sexual behavior in the institutionalized elderly. The author discussed the need to understand the role of nursing staff, physicians, and administrators in recognizing individual needs of patients. He concluded that all of this needs to be done to safeguarding both the residents and the staff from the consequences of unacceptable incidents.

236   Tarbox, Arthur R. (Summer, 1983). The elderly in nursing homes: Psychological aspects of neglect. *Clinical Gerontologist,* *1*(4), 39-52.

The main purpose of the study reported on by the authors was to evaluate the attitudes expressed by medical students toward older adults. Another purpose of the study was to assess the specific effects of medical education on these students' attitudes toward older people. Questionnaires designed to measure attitudes were administered to freshman and senior classes of medical students in 1981 and 1984. To allow comparability, the questionnaire was the same one used by Spence and his colleagues in the 1960s. The questionnaire covered four areas: demographic characteristics and family background; characteristics and traits attributable to old age, the students' attitudes toward different age and sex groups; and the students' attitudes toward the aged in medical situations. Analysis of data revealed that some prejudice against the elderly existed in both medical class samples (1981 and 1984), paralleling negative attitudes toward the elderly expressed by medical students in the 1960's. Compared to students surveyed in the 1960s, medical students surveyed in the 1980s saw the elderly as being economically productive for an additional 10 to 20 years. In both samples (1981 and 1984) seniors expressed more favorable attitudes toward older adults than did freshman medical students. In both years seniors also defined old age as beginning later than did freshmen. Seniors also viewed the elderly more positively in terms of productivity, social significance, and sexuality of the aged than did the freshmen. As the authors conclude, "Taken together, these results indicate that attitudes toward the elderly are becoming more favorable in society and in medical schools in particular and that the medical education process was responsible for the more favorable attitudes expressed by the senior medical students."

237   Tavris, Carol. (July, 1977). The sexual lives of women over 60. *MS, 6,* 62-65.

The author expresses her views on sexuality and older women. She draws on case studies, interviews, and anecdotes involving older women and sexual interest and experience to illustrate her main point which is that many older women continue to have active sex lives. She draws upon the survey conducted by *Redbook* in the 1970s of 100,000 married women published by Delacorte coauthored by Susan Cadd "The Redbook Report on Female Sexuality — 100,000 Married Women Disclose the Good News About Sex."

238   **Traupmann, Jane, Eckels, Elaine, & Hatfield, Elaine. (December, 1982). Intimacy in older women's lives. *The Gerontologist*, 22(6), 493-498.**

The study examined intimacy as a multidimensional concept with particular attention paid to love and sexuality. The study involved a random sampling of 106 married women, ages 50 to 82. Each subject completed an interview and a set of questions dealing with relationships. The author concluded that satisfaction and happiness in a love relationship is a composite of many different factors. Passionate love the women felt for their partners, the compassionate love they felt, and their sexual satisfaction are significantly related to an overall happiness in an intimate relationship.

239   **Wallace, Meredith. (November-December, 1992). Management of sexual relationships among elderly residents of long–term care facilities. *Geriatric Nursing*, 13(6), 308-311.**

This article describes the development of and institutional response to a sexual relationship between two older people in a nursing facility to illustrate the problems and legal issues associated with such relationships in long-term care settings. The author gives several recommendations for managing sexual activity that comply with the residents' legal rights to express themselves sexually, including a sexual function and desire assessment for every resident, compensating for physical changes, preventing the spread of sexually-transmitted diseases, counseling for residents, their families, and staff, and additional staff training. The author suggests that long-term care facilities must develop policies that comply with federal regulations and nursing standards that promote the expression of sexuality among residents while minimizing the risk of potentially negative situations or consequences.

240   **Weinberg, Jack. (April, 1971). Sexuality in later life. *Medical Aspects of Human Sexuality*, 5(4), 216, 223, 226-227.**

This article written by a psychiatrist expresses the view that the transition from a well-stabilized psychological maturity to a state of decline starts at various ages and though it has some basis in physical changes it is primarily psychological. In his view, aging begins when people begin to look back at their past with fond nostalgia and at the future with apprehension and feelings of insecurity. In his experience people begin to think about old age between 45 and 55 at the same time that they are experiencing gradual changes in appearance, graying hair, diminished capacity for physical work, and feelings of sexual decline. It is myths and incorrect assumptions about sexual decline that the author wants to dispel. He cites findings that older people continue to have and enjoy sexual intercourse, that aging does not limit sexual capacities of females. He points out that the studies he cited primarily concern themselves with sexual intercourse and that questions of intimacy, the need for human contact, fantasy, and other sexual behaviors are seldom elicited in these sexual surveys. In older people these behaviors may even be considered suspicious or inappropriate. He concludes that sexual expressions in older people are numerous and diverse and that chronological age is not a barrier to a continued sexual life.

241 Weinberg, Jack. (November, 1969). Sexual expression in late life. *American Journal of Psychiatry, 126*(5), 713-716.

This article discusses the effect of advancing chronological age on sexual activity. The author states that if sexual activities are denied then difficulties may arise for older men. Older men's efforts to establish relationships are usually misinterpreted and rejected, by both the nursing staff and the opposite sex. The men may be forced to regressed behavior. He utilized two case studies to illustrate his points on sexual behavior. The author concludes that others must learn to understand and place in proper perspective the sexual needs of the elderly male and that age is no barrier to continued sexual activity if the opportunity and sanction is present.

242 Weinstein, Stellye, & Rosen, Efrem. (1988). Senior adult sexuality in age segregated and age integrated communities. *International Journal of Aging and Human Development, 27*(4), 261-270.

The authors investigated the relationship between living arrangement and sexual activity and sexual interest, sexual attitudes, and liberal sexual attitudes. One group consisted of people who lived in an age-integrated community in the Greater New York Metropolitan area (N = 159). The second group lived in a year-round age-segregated leisure-type retirement community of apartments in southern Florida (N = 155). Both groups included individuals ages 60 and older with middle class incomes. Questionnaire data from respondents on a senior adult sexuality scale were analyzed. The authors found that the subjects who selected to live in age-segregated leisure-type retirement communities exhibited significantly more sexual interest, sexual activities, and liberal sexual attitudes than those subjects living in age-integrated mainstream communities.

243 **Weizman, R., & Hart, J. (February, 1987). Sexual behavior in healthy married elderly men.** *Archives of Sexual Behavior,* **16(1), 39-44.**

The authors studied the sexual behavior of 81 men; 34 of the men were ages 60 to 65 and 47 were ages 66 to 71. Subjects consisted of Israeli men from two community health clinics who were married, physically healthy, and with no psychopathology or marital problems. A self-report three-point rating scale questionnaire evaluated sexual function for men. The researchers reported that 36% were impotent, with no significant difference between the two age groups. About half of the total population reported regular masturbatory activity in both age groups. The authors noted a decline in frequency of sexual intercourse and an increase in frequency of masturbation in subjects ages 66 to 71 years as compared to subjects ages 60 to 65. The authors suggest that the interest in sexuality continues in elderly men although the form of sexual expression changes from active sexual intercourse to a self-pleasuring form. The authors concluded evaluation of sexual activity in advanced age is recommended and appropriate therapy in case of sexual dysfunction should be offered to elderly men.

244 **West, Norman D. (December, 1975). Sex in geriatrics: Myth or miracle?** *Journal of the American Geriatrics Society,* **23(12), 551-552.**

In this article, West, a medical doctor, shares experiences from a 12-year practice involving geriatric residents ages 68 to 98 living in a 50-bed nursing home. He hopes this article will help people reassess their concepts of the sexual needs of older people and understand the appropriate modifications they may use to fulfill those needs. From taking a sexual history of each of the residents he learned that sexual desire and sexual activity exist in a significant number of elderly people; that aged people are willing to substitute other forms of sexual activity when necessary; that elderly people who have lost sexual desire are not upset by that loss; and that the important component needed to make sex gratifying is love.

245   White, Charles B. (February, 1982). Sexual interest, attitudes, knowledge, and sexual history in relation to sexual behavior in the institutionalized aged. *Archives of Sexual Behavior, 11*(1), 11-21.

The author provides an overview of the literature on sexuality and aging as a preface to a study of the sexual needs and behaviors of institutionalized elderly people. The author interviewed 84 male and 185 female residents in 15 Texas nursing facilities. The interview included the *Aging Sexuality Knowledge and Attitudes Scale* (ASKAS) and four questions assessing current and past sexual behavior. Of those subjects who completed the interview, 91% had not masturbated or had intercourse in the month prior to the interview. Among these sexually-inactive subjects, 17% indicated an interest in sexual activity, but said they lacked an available partner, sufficient privacy, or other opportunity. Sexual activity in this sample was related to attitudes and behavior, as well as their interest in sex and history of frequent sexual activity. The author suggests that residents in nursing facilities evidence sexual needs which are often precluded by the lack of privacy or suitable partners in their institutional setting.

246   Wood, Vivian. (Winter, 1971). Age-appropriate behavior for older people. *The Gerontologist, 11*(4), 74-78.

The purpose of this review of the literature is to investigate what is known about age-appropriate behavior for older people. Wood points out that in youth, the individual's role or loss of role are determined largely on the basis of age. For older people there are few clear-cut norms and expectations. The article includes descriptions of age norms suggested in the literature for older husbands, older wives, widows, parents of adult children, grandparents, and voluntary association members. The author points out that there is an emergence of people retiring earlier than 65 who are in good physical condition and who have more experience with leisure and mobility than earlier generations. New and different life-patterns in retirement are developing. She recommends studying subcultures such as retirement communities and housing developments. The article concludes with a list of research questions for future scientific investigation.

247   **Woods, Nancy Fugate. (1987). Toward a holistic perspective of human sexuality: Alterations in sexual health and nursing diagnoses.** *Holistic Nursing Practice, 1*(4), 1-11.

The purposes of this article are to explore sexual health from a holistic perspective and to propose a nursing diagnostic taxonomy that encompasses sexual function, sexual self-concept, and sexual relationship within the sexual health perspective. The ways that sexual health are perceived are clinical (absence of health problems), functional (ability to function), adaptive (ability to cope with changes), and eudaemonistic (feeling of well-being and ability to actualize potential). Sexual development includes gender identify and gender role. Woods reviews Masters and Johnson's studies of human sexual response and Kaplan's revision of their original concept which includes three phases: desire, arousal, and orgasm. Woods discusses the interrelationship between sexual function, sexual self-concept, and sexual relationships in aging individuals. She says that sexual activity is part of life for elderly people with 10% to 20% of people over 75 being sexually active. She includes a discussion of alterations in sexual health including changes in sexual desire, sexual arousal, orgasm, sexual self-concept, and sexual relationships.

248   **Wright, Dominique. (July 31, 1985). Sex and the elderly.** *Nursing Mirror, 161*(5), 18-19.

This article reviews the literature and examines the importance of sexuality for emotional and general well-being as well as for procreation. Despite evidence to the contrary, the author has observed the myth that sexual interest and capacity steadily wanes in later-middle-age and stops altogether after retirement. She points out that sexuality is not only expressed in terms of orgasm but also in the ability to give and receive warmth and affection. She points out that inhibiting factors regarding elderly sexuality are more likely to be psychological and social than physical. The author cites findings from the Kinsey, Masters and Johnson, and the Duke studies which provide evidence of continued sexual interest and activity among the elderly. Wright briefly discusses the effects of high blood pressure, heart attacks, diabetes, and long-stay hospital admission and residential care on sexuality. She concludes with a call to health workers to examine their own sexuality and biases and to allow elderly people to express their sexuality with impediments.

249 Yeaworth, Rosalee C., & Friedeman, Joyce Sutkamp. (September, 1975). Sexuality in later life. *Nursing Clinics of North America, 10*(3), 565-574.

The authors discuss biological and social aspects of sexuality among older people. Physical changes associated with aging affect sexual organs and the strength of sexual urges. Sexual interest and thoughts decline, but do not disappear. Sexual interest and activity in later life are affected by the availability of partners and youthful attitudes. Research has shown that keeping sexual activity regular in later life is the best way for older men and women to retain sexual capacity and performance. The author suggests that nurses and other health professionals should help older people struggling with sexual problems to overcome them, and should take a more active role in counseling the elderly and changing attitudes toward elderly sexuality.

250 Zeiss, Antonette M. (February, 1982). Expectations of the effect of aging on sexuality in parents and average married couples. *The Journal of Sex Research, 18*(1), 47-57.

The purpose of the present study was to examine the differences between estimates of parents' sexual activity and estimates of the activity of married couples other than one's parents from ages 20 to 80. The sample consisted of 205 subjects who completed a questionnaire asking them to estimate sexual frequency, at different ages, of either their parents or married couples on the average. After the questionnaire was completed the subjects then completed the *Profile of Mood States* (POMS) which measured six moods: anxiety, depression, hostility, vigor, fatigue, and confusion. The results indicated that in all decades but the 1970s and 1980s, subjects who estimated intercourse frequencies for their parents reported significantly lower means than the group who estimated married couples on the average. Subjects who estimated parental intercourse are significantly more anxious and depressed on the POMS than subjects who estimated married couples on the average. Effects for confusion and hostility are in the same direction but of borderline significance. There is also a dramatic main effect for age, with subjects expecting a steep linear decreasing pattern for intercourse frequency and age. The author concluded that psychologists need to set aside simplistic theories about the effect of stereotypes and look more carefully at exactly how beliefs about sexuality and aging might affect behavior.

10

Staff Responses to Sexual Behavior of the Elderly

A few researchers have investigated staff behaviors and responses toward elderly sexuality. In this chapter, articles which examine the role of the staff in promoting sexuality are presented. Although the role of staff is considered critical in supporting expression of sexuality, evidence suggests that the elderly, especially those in institutions, have little freedom of expression. Several writers have investigated staff behaviors or discussed their views of what staff behavior should be (Gochros, 1972; Lyder, 1990; Woodard & Rollin, 1981).

A second aspect of staff behavior is the willingness of nurses and other health care workers to provide information to older people regarding their sexuality. This topic is discussed by several writers in this chapter (Cook, 1994; Parsons, 1981; Pollard, 1985; Smedley, 1991).

Other writers have discussed ways in which nurses can provide the intimacy and touching that older people living alone need (Barnett, (1972) and also how nurses can react appropriately to sexual behaviors of their patients (Peace, 1974; Sloane, 1993).

251 Barnett, Kathryn. (March-April, 1972). A theoretical construct of the concepts of touch as they relate to nursing. *Nursing Research, 21*(2), 102-110.

The purpose of this investigation was to identify the basic and accepted theories of touch as they relate to nonverbal communication in an area of patient care and to develop a theoretical construct of the concepts of touch as they relate to nursing. The author discussed the universals of touch communication, as observed in American culture today. She identified four broad areas. They are: a fundamental mechanic of communication, a vital means of communicating, a basis for establishing communication, and as an important means of communicating emotions and ideas. She stated that the act of touch is an integral part of nursing intervention and is to be used judiciously between nurse and patient, health team and patient, and health team and nurse. She concluded that touch should not be overlooked by health care providers and be thought of not as a problem but as a cure.

252   Cook, Marilyn J. (September, 1994). Nursing assessment for the older woman. *RN, 57*(9), 40-43.

This brief article, written by a gynecological nurse and directed at nurses working with female patients 45 years and older, provides advice on doing a sexual assessment in this population. The author points out that middle-aged women may have concerns about the psychological and physical changes associated with menopause. Older women may have difficulty satisfying their sexual needs or may be ignoring them completely, yet they may not feel comfortable discussing these concerns. The author emphasizes the importance of sensitive interviewing in a private location and of using simple, straightforward language and speaking calmly and slowly. Cook provides specific guidelines on what to include in an assessment and gives sample questions. She recommends probing for factors related to decreases in sexual activity such as physical changes, hormonal imbalances, lack of a partner, and a psychological response to these changes. It is also important to review the patient's medication regimen since some drugs affect sexual performance. She concludes with a discussion of strategies to reduce sexual problems such as exercise, estrogen replacement therapy, masturbation, and touching. The author recommends that nurses include questions about sexuality when they take a history. Despite openness of the last few decades, many middle-aged and elderly women have a lot of misconceptions nurses can clear up.

253   Gochros, Harvey L. (March, 1972). The sexually oppressed. *Social Work, 17*(2), 16-23.

The author of this article discussed the problems experienced by the sexually oppressed, who are handicapped by contemporary society's sexual confusion, stereotypes, and anxieties. This large, diverse group of people has been denied its rights essentially by society. Social work efforts on behalf of the sexually oppressed can involve practice in many settings and call for professional in all levels of society. The author concludes that if social workers are to deal with sex related problems, its highest priority might well be intervention on behalf of these groups too often ignored by others.

254 Lyder, Courtney H. (September, 1992). NPs play major role in promoting sexuality among institutionalized elderly. *Nurse Practitioner, 17*(9), 10, 13.

Because the attitudes of nursing facility staff toward the sexuality of elderly residents have an impact on the behavior of residents, the author suggests that gerontological nurse practitioners (NPs) can produce an environment that is supportive of the residents' right to express themselves sexually. To accomplish this goal, the author recommends that NPs teach staff accurate information about sexuality and aging, facilitate staff members' awareness of their own sexuality, and promote an environment that encourages sexual freedom among residents. Once staff members understand that nursing facility residents should be supported and not deprived of their sexual rights, the author suggests that the subject will no longer be a taboo for staff.

255 Parsons, Virgil. (1981). Assessment of the older clients' sexual health. In Irene Mortenson Burnside (Ed.), *Nursing and the aged, 2nd ed.* (pp. 374-380). New York: McGraw-Hill Book Company.

In this chapter, the author says that sexual health care includes three basic elements: a capacity to enjoy and control their own sexual and reproductive behavior, freedom from psychological factors inhibiting sexual response, and freedom from organic disorders and diseases. He presents common questions of nurses about elderly sexuality and provides responses to basic who, where, when, what, and how questions. He identifies factors that present sexual interest and activity in older people. He explains methods for assessment of older client's sexual health status and outlines a plan for using information for sexual health assessment in intervention and evaluation of nursing care. The author recommends that sexuality should be introduced early in the nurse-client relationship to reinforce the belief that sexual health is an appropriate component of the client's health.

256   Peasé, Ruth A. (April, 1974). Female professional students and sexuality in the aging male. *The Gerontologist, 14*(2), 153-157.

This article explored examples of female student nurses involved with the elderly and their outcome. Female professional students often receive overt or covert sexual overtures from their elderly male patients. The author examined three such cases with an emphasis on the stereotypical thinking that the young often hold regarding the sexual needs of older men. They illustrated the feelings, nonverbal communication, and sociocultural background of what nurses need to look at while caring for older patients. The author also examined literature on sexuality in aging men. The author concluded with helpful teaching approaches that are outlined along with curricular suggestions for professional health workers.

257   Pollard, Marcia Swistock, & Barker, Elizabeth Dawson. (February, 1985). Straight talk on sex for the older patient. *RN, 48*(2), 17-18.

This article suggests ways a nurse can interact with a patient that is having a sexual problem. The authors suggest three steps to get a patient to talk about the problem. After establishing that a sexual problem is bothering a person, the nurse must first build the patient's trust before discussing the subject. The first step is to talk about the problem in a quiet private place where the patient feels comfortable. Second, the nurse must communicate effectively to the patient keeping a calm voice and being considerate. A nurse who raises her voice or has a more comical voice is more likely to discourage a patient. The last step involves moving onto the problem slowly. Working on smaller and more broad questions will help the patient feel more comfortable. As time progresses, more confined questions should be asked to determine the problem. On some questions, generalization may help alleviate any pressures a person has about sexual topics. The authors concluded that by showing a more positive attitude the nurse will be able to offer better support on sexual issues to older patients.

258   Sloane, Philip. (October, 1993). Sexual behavior in residents with dementia. *Contemporary Long Term Care, 16*(10), 66, 69, 108.

The author discusses staff responses to sexual behavior in

residents with Alzheimer's disease and related disorders. He states that these residents often maintain and express sexual feelings. Common behaviors are displays of affections (hand-holding, hugging, and kissing), self-stimulation behaviors (masturbation, reading sexually explicit materials, public exposure), making unwanted verbal or physical advances toward other residents, and expressing sexually intimate behaviors generally reserved for private settings (prolonged kissing, touching, sexual intercourse). Sloane reports the actions of one facility which developed guidelines to manage sexual behaviors. The general principles are summarized in the article. The article also includes a recommended intake sexual history. Assistance in evaluating a sexual behavior problem is also provided. The recommended steps in managing sexual behavior are: describe and document the behavior, develop a plan of care to manage the behavior, and monitor the plan of care.

259   Smedley, Grace. (January-February, 1991). Addressing sexuality in the elderly. *Rehabilitation Nursing, 16*(1), 9-11.

The purpose of this article is to help rehabilitation nurses overcome their prejudices concerning sexuality and the elderly and provide their patients with appropriate sexual counseling and information. Topics discussed are attitudes toward sexuality in the elderly, the nurses' role in attitudinal change, and the PLISSIT model to sexual counseling. The PLISSIT model is P—giving permission; LI—limited information, SS—specific suggestions, and IT—intensive therapy. Smedley discusses each of these steps. She also provides guidelines for taking a sexual history and a reprint of the complete PLISSIT model. Smedley points out that the continually increasing numbers of elderly people mean that rehabilitation nurses will be dealing with greater proportions of older people and therefore need to become familiar with the literature related to elderly sexuality. They also need to examine their own feelings and concerns by attending inservice programs, professional workshops, and seminars so that they can address sexual issues without the influence of societal myths and stigmas.

260   Woodard, Wallace S., & Rollin, Stephen A. (October, November, December, 1981). Sexuality and the elderly: Obstacles and options. *Journal of Rehabilitation, 47*(4), 64-68.

This article examines aspects of human sexuality and sexual counseling for rehabilitation counselors who work with disabled elderly clients. The authors discuss obstacles to normal sexual expression and options to help disabled elderly people achieve adequate sexual relationships. Woodard discusses consequences of aging on sexual activities of elderly disabled persons. In his view all individuals deserve the right to enjoy recreational sex if they choose. He lists several commonly held beliefs which he says are all false: (1) that older disabled persons are not interested in sex; (2) that they should adjust to a life of celibacy; (3) that those who think about sex are childish; (4) that masturbation by older disturbed people is unhealthy; (5) that disabled men experience permanent impotency; (6) that menopause is the end of sexual interest for older women; (7) that older disabled women do not experience orgasm; (8) that intercourse is the only normal method of sexual activity; and (9) that sexual activity for older people is immoral. He recommends that counselors adopt a list of positive beliefs. Two of which are that ignoring or denying sexual feelings will not solve the problem, and sexual feelings are individual. Woodard provides a discussion of essential components of effective counseling. He stresses the importance of asking questions, trusting the client, and approaching sexuality, disability, and aging concerns as those they were related. He concludes with a discussion of changing sex roles among older disabled persons. He recommends that nursing homes and institutions increase privacy and provide acceptance and instruction on self-pleasuring.

11

Marriage, Divorce, and Living Arrangements

This chapter includes a wide variety of topics associated with living arrangements. The writers discuss marriage, remarriage, widowhood, divorce, living together without marriage, house-sharing, companionship, and friendship. Also included here are articles about marital satisfaction and adult socialization patterns and adaptation among the elderly both in the community and in long-term care institutions. Many elderly people live alone and studies of that population are also included in this chapter.

Many researchers have investigated problems associated with widowhood. Included in the chapter are investigations of the psychological and social differences between married and widowed older people, friendships among older married and widowed women, suicide rates among widows, and bereavement.

Data for these studies has been collected via questionnaires and interviews.

261 Ade-Ridder, Linda. (1990). **Sexuality and marital quality among older married couples. In Timothy H. Brubaker (Ed.),** *Family relationships in later life, 2nd ed.* **(pp. 48-67). Newbury Park, CA: SAGE Publications.**

The author studied 670 married elders concerning their sexual interest and sexual behavior and their relation to marital quality. The respondents averaged 72 years of age and had been married more than 40 years on average. The respondents scored high on general sexual interests and feelings, yet most reported frequencies of intercourse that were substantially lower than during the early years of marriage. The author concluded that carrying sexual interest through to completion in intercourse is not as necessary to marital quality in the later years of marriage compared to the earlier years. Most of the couples were in their early 1960s when they noticed a decline in sexual behavior, and most of the time dramatic changes were brought on by the husband's declining capacity for physical sexual arousal. The author found those marriages in which sexual behavior had not noticeably changed tended to be happier compared to marriages in which there had been a marked decline in sexual behavior. But happier marriages were also typified by higher levels of sexual interest, too.

262   Atchley, Robert C. (April, 1975). Dimensions of widowhood in later life. *The Gerontologist, 15*(2), 176-178.

The author studied the various social and psychological differences which occur between married and widowed older people. He also studied the differences which appear between widows and widowers. Subjects were 902 respondents to a mail-in questionnaire. They consisted of retired employees of a large midwestern telephone company and retired public school teachers. A total of 233 respondents were the correct age (70 to 79) and martial status (married or widowed). The author concluded from the data that no generalizations about the social psychological effects of widowhood could be made that hold for all subgroups. He found that among working-class women, widowhood is associated with income inadequacy, which is associated with lower automobile use, lower social participation, and higher loneliness and anxiety. He suggests that as compared to other subgroups, widowhood has a much less pronounced social impact.

263   Babchuk, Nicholas, & Anderson, Trudy B. (1989). Older widows and married women: Their intimates and confidants. *International Journal of Aging and Human Development, 28*(1), 21-35.

This study investigates the extent to which widows cultivate new friendships upon the death of their spouse. The authors also explored friendship patterns that characterized older married women and their patterns of association with intimates as compared to those maintained by women who had lost their spouses. The subjects were a group of white, noninstitutionalized, elderly married women and widows ages 65 to 98 (mean = 73.5). The researchers interviewed the women in their homes over a 3-month period. Widows were significantly older than the married women. Primary friendship involvement was measured by asking each respondent to identify her acquaintances. From these, she was asked to list those to whom she felt close. Frequency of contact, type of activity, affectivity, exchanging of confidences, and demographic characteristics of friends were determined through follow-up questions. The number of friends ranged from zero to fifteen (mean = 5.69). About 8% of the women said they had no close friends. About 20% named ten or more close friends. Four women identified as many as 15 close friends. For widows, those who were younger had more friends. Among married women, age was not a factor in determining number of friends. Proximity was important in establishing friends. The neighborhood was the most opportune setting for establishing close ties with others. Other places where they met friends were church, work, voluntary associations, and school. Most met through self or neighbors, through relatives, or mutual friends. About one-fifth of the subjects (married and widows) reported one or more men as close friends. Most of these men were married to women who were listed in that subject's close friends. About 23% of widows and 37% of married women did not have a relationship with anyone in which they could confide. The others had between one and four or more people in whom they could confide. The authors concluded that married women and widows have a comparable number of primary friends, about five. Being over the age of 74 influences the size of the friendship network for widows, but not for married women. The old-old widows had fewer friends than the young-old widows. For this sample, the majority of the people had lived in the community for a long time (mean = 50 years). Having cross-sex friends was uncommon. Widows relied on friends as confidants to a greater extent than married women. Confidants were used when individuals are depressed, ill, or worried, but almost never in a financial crisis.

264   Bock, E. Wilbur, & Webber, Irving L. (February, 1972). Suicide among the elderly: Isolating widowhood and mitigating alternatives. *Journal of Marriage and the Family, 34*(1), 24-31.

This article reports the results of a study of the relationship between widowhood and suicide. Information was obtained from two sources: (1) a random sample of the noninstitutionalized aged population in one county in Florida; and (2) a group of persons ages 65 and over who had committed suicide in that county between 1955 and 1963. This procedure resulted in 188 suicides being compared with 2,544 elderly respondents. Data were gathered through interviews with respondents; and suicide data was obtained from death certificates and files of funeral directors. Suicide rates were calculated for various categories of married and widowed elderly people. Analyses of data revealed that suicide rates are higher for widows and widowers than for married elders. Widowed males, in particular, are much more likely to commit suicide than husbands. Analyses revealed that compared to married males, widowed makes were significantly more socially isolated. Widows, on the other hand, are different from widowers and are more likely to remain socially active and involved. Bock and Webber note that "the relational system has a strong negative connection with the suicide rate: the stronger the relational system, the lower the rate of suicide." This association was found for all categories of sex and marital status. Analyses revealed that the largest difference between the widowed and the married occurs under conditions of social insulation, and the smallest difference appears under the conditions of isolation. The article concludes with a recommendation that programs for the prevention of elderly suicide direct special attention toward the widower.

265   **Bograd, Ruth, & Spilka, Bernard. (1996). Self-disclosure and marital satisfaction in mid-life and late-life remarriages. *International Journal of Aging and Human Development*, 42(3), 161-172.**

This study investigated self-disclosure and marital satisfaction among 125 males and females who were in their first remarriage. The purpose was to compare people remarrying in midlife (ages 30 to 45) with people in their late-life (ages 60 to 75). Participants completed the *Wheeless Self-disclosure Scale*, the *Locke-Wallace Marital Adjustment Scale*, and the *Marlowe-Crowne Social Desirability Scale*. Researchers found that second marriages begin with a different premise than a first marriage. Marital satisfaction and self-disclosure was positively associated in both mid-life and late-life remarriages. Age is negatively associated with self-disclosure. The amount and depth of disclosure appear greater in mid-life than in later-life remarriages. Men in this sample had higher levels of marital satisfaction than females in both mid-life and late-life marriages, a finding which is well supported in the literature. Marital satisfaction was greatest for late-life remarriages due to the high level of male satisfaction in this age group. With more older persons remarrying, the authors believe there is a need for additional longitudinal and cross-sectional research on remarriage.

266   Brothers, Dr. Joyce. (1990). *Widowed.* New York: Simon and Schuster.

This book relates the story of Dr. Joyce Brothers, her marriage and then her experience as a widow. She discusses her coping with loss and her struggle with grief and loneliness. Included in this honest portrayal of life as a widow is a frank discussion of her need for companionship, intimacy, and sexual expression. In her list of suggestions for widows she includes masturbation as an easy and natural way of dealing with sexual needs.

267   Burr, Jeffrey A. (December, 1990). Race/sex comparisons of elderly living arrangements: Factors influencing the institutionalization of the unmarried. *Research on Aging, 12(4),* 507-530.

This article describes trends in the total institutionalization rates among the unmarried population, by race and sex. The author analyzed United States Census data from the 1960, 1970, and 1980 Public Use Samples for the population ages 55 and over. Burr found that black and white population groups became more alike during the 1960s and 1970s in their rates of institutionalization. For both white and black females, those in institutions have fewer children, on average, than those who are not in institutions. Other differences by race are still substantial. Almost 13% of unmarried white females with no children are in institutions, whereas for comparable black females only 7.6% are in institutions. While 31.7% of disabled white females are in institutions, only 14.6% of black females who are in a similar situation are in institutions. As with females, the same general patterns of relationships regarding disability and male institutional status were found. For white males and females, being widowed decreases the probability of institutionalization but not for black males or females. The author discusses policy considerations that are affected by these findings.

268   Carey, Raymond G. (1977). The widowed: A year later. *Journal of Counseling Psychology,* 24(2), 125-131.

This article reports the results of a study of 78 widows and 41 widowers, who were interviewed 13 to 16 months after they were widowed. The purpose of the study was to develop a single self-report measure of adjustment capable of measuring the degree of adjustment and to identify correlates of adjustment that will keep caregivers predict which spouses will have the greatest difficulty during bereavement. Structured interviews were conducted with widowed individuals (N = 119) and with 100 married people approached randomly in or near a hospital. An *Item Adjustment Scale,* an 8-item self-report measure of adjustment depression was developed from the 40 questions the widowed were asked regarding their feelings and attitudes. The type of items included were: Is loneliness a serious problem for you? Results indicated that married people were significantly better adjusted than widowed people. Contrary to expectations, widowers were better adjusted than widows. The widowed who had forewarning about the approaching death of their spouses had a significantly higher level of adjustment than the widowed who had no forewarning. Age was a significant factor. Widowed people over the age of 57 were better adjusted than their counterparts under age 57. Education was also a factor in adjustment, with those who had more education scoring significantly higher than widowed persons with less education. Similarly, higher income was positively related to adjustment. Happiness in marriage was not significantly related to adjustment. Neither were religious orientation or employment. Sex and forewarning were the two main predictors of adjustment (R = .30). Based on these findings Carey concludes that counselors in a medical setting are well advised to give special attention to the importance of anticipatory grief in women.

269   Clayton, Paula J. (1974). **Mortality and morbidity in the first year of widowhood.** *Archives of General Psychiatry,* 30(6), 747-750.

This article reports results of a study of 109 widowed people (mean = 61 years) and 109 married people. The widowed people were identified and interviewed by a psychiatrist shortly after widowhood. The married individuals, who were matched on sex and age, were interviewed mainly about their physical and mental health by a psychiatrist, nursing instructor, and medical student. After 13 months, 90 widowed people and 90 married controls were interviewed again. Results showed no difference in the mortality rates of the recently widowed and the controls. Four widowed people and five controls died. The bereaved, however, experienced significantly more psychological and physical depressive symptoms than their nonbereaved counterparts. There were no differences between the two groups in numbers of physician visits, hospitalizations, or use of tranquilizers.

270   Cleveland, William P., & Gianturco, Daniel T. (1976). Remarriage probability after widowhood: A retrospective method. *Journal of Gerontology, 31*(1), 99-103.

This paper reports on a procedure developed to estimate age-specific remarriage probabilities and results of using the procedure with North Carolina data. The authors reported that re-marriage probabilities decrease faster for widows than widowers. Less than one fourth of men widowed after age 65 ever remarry. Less than 5% of women widowed after age 65 ever remarry. Men remarry more quickly than women. The median interval to remarriage was 1.7 years for men and 3.5 years for women.

271   Connidis, Ingrid Arnet, & Davies, Lorraine. (1990). Confidants and companions in later life: The place of family and friends. *Journal of Gerontology, 45*(4), S141-S149.

This article reports on results of a study of 400 community residents ages 65 and older living in London, Canada. The aim of the study was to examine and compare the confidant and companions networks of older people, and to determine whether the networks differed from one another. The sample was a stratified random sample. Face-to-face interviews were conducted with respondents. Closed- and open-ended questions were asked about ties with family and friends, health and well-being, employment history, service needs and subjective views of aging. Independent variables included gender, marital status, and geographic proximity to children among those who are parents. Dependent variables were those who are companions and those who are confidants to respondents. Asking people in whom they "trust and confide" provided the basis for determining if an individual was a confidant or merely a companion, who shared activities and time with the respondent. Authors predicted that confidant networks and companionship networks would differ. Those living in closer proximity were assumed to more likely to be companions. Analyses of data revealed that for older respondents in this study, children and friends are the dominant tie in the confidant network, while friends and spouses are the key relationships in the companion network. Differences were found between men and women and between those who where married and single and those who had children or were childless. Children make up a larger proportion of the confidant network of men (43%) than of women (35%). Friends make up a much larger proportion of the confidant network of women (one third) than of men (one fifth). Analyses further revealed the greater dominance of children in the confidant than companion network. Among those with children, the greater dominance of friends in the companion than confidant group for all groups, and the greater dominance of siblings and other relatives in the confidant than companion network for all groups. For a single woman, however, siblings make up one quarter of the companion network, indicating the far greater importance of siblings to the lives of older, single women. Childless women tend to develop ties with friends as both companions and confidants to a greater extent than other groups. Childless men also rely more on friends, but only as companions. Finally, based on their analyses these researchers conclude that "findings from this study suggest that single and previously married without children, especially male, may be at risk of not having diverse enough social networks to ensure that their needs are met regularly.

272   **Dean, Stanley R. (1966). Sin and the senior citizens.** *Journal of the American Geriatrics Society, 14(9),* **935-938.**

The purpose of this paper is to present a review of the psychological pressures that would lead older people to "defy the law" in order to collect Social Security pensions. The author discusses the sociological phenomena of older unmarried people living together due to the provision in the Social Security Act that a widow will receive 82.5% of her deceased husband's benefits only if she does not remarry. Should she do so, she could lose her benefits or receive a substantially reduced amount. The author expresses his concern with the ethical, moral, and social implications of this dilemma. As a result of a previous article by the author on this topic, Congressman Claude Pepper introduced a bill that would allow a widow who remarried to retain her previous allotment or change it in accordance with her new husband's benefits, depending upon which sum is greater. The author comments that the change in law affecting old people is only a start. There are still loopholes that need to be closed and similar deficiencies in Veteran's pensions and in the Railroad Retirement Act.

273 Depner, Charlene E., & Ingersoll-Dayton, Berit. (1985). Conjugal social support: Patterns in later life. *Journal of Gerontology,* 40(6), 761-766.

This article reports on a study of conjugal social support in 412 married respondents 50 years and older. Data were from the Social Networks in Adult Life Survey, a national sample survey. Interviewers were conducted with respondents to gather data on social networks, emotional support, respect, and social support (i.e., confiding, reassurance, respect, care when ill, talk when upset, and talk about health). Health support was also assessed. Data were analyzed using two multivariate analyses of variance (MANOVA), one on support received from the spouse and the other on support provided to the spouse. Analyses revealed no overall age differences in social support received from the spouse. There was a significant univariate effect of age on support provided by the respondent to the spouse. Univariance tests of age effects in the provision of all forms of support were significant, specifically emotional support and health support. The multivariable test of the effect of sex on the receipt of conjugal support was significant. Women were less likely than men to report that they received emotional support, respect, or health support. The multivariate effect of sex on provision of conjugal support was also significant, with women less likely than men to provide their spouses with emotional support and health support. Analyses revealed that support is decreasingly prevalent in the marriages of older people. Support is less plentiful for women (giving and receiving) than for men. The authors suggest that even though there is a greater need for support in later life, as time passes the capacity of the spouse to respond to increased needs may be constrained by limits in personal resources and nurturing skills.

274 Gilford, Rosalie. (1984). **Contrasts in marital satisfaction through-out old age: An exchange theory analysis.** *Journal of Gerontology,* 39(3), 325-333.

This article presents the results of a quasilongitudinal study of marital satisfaction in 318 married people ages 55 to 90 years. The study tests Homans' (1974) exchange theory as it applies to the marital relationship. Exchange theory postulates that individuals will maintain interaction as long as the rewards (benefits) outweigh the costs. In marriage the rewards are positive interaction and sentiment. Data were gathered through mail question-naires sent to those who were members of intact, three-generation families. The sample of 318 consisted of 69% married couples, 16% husbands and 15% wives exclusive of their respective spouses. Respondents were divided into age groups: ages 55 to 62 (N = 90); ages 63 to 69 (N = 132); and ages 70 to 90 (N = 96). The sample was exclusively Caucasian, mainly Protestant, with a blue-collar, labor-union background living in the Los Angeles area. The questionnaire included 10 marital satisfaction items. Marital satisfaction, the dependent variable, was determined by the respondent's evaluation on two dimensions: positive interaction and negative sentiment. The analysis employed 19 independent variables including social variables such as age and gender and personal variables such as happiness, perceived health problems and financial problems. Stepwise multiple regression analysis was performed. Results indicated differences in marital satisfaction among the different age groups, with those aged 63 to 69 reporting the highest levels of positive interaction and lowest levels of negative sentiment. Results also indicated that some of the 19 independent variables accounted for differences in marital satisfaction, particularly for the youngest age group ages 55 to 62. Positive interaction appeared to be more influenced by resources that set marital exchange rates than was negative sentiment. The following were rewards in older marriage and associated with positive interaction: happiness, good health, familistic attitudes, both spouses being home, affectual solidarity with child, greater age, religiosity, being a man, and education. Costs associated with marriage in late life and with reports of negative sentiment were: low psychological well-being, low income, low effectual solidarity with a child, contemporary orientation to sex and marriage, financial problems, both spouses not being home, low humanism, and being a man. Analyses revealed that fewest predictors and least productivity of marital satisfaction emerged for the oldest age group ages 70 to 90.

275   Gilford, Rosalie. (Summer, 1986). Marriages in later life. *Generations, 10*(2), 16-20.

This paper reviewed the literature on older marriages for the purpose of identifying their special strengths and strains. The evidence was examined from the perspective of three questions: (1) What are the strengths of older marriages? (2) What strains do older marriages endure? (3) And what insights can service providers and planners gain from an understanding of long-lived marriages? Strengths include enhanced quality of life for spouses, opportunities for intimacy, shared resources, and a sense of belonging. Strains include stress and conflict in some situations and especially at retirement and dealing with health problems of an aging spouse. Service providers need to provide social and professional support for older couples.

276 Harvey, Carol D., & Bahr, Howard M. (February, 1974). Widowhood, morale, and affiliation. *Journal of Marriage and the Family, 36*(1), 97-106.

This article reports on a cross-national study of attitudes and interaction patterns of widowed people in five nations. Data were derived from three large sample surveys, which include respondents from five nations, including the United States, Italy, Germany, Mexico, and the United Kingdom. The surveys are described in detail. Each included different measures of positive and negative feelings and attitudes, affiliation, and happiness/ morale. Based on their analyses, Harvey and Bahr conclude that the negative impact sometimes attributed to widowhood (unhappiness, low morale, and so forth) derives not from widowhood status but rather from socioeconomic status.

277 Heinemann, Gloria D., & Evans, Patricia L. (1990). Widowhood: Loss, change, and adaptation. In Timothy H. Brubaker (Ed.) *Family relationships in later life, Second edition.* Neubury Park, CA: SAGE Publications.

The purpose of this chapter is to place widowhood in a larger context of loss, change, and adaptation. The authors describe the loss and change model and discuss each of its components: preparation, grief and mourning, and adaptation. They discuss the stages of preparation for widowhood: socialization, life stage rehearsal/planning, and anticipatory grieving. The authors also discuss grief and mourning in widowhood including response to death of spouse, coping strategies, social supports in grief and mourning and adaptation to widowhood including reorganization and life style choice, support, well-being and morale among the widowed. Findings derived from the data from the Quality of American Life Survey are discussed. Subjects for this survey were 289 widows and 446 married women ages 50 to 79.

278 Johnson, Colleen Leahy. (February, 1985). The impact of illness on late-life marriages. *Journal of Marriage and the Family, 47*(1), 165-172.

This article reports on a qualitative study of 76 late-life marriages (ages 65 years and older) in which one spouse was recuperating from a hospital stay. Couples in the San Francisco Bay Area were interviewed. Open-ended questions were asked about social supports used to elicit help from a spouse or other relative, the quality of the marriage, and questions about the illness and how it affected the marriage. The *Activities of Daily Living Scale* (ADL) was used to determine functional status of the patient. Quality of the marriage was evaluated on the basis of self-reports on satisfaction with marriage, the extent of conflict, shared interests and activities, power distribution, and emotional interdependence. Interviews revealed that most couples were satisfied with their marriage, and had a companionate type of marriage. Dissatisfaction, while rarely reported, was usually traced to the problems of the illness and burdens of care. Johnson categorized expressions of marital satisfaction into four general items: sense of survivorship; shared experiences, traditionalism, and interdependence. One source of tension in the marriage was related to fears of a spouse's death and feelings of loss and abandonment it would entail. Some wives expressed their fears through elaborate health promotion (e.g., regulating the spouse's diet, exercise, and so forth), which sometimes produced anger and resentment in the husband. Conflict was generally handled through joking. One interesting finding reported was that socioeconomic status and gender had no significant effect on levels of conflict or emotional interdependence in the marriages, or in the strain and ambivalence experienced by caregivers. Degree of functional impairment (as measured by ADLs) also had no effect. However, caregivers of the more disabled did report significantly more strain. Another noteworthy finding is that among those families in which the spouse was the primary caregiver, members of the social network were significantly less involved than among those in which another family member had these responsibilities.

279   **Lawton, M. Powell, Moss, Miriam, & Kleban, Morton H. (September, 1984). Marital status, living arrangements and the well-being of older people.** *Research on Aging, 6*(3), 323-345.

The purpose of the present study was to take advantage of the availability of several data sets that are both large and rich in variables representing behavioral competence, perceived quality of life, and psychological well being. Three large data sets are used for analysis. The sets come from The National Senior Citizens Survey, The Harris Survey of 1974, and a local random sample of people from a list of social security recipients. This study sampled, from the three sources, 8,062 individuals ages 65 and over by personal interviews. The samples of older people were analyzed in terms of the relationship between marital status and living arrangements, and a variety of indicators of well-being including cognitive functioning, health, family interaction, and other aspects. With other background factors controlled, the major effect of marital status was seen in the favorable situation of the presently married. Effects associated with living arrangements are stronger. Those living alone are healthier but notably lower in all types of subjective well being. Living with children was associated with lower basic competence and subjective well being, but being married had generally favorable consequences whether or not other people lived in the household.

280   Lee, Gary R. (February, 1978). Marriage and morale in later life. *Journal of Marriage and the Family, 40*(1), 131-139.

This article reports results of a study on the effect of marital satisfaction on morale of married people ages 60 and over in Washington State. A total of 870 individuals completed a mail questionnaire (341 males and 247 females). The sample from whom complete data were available on all variables consisted of 258 married males and 181 married females. Morale, was measured using a 6-item scale, including items such as "On the whole, life gives me a lot of pleasure." Marital satisfaction was indexed by a five-item scale consisting of items such as "If you had it to do over again, would you marry the same person?" Data were analyzed by means of multiple regression. Results indicated that marital satisfaction is a significant correlate of morale, which is more true for women than for men. For men and women, the strongest correlates of morale are health and satisfaction with standard of living and, to a lesser extent, education. Age and length of marriage have negligible effects in morale.

281   Liang, Jersey, & Tu, Edward Jow-Ching. (October, 1986). Estimating lifetime risk of nursing home residency: A further note. *The Gerontologist, 26*(5), 560-563.

The authors calculate the lifetime risk of living in a nursing home. At any given time, approximately 5% of older people live in long-term care. Over a lifetime, the risk of being institutionalized is 29.7% The probability of a person aged 65 entering a nursing home is 35.6%. The probability of institutionalization increases from .297 to .456 between ages 0 to 90. After 90, the risk declines somewhat. The authors provide a detailed description of their mathematical analysis and several tables.

282   Lloyd, Sally A., & Zick, Cathleen D. (Spring, 1986). Divorce at mid and later life: Does the empirical evidence support the theory? *Journal of Divorce, 9*(3), 89-102.

This article examines existing literature on divorce at midlife and later life to test the applicability of two very similar theories of divorce. Divorce in midlife and later life is an important concern, considering that over 20% of all divorces in the United States occur in mid-life and later life. Most research reported has been conducted on marriages lasting less than 10 years and on individuals under 35 years of age. Two exchange-oriented models of divorce, which are tested, are those proposed by Levinger (1976) and Becker (1981). Both models argue that the costs and benefits of marriage are weighed against the cost and benefits of divorce. Four factors considered in the divorce decision are positive attractions of the marriage, costs of remaining married, barriers to divorce, and alternatives to marriage which are available. Each of these factors changes over time. For example, in the early years of marriage the presence of children is a major barrier to divorce; however, in mid-life or later when children have left home, this barrier is removed. This article focuses on the four factors specified in the conceptual models as they apply to marriage and divorce in mid-life and later life. The primary benefit of long-term marriage is companionship. Communication becomes an important source of marital satisfaction as partners become more dependent on one another over time. Other reported benefits of long-term marriages include affection and sexual expression, social approval, shared religious beliefs, health, presence of children, shared memories, and financial security. The main costs of long-term marriage cited in the literature are changes in the original contract, unfulfilled goals, sexual problems, and physical disability. The main barriers to divorce in midlife and later life cited in the literature are financial expenses, obligations toward the marital bond, religious constraints, community pressure, and feelings toward children. Two major barriers to divorce are the large investment in terms of time, money and emotion that has been made to the relationship; and fear of social isolation. Major alternatives to marriage or benefits of divorce in midlife and later life fall into two categories: other partners who are perceived to be more rewarding than the current partner and the perceived availability of a more rewarding life style. The authors conclude that both theories are useful explanations of divorce in mid-life and later life. They cite the need for more systematic investigation of the factors. They argue that age at divorce and duration be differentiated in future research.

283 Lopata, Helena Znaniecki. (Spring, 1971). Widows as a minority group. *The Gerontologist, 11*(1), 67-77.

This early article, which is now viewed as one of the classic pieces on widowhood, offers a comprehensive review of the subject of widows. Lopata argues that widows in America represent a minority group for several reasons. First, they are demeaned by having to socialize only with other widows. Second, they feel they are "second-class citizens" because friends avoid them in an attempt to ignore the subject of death and grief. Third, widows are women, the "lesser sex" in a male-dominated culture. Fourth, most widows are older and, thus, suffer from the prejudice and discrimination facing older people in youth-oriented America. Fifth, many widows are members of other minority groups, particularly ethnic or racial groups. Sixth, many widows are poor, which places them in a minority group. Finally, many widows are ignorant of how to function on their own in the larger society. Lopata also reviews data on widows from a variety of sources. Based on existing literature, Lopata concludes that three sets of factors influence the life style of a widow: the social structure and culture of the society and community in which she lives; the family institution, especially the norms surrounding the role for wife, mother, and kin member; and her personal characteristics (e.g., age, number and location of children, sources and amount of income, employment, and friendships). Lopata also describes characteristics of widows such as total number, age, distribution, living status, economic status, employment status, and others. Lopata calls for more longitudinal and cross-cultural studies of widows. Finally, she calls for action to benefit widows. She suggests that widows be trained to live independently and challenges housing managers to provide occasions which facilitate friendship and other forums of social engagement.

284 Lowenthal, Marjorie Fiske, & Haven, Clayton. (1968). Interaction and adaptation: Intimacy as a critical variable. *American Sociological Review, 33*, 20-30.

This study is devoted to the analysis of the relation between adult socialization patterns and adaptation. Panel data collected for an older sample are drawn upon to document further the equivocal nature of this relationship when conventional measures of social role and interaction are compared with three types of indicators of adaptation. The comparative importance, respectively, of social privilege and social deprivation for adaptation varies according to the subjectivity of adaptive measure used. It also differs for self as compared with professional appraisals of well-being. Regardless of the overall pattern of these interrelationships, deviant cells are sizable. The introduction of a variable bearing on the quality of social relationships, in this case the presence of an intimate relationship serves as a buffer both against gradual social losses in role and interaction and against the more traumatic losses accompanying widowhood and retirement. They conclude that age and sex differences may have implications for the differential in the survival rates of men and women.

285   McAuley, William J., Jacobs, Mary D., & Carr, Carol S. (January, 1984). Older couples: Patterns of assistance and support. *Journal of Gerontological Social Work, 6*(4), 35-48.

The authors examined the degree to which older, noninstitutionalized husbands and wives are involved in providing various types of assistance, the likelihood of providing assistance to one's spouse and to others, and the characteristics associated with giving more forms of help. Selected for this survey were subjects from the statewide Survey of Older Virginians, a survey of 2,146 people over 60 in 1979. A total of 85% of the original survey took part in this survey. Subjects completed an individual interview with a researcher. The questions asked were based on the OARS multidimensional functional assessment instrument developed at Duke University. The authors' findings suggested that older wives are more likely than older husbands to provide most of these forms of assistance. They also suggested that husbands are more likely to help their spouses, while wives are more likely to help people outside the pair. Their analysis concluded that the ability of the potential recipient spouse to perform daily living tasks is a key factor in determining number of forms of help provided by the potential helping spouse.

286   Reedy, Margaret Neiswender, Birren, James E., & Schaie, K. Warner. (1981). Age and sex differences in satisfying love relationships across the adult life span. *Human Development, 24*(1), 52-66.

The purpose of this research was to identify age and sex differences in the major characteristics of satisfying heterosexual love relationships. Subjects were 102 happily married young (mean age = 28.2), middle-aged (mean age = 45.4), and older (mean age = 64.7) couples who completed a 108 statement Q-sort of love experiences. Subjects were mostly white (N = 198); six were black. Scores were determined for six components of love: emotional security, respect, help and play behaviors, communication, sexual intimacy, and loyalty. Statistical analysis showed that older lovers had higher ratings for emotional security and loyalty and lower ratings for sexual intimacy, while young adult lovers had higher ratings for communication. Men were found to have higher ratings for loyalty, while women had higher ratings for emotional security.

287 **Rubenstein, Robert L., Kilbride, Janet C., & Nagy, Sharon. (1992).** *Elders living alone: Frailty and the perception of choice.* **New York: Aldine De Gruyter.**

The material in this book derives from a project funded by the Commonwealth Fund Commission on Older People Living Alone. The project titled "The Personal Surrounds of Frail Elders Living Alone: An Empirical Inquiry" was one of three research programs selected to examine how frail and functionally impaired older people who live alone manage against great odds to maintain themselves independently. The project was designed to answer the questions: Who among the severely impaired elderly people will be able to manage at home and avoid nursing care? *and* How do frail elders maintain themselves successfully outside nursing homes? The authors state that the term "frailty" links objective health status with both objective and subjective personal efficacy and viability. The authors examined the personal surroundings of individuals and their home environment. They examined the effects of choice; independence and aging; factors limiting choices among the study population; the altered ethos of choice among frail elders living alone; the world at home; life history and individual choice; and choice and successful aging. The book consists of many case studies resulting from interviews conducted by the authors in Philadelphia. Most of the subjects were poor elderly living on Social Security and in subsidized houses.

288   Silverstone, Barbara, & Wynter, Lolita. (February, 1975). The effects of introducing a heterosexual living space. *The Gerontologist, 15*(1), 83-87.

This paper reports on the integration of an all-male floor and all-female floor in a geriatric institution for the purpose of providing a healthier climate for the 62 elderly residents involved. The mean age of the subjects was 87.1. The mean duration of their residency in the home was 3.6 years. The subjects suffered in varying degrees from physical and/or mental disability. Most were Jewish and all but a few were widowed. Reactions of the residents to the change were assessed and the effects evaluated and measured. Initial resistance to the change gave way to group acceptance and a more cheerful floor life. A control group in the same facility was established. Assessment involved administering the *Oberleder Attitude Scale* (OAS), a 25-item questionnaire involving attitudes about aging and the *Ward Behavior Inventory* (WBI) designed to estimate severity of disturbances and assess changes over time for hospitalized patients. Both instruments were administered as pre- and posttests to nursing staff on each floor. Quantitative findings suggested significant improvements in the social behavior of the males eight months later. Physical changes such as improved grooming and less use of profane language. The author describes specific situations that developed related to the integration of the floors.

289   Stephens, Joyce. (August, 1974). Romance in the SRO: Relationships of elderly men and women in a slum hotel. *The Gerontologist, 14*(4), 279-282.

This study was an attempt to investigate characteristics and patterns of interactions between aged men and women living in a hotel in the central core of a large midwestern city. The study population was 92 men and 11 women. Stephens reports that elderly women are considerably less likely to live in slum hotels because they tend to be living with family members or in their own homes or apartments. Women living in this hotel were significantly different from men. She found that the men were wary and suspicious; the women were bitter and resentful. Each sex thought the other was trying to use or exploit him or her. Women were more likely than men to have been married, had children, and been linked up to a conventional life style. Women were more vulnerable, less successful at coping, and unreconciled to their present life style. The sexual life of the men usually involved prostitutes with some involvement with women living in the hotel. Men were very interested in discussing sex. The women did not get along with each other well and provided each other with little support. The data in this study were obtained for the author's doctoral dissertation, "Loners, losers, and lovers," Wayne State University (1973).

290 Tobin, Sheldon S., & Neugarten, Bernice L. (1961). Life satisfaction and social interaction in the aging. *Journal of Gerontology, 16*(4), 344-346.

The purpose of this article was to investigate the relationship between disengagement and psychological well-being in the aged. The study population was a group of persons ages 50 to 70 and a group of people ages 70 to 80. The first group was interviewed in 1956; the second group joined the study at a later time. The total 187 cases were divided into two age groups: those ages 50 to 69 and those ages 70 and over. All measures are based on data from interviews obtained at 6-month intervals. Measures of social interaction were the *Interaction Index*, the *Social Life Space*, the *Role Count, and Perceived Life Space*. Psychological well-being was measured using the *Life Satisfaction Ratings* (LSR). The authors found that aged persons in this sample who perceive their life space as large are low on social interaction. Social interaction is positively associated with life satisfaction for all ages included in this study population and with advanced age this association is increased. These findings indicate that engagement, rather than disengagement, is more closely related to psychological well-being.

291 Travis, Shirley S. (June, 1987). Older adults' sexuality and remarriage. *Journal of Gerontological Nursing, 13*(6), 9-14.

Nurses now find themselves the primary information/education source for older, healthier, sexually active, married, unmarried, and remarried older adults. This review of the literature summarizes information on aging sexuality from the *Kinsey Report* and Masters and Johnson's ground breaking studies. The author discusses changes in the aging female and male. She also discusses the difference between sexual intercourse and sexuality and points out that people have emotional needs which may be met by holding, touching, and closeness. She states that contactual relationships may be more important than sexual relationships for aging individuals in their later years. Remarriage in later years is an important issue. Since there are five times as many women as men, remarriage is more available to men. She summarizes the results of several studies of older couples. She finds that many older couples who marry knew each other for many years during previous marriages. She concludes that a great deal of the information used today to plan for the elderly is based on studies of people two decades ago. She calls for additional studies and discussions of issues such as privacy in nursing homes. She questions the ability of nurses to effectively counsel the elderly in matters of sexuality without more current research information.

292   **Treas, Judith, & VanHilst, Anke. (April, 1976). Marriage and remarriage rates among older Americans.** *The Gerontologist,* **16(2), 132-136.**

This analysis is based on published data from marriage certificates sampled for 47 states and the District of Columbia in 1970. The authors found that about 60,000 people ages 65 and older were married in 1970 which was 3 brides out of every 1,000 single women and 17 grooms per 1,000 single men. Of all marriages, 1% involved older brides and 2% older grooms. Marital prospects for women decline at every 5-year interval of life. Comparisons with 1960 data indicate little change in numbers of older marriages. Divorced people are the most likely to remarry followed by widows and last by never-married. First marriages constitute only 6% of all marriages for older brides and grooms. In the South and West, older men and women are about two times more likely to marry than in the Northeast and North Central states. The most likely senior citizen to marry is a 65-year-old divorced man residing in the Southern or Western United States. The authors discuss advantages of marriage in old age and cultural impediments.

293   **Uhlenberg, Peter, & Myers, Mary Anne P. (June, 1981). Divorce and the elderly.** *The Gerontologist, 21*(3), **276-282.**

The authors examined levels of divorce among the elderly now and in the future using data collected from the decennial censuses and the annual March *Current Population Reports* which report marital status by age. While divorce among the current elderly cohort is uncommon and relatively few have ever experienced a divorce, the proportion who will have been divorced before reaching old age in future cohorts will increase rapidly. Reasons for the expected increase are: the national trend toward divorce, a large increase in second marriages (which have a higher chance of divorce), longer life expectancies, and increase in economic independence for both male and female. Knowledge about the effects of marital status upon well-being suggests that being divorced or separated is detrimental to one's social and economic welfare in old age.

294   Usher, Carolyn E., & McConnell, Stephen R. (May, 1980). House-sharing: A way to intimacy? *Alternative Lifestyles, 3*(2), 149-166.

The authors investigated the role that social resources play in determining favorable attitudes toward housesharing in older people. They also investigate the reasons why older people might wish to house-share, whether to acquire companionship and/or an intimate partner. Eighty-five subjects ages 55 to 80 who owned their own homes were interviewed over a 3-month period by an individual close to the age of the subjects. The interview consisted of questions that dealt with the homeowner's present living arrangement, social interactions, and others. The authors concluded that subjects who have had unpleasant experiences in the past were more likely to want to live alone. Subjects who have had and still have an integration in a social group were more likely to want a companion at home close to their own ages. Older homeowners did not view housesharing as a way to become intimate but more of a codependency on each other in need of home services or additional income.

295   Wax, Judith. (September 19, 1975). Sex and the single grandparent. *New Times, 5*(6), 43-47.

This article discusses the trend toward living together by couples over 65, an estimated 18,000 couples according to the United States Census Bureau. The reasons for this 1970s trend included potential loss of income by widows, remnants of the sexual revolution, and increased numbers of older people, single and desiring companionship but not marriage. Wax discusses the interest in sexuality of these older couples who report sexual desire on the parts of both men and women. The author cites case studies and contemporary research to illustrate her perspective which is supportive of the trend.

12

Alternative Life Styles in Old Age

The most noticeable change in the literature between the 1970s and the 1990s is the proliferation of research about the effects of aging on the gay and lesbian communities. In 1979, Martin Berezin remarked that "Studies on the aging homosexual are extremely rare." The number of books and articles in this chapter illustrates the growing body of research in this area.

As the gay population increases its visibility in all aspects of life in the United States, elderly gay people also are becoming more visible. Several organizations, whose members consist of professional researchers, gerontologists, and health care professionals, have created special interest groups in response to this growing interest. Lesbianism has been suggested as a way of meeting the sexual and affection needs of the disproportionate number of women in the older population. Researchers have investigated the adjustment of gay people in later life, issues of loneliness and family interaction. A few of the writers have also included bisexuals in their investigations or discussions.

Like elderly sexuality in general, there are many myths and misconceptions associated with aging and the gay community. The writers whose work is listed in this chapter have identified the stereotypes and attempted to refute them. Many writers have set out to educate nurses and other health care professionals about gays and lesbians much as other writers have tried to educate nurses and physicians about the aging heterosexual population.

The sexual practices and changes in behaviors and interests are addressed in only a few of these works. That subject is addressed in Adelman's collection of autobiographical pieces by aging lesbians titled *Long Time Passing* (1986). Friend's article (1987) addresses normal changes in sexual response related to age in gays and lesbians.

Study populations include acquaintances of the writers, friendship networks, members of gay social organizations, support groups, churches, senior centers, and personal advertisements.

296   **Adelman, Marcy. (1991). Stigma, gay lifestyles, and adjustment to aging: A study of later-life gay men and lesbians.** *Journal of Homosexuality, 20(1),* **7-33.**

This study examined adjustment to later life and coping with stigma among 27 older gay men and 25 older lesbians. Subjects were interviewed concerning their health, work/retirement, leisure activities, relationships, sexual behavior, living arrangements and perspectives on the life course. The data for this study were taken from 11 questions from these interviews. Adjustment to later life was significantly related to the subject's satisfaction with being gay, and the sequence of early events in the subject's gay development. The author also discussed other social styles, such as styles of disclosure, in relation to adjustment - to later life and aging, and suggested that the findings of this study raises questions to be answered by future research.

297   **Adelman, Marcy (Ed.). (December, 1986).** *Long time passing: Lives of older lesbians.* **Boston: Alyson Publications, Inc.**

The book is a collection of autobiographical remembrances of older lesbian women. Many of the women had been married and had children. Most had early sexual experiences with women as well as men. The author conducted research on lesbian aging and co-directed a National Institute of Mental Health grant on the subject. The study compared heterosexual men and women to gay men and lesbians over 60 in terms of their adjustment to aging. To acquire the stories for this book, the author sent out letters to acquaintances in the lesbian community asking for their personal reflections on their own aging process. This book was the result of that request.

298   **Bennett, Keith C., & Thompson, Norman L. (October, 1980). Social and psychological functioning of the ageing male homosexual.** *The British Journal of Psychiatry, 137,* **361-370.**

The authors discussed the stereotype of the older male

homosexual as one of disengagement from the homosexual world, loneliness, rejection, depression and unhappiness. This typical picture of the aging homosexual is not supported by the findings from 478 homosexual men in Australia with diverse backgrounds. The men completed an 18-page questionnaire on several aspects of homosexual and heterosexual behavior. They found that there are no age differences in psychological well-being and involvement in the gay community. They reported that older homosexuals believe they lack control for their sexual orientation. The older homosexual attempts to hide his homosexuality more than his younger counterpart. These findings appear to be generational differences. The authors discussed the implications of their findings for professionals working with homosexuals and their parents.

299   Berger, Raymond M. (May, 1982). The unseen minority: Older gays and lesbians. *Social Work, 27*(3), 236-242.

The author discusses the need for those in the social work profession to acknowledge the existence and special needs of the large but often ignored group of elderly gay men and lesbians. This group comprises 8% of the adult population which is equal to over 1,750,000 people. At one point a majority of this group will need to speak with a social worker, and social workers need to know how to deal with this group. According to the author, until recently a total lack of awareness of and information about homosexuals has existed, especially about older homosexuals. Most homosexuals have been hiding their sexual preferences for years and it is the social workers need to be aware of this. They must take appropriate actions because older homosexuals will usually not talk about their sexual preference except to certain people. The author concludes that older homosexuals face problems from areas such as institutions, legal, emotional, and medical and suggests ways that social workers can provide services that meet this group's needs.

300   Dorfman, Rachelle, Walters, Karina, Burke, Patrick, Hardin, Lovida, Karanik, Theresa, Raphael, John, & Silverstein, Ellen. (1995). Old, sad, and alone: The myth of the aging homosexual. *Journal of Gerontological Social Work, 24*(1/2), 29-44.

This study examined the relationship between sexual orientation, depression, and social support, testing the assumption that older lesbians and gay men are more depressed and socially-isolated than heterosexuals of the same age. The authors distributed 200 questionnaires to gay and lesbian elderly organizations, support groups and churches, and at gay and lesbian events, and senior citizens' centers in large urban settings. The subjects consisted of 133 people who returned questionnaires of whom 28 were dropped for insufficient data. The final sample of 108 consisted of 55 women and 53 men ranging in age from 60 to 93 (mean 69.3 years). There were 56 homosexuals (23 females, 33 males) and 52 heterosexuals (32 females, 20 males). The questionnaire assessed sociodemographic-demographic information, level of depression, social support networks, and gay and lesbian group identity attitudes. The *Geriatric Depression Scale* (GDS) was used to measure depression. The *Lubben Social Network Scale* (LSNS) was used to measure social support. Data analysis revealed no significant difference between homosexuals and heterosexuals on depression. They found that 15% of the total sample was depressed which was consistent with other studies on elderly samples. Higher social network scores were positively related to lower depression scores. There was no significant difference between homosexuals and heterosexuals in overall social support. Both group means were above 28 points on the LSNS which indicates high social support. There were differences in type of support. Gay males had significantly less family support. Heterosexual females had the most family support. Friend support was greater for gay males and to some degree for lesbian females than for heterosexuals.

301   Eliason, Michele J. (May-June, 1996). Working with lesbian, gay, and bisexual people: Reducing negative stereotypes via inservice education. *Journal of Nursing Staff Development, 12*(3), 127-132.

In this article, the author provides guidelines and information that could be used to develop and present an inservice program for nurses that deals with lesbian, gay, and bisexual issues. Eliason says that because negative attitudes about sexuality are deeply ingrained from early childhood, this education must include factual information to correct misinformation and provide an opportunity to explore affective reactions such as fear, disgust, guilt, anger, or general discomfort. Eliason includes suggestions for workshop preparation, format and content. She includes common stereotypes about lesbian, gay and bisexual people and research findings that dispute certain myths. She says to expect opposition for having the workshop and to be prepared to justify the program. She recommends embedding the workshop in a series on cultural diversity. Topics recommended for program content are breaking down stereotypes such as the myth that homosexuals are oversexed, that they are all at high risk for AIDS, and that homosexuality is immoral or unnatural, that homosexuality can be "cured" or changed, and that they are a threat to society or family values. Eliason also discusses bisexual myths and stereotypes. She stresses the importance of presenting factual information and pointing out the irrational basis of most stereotypes.

302 Friend, Richard A. (1987). **The individual and social psychology of aging: Clinical implications for lesbians and gay men.** *Journal of Homosexuality, 14(1/2),* 307-336.

This article examined issues regarding aging for homosexual people in an attempt to provide a more comprehensive understanding and appreciation of the meaning age has for women and men in society. The author discusses case examples, clinical concerns and interventions as related to three areas: (1) the interrelated effects of ageism and heterosexism; (2) normal changes in sexual response with age; and (3) accelerated aging. The relationship between social context and individual psychology provides the framework for this study. The author observed that there was a great deal of diversity among homosexual women and men in their experiences with aging. He concluded that the strengths and insights that characterize many older homosexual men and women, provide valuable lessons for all men and women.

303 Friend, Richard A. (1991). **Older lesbian and gay people: A theory of successful aging.** *Journal of Homosexuality, 20(2),* 99-118.

The author describes a theory for successful aging among homosexuals which is based on an analysis of three groups illustrating the continuum of ways in which older people determine their identity as gays or lesbians in response to heterosexist society. The first group, referred to as "stereotypic," represents those who have internalized the homophobia around them. The people in this group are at one extreme of the continuum, and are characterized by the stereotypes of loneliness, depression, and alienation. The second group, the "affirmative," have responded to society by reconstructing homosexuality into something positive. This group is the other extreme, described as psychologically well-adjusted, vibrant, and adapting well to the aging process. The third group, the "passing," are those who respond by accepting some aspects of homosexuality, but still believe that heterosexuality is inherently better. This group is the middle of the continuum, often has a strong investment in passing as heterosexual, but may under certain circumstances label themselves as lesbian or gay. The author suggests that aging can also be viewed as a continuum from successful to unsuccessful. According to his theory, lesbian and gay people who fall toward the affirmative end of the identity continuum will also age more successfully than those who are passing or stereotypic. Because the stereotypic and passing groups are least represented in the literature, the author suggests that additional research is needed, and recommends that future research verify this theory.

304   Gray, Heather, & Dressel, Paula. (February, 1985). **Alternative interpretations of aging among gay males.** *The Gerontological Society of America*, 25(1), 83-87.
        The authors investigated the impact of age and length of homosexuality stereotypes on over 50 gay males. Subjects completed a questionnaire they received from various methods. Methods included distribution at known gay bars and clubs, distributed by gay men through homophile organizations, published in the *Blueboy*, and mailed to men's names bought through a mailing company. A total of 4,212 gay males returned the questionnaire. The findings suggested the variability of several key factors effects a gay male's life. The authors suggested that as a male ages in the homosexual community, he generally starts to lose self-esteem regarding his looks and ability to please other gays. The authors discussed the most influential aspect of a gay's community is youth. All aspects surround the ideas of youth: looks, performances, and attitudes. They concluded that the stereotypes imbedded in the gay culture are influenced mostly by age because the reflect attitudes and behaviors of the individual not the whole group.

305   Harry, Joseph, & DeVall, William. (June, 1978). **Age and sexual culture among homosexually oriented males.** *Archives of Sexual Behavior*, 7(3), 199-209.
        The authors explored the often reported observation that the culture of homosexually oriented males is heavily youth-oriented to the greatest disadvantage of the older members. This study utilized data from 243 males from the Detroit area in 1975. Data was collected by a 12-page questionnaire distributed to gays by several means: gay bars, known homosexual organizations, and

friendship networks. The researchers found that a majority of males ages 18 to 24 prefer a male partner who is older, a majority of those ages 25 to 34 years prefer a same-age person, and those over 35 prefer a younger partner. They found that these relationships are especially strong among those segments of the sample who attend gay bars infrequently or who are of lower occupational levels. They also found that a higher occupational status was associated with preference for the younger partner, independent of age. The authors suggested that, because of the heterogeneity of the homosexual community, the degree of emphasis on youth will be found to vary with social setting.

306   Kehoe, Monika. (1991). Loneliness and the aging homosexual: Is pet therapy an answer? *Journal of Homosexuality, 20*(2), 137-142.
        This article, written by a well-known, respected researcher on homosexuality, suggests pet therapy as a major therapeutic technique to help older lesbian women deal with problems of loneliness, depression, and loss of a partner, and possibly prevent suicide. Loneliness, as Kehoe defines it, is "more of a state of mind, a genre of forlornness, a feeling of abandonment where one is separated from others by barriers or handicaps." She suggests that the typical methods of combating loneliness (e.g., greater rapport with others, more friends, more social groups, more joining groups) may not be as readily available as therapeutic agents. Animals offer unconditional love, fuzzy creatures that provide sensory stimulation through touch, and a source of love that offers no hurtful words. Kehoe refers to the research study, but does not describe the study in this article. Based on this "study," she found that 73% of the older lesbian women studied never had children and named loneliness as their major problem. Kehoe suggests pets as a practical solution to a solitary, lonely old age for these women.

307   Kelly, Jim. (August, 1977). The aging male homosexual: Myth and reality. *The Gerontologist, 17*(4), 328-332.
        This article discusses findings from a study of 241 gay men ages 16 to 79 years living in the Los Angeles metropolitan area. The study examined the attitudes, stereotypes, and characteristics of these men in reference to aging. Data were collected over a 2-year period through participant observation, interviews, and questionnaires. The author notes that in the "hazy folklore" there are myths and stereotypes about the participation of older gay men in gay subculture activities, about their interpersonal

association with other gay men, about their self-identifications as gay people, and about their sexuality. Kelly describes one composite stereotype of the aging gay male as "an individual who no longer frequents gay bars, having lost his physical attractiveness and his sexual appeal to the young man he craves, is oversexed but has a very unsatisfactory sex life, is seldom sexually active and has no regular partner but only has sex in tea rooms." Kelly did not find support for this stereotype of the aging gay male in his research. Results of his study revealed that older gay men seldom frequent gay bars or tea rooms. His subjects ranked their association with other gay men as "moderate" (44%) to "high" (42%). The gay male's main concern about disclosure is related to his many years of working in a profession where known gays are not tolerated. In contrast to the accepted stereotype, Kelly found that older gay men he studied were quite satisfied with their sex life. Eighty-three percent of those ages 65 and older reported being sexually satisfied. The number of persons involved in liaisons increases with age peaking in the 46 to 55 year age group, then declines to almost none. Loss of a partner through death and rejection if the idea of having a single life-long lover were the reasons cited for the decrease. The older gay men studied did not consider themselves effeminate nor like to define themselves in terms of gay labels. Kelly found that older gay men face many of the same problems faced by aging heterosexual males; stigmatization on the bases of age; loss of people emotionally important to them; and fear of institutionalization. In addition, older gay males face unique discriminations related to the stigmatization of their sexual identity; denial of life insurance; no children to help provide for economic, emotional, and physical security in late life; legal discrimination when a partner dies; and personal prejudice of his dead loved one's family.

308   **Kimmel, Douglas C. (1979-1980). Life-history interviews of aging gay men.** *International Journal of Aging and Human Development, 10*(3), 239-248.

This study focused on the life style and life history of 14 white gay men from New York City ages 55 to 81, mean = 64.9. The author interviewed each man for one and a half to two hours. Kimmel found that the men led a variety of life styles. Ten lived alone, three had lovers, and one lived in a nonsexual relationship with a man who had been his lover several years before. Some of the men had been married and had children; others had been exclusively homosexual all their lives. All of the subjects felt that sexuality was important and nearly all were sexually active. Half of the men said that sex was less important than it was when they were younger. Kimmel summarizes the subjects' responses to questions about their current life styles and life histories. The author concluded that growing old as a gay person does not necessarily lead to despair, loneliness or other negative stereotypes often associated with homosexuality.

309   Kimmel, Douglas C. (Summer, 1978). **Adult development and aging: A gay perspective.** *Journal of Social Issues,* 34(3), 113-130.
       The author studied the need to provide a model for understanding gay adult development and aging. The information in this article comes from interviews with 14 white gay men and from patient to therapist conversations with older gay patients. He found that stereotypes of lonely, depressed, sexually frustrated, aging gay men are not true for the majority of respondents studied. The author concludes that gays do have particular needs such as support during bereavement, assistance if physically disabled, and a reduction in stigmatization as they age and become dependent on others.

310   Laner, Mary Riege. (October, 1978). **Growing older male: Heterosexual and homosexual.** *The Gerontologist, 18* (5), 496-501.
       The author analyzed age-related materials in the "personals" advertisements of heterosexual and homosexual men. She investigated the differences between these groups in terms of accelerated aging (in homosexual men) and a special preference for young partners (among homosexual men). Personal advertisements came from *The Advocate* and *National Singles Register,* both nationally circulated newspapers. One issue from each publication yielded 353 heterosexual male ads and 359 homosexual male ads. The author concluded that stereotypic notions are not supported by the analysis of ads collected. The findings of this study while limited to nonreactive data (newspaper advertisements) supported the normalcy of the process of homosexual aging.

311   Lee, John Alan. (Summer, 1987). **What can homosexual aging studies contribute to theories of aging?** *Journal of Homosexuality, 13*(4), 43-71.
       This sensitive, insightful article, written by a homosexual researcher interested in aging and sexuality issues among older homosexuals, examines homosexuality and aging in a theoretical context. Several theories of aging are discussed and questions on

homosexual aging are posed for each theory. Theories discussed include: disengagement, activity, continuity, social exchange, subcultural, symbolic interactionism, stratification, and conflict theory. The article also reports the results of a 4-year study of 47 homosexual men over 50 years of age. The author gathered data, through in-depth personal interviews and questionnaires. Measures included life satisfaction, self-image, self-description of personality, role count, activities, family and friendships networks, achievement of career and personal goals, celebrations of major festivals, stressful events, and self-portraits of personality traits. Following the final interview, respondents were scored according to their responses to questions about current life satisfaction and their adjustment to aging as very happy, fairly satisfied, satisfied, dissatisfied, or very unhappy. Age made no difference in life satisfaction. Lee provided a test of the questions of crisis competence, whether dealing with the crisis of homosexuality earlier in life is functional to the aging process or accelerates aging toward a lonely, miserable old age. To answer the question, Lee compared life satisfaction scores with numbers of life crises and stressful life events encountered. He found that men who managed to avoid life crises, even if it meant staying a "closet" homosexual to do so, were the happiest. As Lee notes: "But the general tendency went against crisis competence. Instead, the lives of these 47 men suggested that the best coping strategy in earlier life that leads to confidence in coping with the crises of age is one in which earlier life crises are avoided as much as possible." Lee also examined the question of whether older homosexuals are more similar than different. His analysis revealed more similarities than differences. As research on aging heterosexuals has confirmed, in homosexual males the most important predictors of life satisfaction in late life or "successful aging" were health, wealth, and contentment with your "lot in life." Those who were healthier and wealthier, and those who rated their standard of living as "well above" or "above" normal were happiest. Education was the most dramatic social class predictor of happiness in homosexual old age. Based on his analysis, Lee concluded that "it was obvious that social exchange, stratification, and conflict approaches, produced a more insightful explanation of homosexual aging than the functionalist–interactionist models applied by most researchers hitherto of homosexual aging. The final question addressed by Lee is whether or not young and old gay males are allies or adversaries. Lee found that most of the men in this sample, particularly those with higher incomes and other resources and socioeconomic advantages, preferred younger partners. Lee pointed out that many heterosexual men also prefer younger women.

312 **MacDonald, A. P., Jr. (Spring, 1981). Bisexuality: Some comments on research and theory.** *Journal of Homosexuality,* 6(3), 21-35.

The purpose of this article was to examine issues related to conducting research on bisexuality. The author comments that researchers include homosexuals in samples when studying bisexuality and bisexuals in samples that are supposed to be homosexual. One problem is that homosexuals are more visible than bisexuals. Bisexuals have no organizations; they do not meet formally to discuss matters related to their sexual behaviors and concerns. Also there is a crossover in the two populations. The author concludes that it is necessary to look at bisexuals, homosexuals and heterosexuals separately to meaningfully come to terms with sexual orientations. Because previous studies usually have not made the necessary distinctions, they are tainted and their results questionable.

313 **Pope, Mark, & Schulz, Richard. (1991). Sexual attitudes and behavior in midlife and aging homosexual males.** *Journal of Homosexuality,* 20(2), 169-177.

This article reports findings from a study of gay males ages 40 to 77 in the Chicago metropolitan area. Data came from questionnaires mailed to 235 members of Maturity, a social group for gay men ages 40 and older. Of the 235 questionnaires mailed, 101 were returned. Twenty-four percent of the respondents were ages 60 and older. Compared to respondents in the 40 to 49 age group and the 50 to 59 age group, those 60 plus reported having sex much less frequency. However, 86% of those 60 and older reported that they were still sexually active. In all age groups respondents reported a moderate to strong interest in sexual relations, with the 60 and older group reporting less interest than the younger men. Sixty-nine percent of respondents reported no change in their enjoyment of sex, and no difference were found by age. Results of this study confirm that older gay males maintain their interest in sex, as well as their ability to function sexually. The study sample of 101 is considerably larger than most samples of gay men in earlier research studies.

314   Quam, Jean K., & Whitford, Gary S. (April, 1992). Adaptation
       and age-related expectations of older gay and lesbian adults. *The
       Gerontologist, 32*(3), 367-374.
            This article reports results from a study of lesbian women
       and gay men over the age of 50, who are very involved in the
       gay community. The authors note the lack of attention to aging
       lesbians and gay men in research. They offer a brief review of
       literature, noting several methodological problems of past studies
       including: a focus primarily on urban homosexuals living in a
       few major cities; combining all people over 50 into the category of
       aging; and mixing lesbians and gay men. A review of existing
       literature reveals that being homosexual facilitates the aging pro-
       cess. The literature review also shows that integration into the gay
       community results in several positive outcomes: more self-accep-
       tance, less depression, less fear of aging, and greater happiness.
            Quam and Whitford mailed a 32-item questionnaire to a
       sample of 80 lesbian women and gay men over the age of 50,
       who lived in a midwestern metropolitan area and were actively
       involved in the gay community. Three sets of questions were
       included: demographic items; questions on social life of the
       respondent; and measures of life satisfaction. Results indicated
       that close to 64% of the sample were involved in the gay
       community. Thirty-five percent reported going to gay bars (47.5%
       of the males, 23.1% of the women). Seventy-nine percent of the
       sample said they would participate in a social organization for
       older lesbians only or older gay men only. Over half of the
       women reported that most of their closest friends were lesbians;
       however, only 27.5% of the males reported that most of their
       closest friends were gay men. Overall, respondents scored high
       on measures of life satisfaction, current health, and acceptance of
       the aging process. Seventy-one percent described their current
       health status as good or excellent. These findings support those
       reported in earlier studies of older lesbians and gay men.

315   Riley, Matilda White, Ory, Marcia G., & Zablotsky, Diane (Eds.)
       (1989). *AIDS in an aging society: What we need to know*. New
       York: Springer Publishing Company.
            This volume includes a review of the research on sexual
       and AIDS related attitudes and behaviors and a discussion of
       AIDS and older people. Other topics discussed in the text are
       social consequences of the AIDS epidemic, HIV transmission risk
       of older heterosexuals and gays, and problems with AIDS and
       older people.

316   Slusher, Morgan P., Mayer, Carole J., & Dunkle, Ruth E. (February, 1996). Gays and lesbians older and wiser (GLOW): A support group for older gay people. *The Gerontologist, 36*(1), 118-123.

This article describes the Gays and Lesbians Older and Wiser (GLOW) support group which was established for older gay men and lesbians in Ann Arbor, Michigan and supported in part by a grant from the National Institute on Aging. The authors provide demographic data about the older gay and lesbian population. They report that an estimated 3.5 million over the age of 60 live in the United States. The purpose of GLOW is to provide a safe space for older gay men and lesbians where they can meet and engage in mutual support. The authors provide a history of GLOW, explain its recruitment activities, describe its initial structure, and changes in group goals and organization. The authors explain the support functions of the organization. They invite replication of GLOW in other communities as a way to meet the needs of the often invisible population of older lesbians and gay men.

13

Sexual Dysfunction Among the Elderly

Sexual dysfunction among the elderly has a variety of causes, both physiological and psychological. Included as dysfunction are problems with sexual performance, lack of desire, and diminished arousal capacity. Researchers and writers usually include inability to engage in heterosexual activities for any reason in their studies and discussions.

Failure to adjust to normal aging changes and illness are two common causes of sexual dysfunction. Physical causes of sexual dysfunction are often compounded by psychological factors including acceptance by the elderly of negative societal attitudes. Other factors leading to sexual problems are the lack of availability of a sexual partner, mental health problems, chronic pain, substance abuse, side effects of medications, dementia, and a lack of privacy.

Among males, changes in libido and erectile function have been studied extensively. Impotence is the major sexual dysfunction among elderly males although other problems are premature ejaculation, impaired sexual interest, retarded ejaculation, and pain on intercourse.

Among females, the emphasis is on changes occurring after menopause. Decreased estrogen is the most commonly cited cause of problems. The most common sexual dysfunction for females according to some writers is decreased sexual interest. Other problems which interfere with sexual behavior and sexual satisfaction are increases in urinary tract infections, vaginal atrophy, vaginal dryness, reduced libido, vaginismus, dyspareunia, orgasmic dysfunction, and secondary problems caused by illnesses.

Also included in this chapter on sexual dysfunction are those articles and studies dealing with inappropriate sexual behaviors such as physical aggression and public handling of genitals.

Most writers offer suggestions for nurses or physicians in dealing with sexual dysfunction. The most common solutions are education, sex therapy, marital therapy, counseling, and in some cases psychiatric referral. Increasing opportunities for privacy is also suggested. Writers often suggest considering hormone replacement therapy for females but note its risks as well as its benefits. Male hormone therapy has not been shown to be beneficial.

Diseases contributing to sexual dysfunction which are discussed in these articles are diabetes, vascular disease, heart disease, hypertension, post operative dysfunction, prostate cancer, and depression. Articles dealing specifically with health problems and disabilities that interfere with sexuality in the elderly are included in Chapter 14.

317   **Barber, Hugh R. K., Lewis, Myrna, Long, James, Whitehead, E. Douglas, & Butler, Robert N. (March, 1989). Sexual problems in the elderly, II: Men's vs. women's.** *Geriatrics, 44*(3), 75-78, 86.

This article is a summary of a panel discussion of professionals in the geriatric field discussing sexual dysfunction. The major sexual dysfunctions discussed were impotence, diabetes, vascular disease, and psychological problems. As men and women age, each sex finds a particular type of sexual dysfunction becoming more prevalent. For each dysfunction the primary care physician has a management role. Major sexual dysfunctions (impotence, diabetes, vascular disease, psychological problems), and what to do about them are reviewed.

318   **Bishop, Gene. (November, 1989). Sex and UTI in older women.** *Medical Aspects of Human Sexuality, 23*(11), 65-66, 68-69.

This study examined the relationship of sex and urinary tract infections (UTI) in postmenopausal women. Sexual intercourse and urinary tract infections are related due to (1) rapid migration of bacteria into the bladder; (2) trauma to the urethra; and (3) behavior factors. The author stated that the relationship between UTIs and sexual activities is not well understood by women and doctors. The author suggests that physicians include a sexual history at the time of examinations. A better sexual history can lead to better treatment along with counseling to help women deal with this infection.

319　Bowers, L. M., Cross, R. R., Jr., & Lloyd, F. A. (July, 1963). Sexual function and urologic disease in the elderly male. *Journal of the American Geriatrics Society, 11*(7), 647-652.

This survey conducted by a group of medical doctors working at Veterans Administration Hospitals concerns the sexual function and medical status of a population of elderly men who were not patients. The subjects were 157 men ages 60 to 74 of whom 55% were potent. Potent was defined as having coitus even once annually. With the increase in age the incidence of impotence increased from 28% to 61%. Among the potent men the average frequency of coitus per year was 20.7 and no decline in sexual activity with advancing years was evident. Among the impotent men, the average age at the time of the last coitus was 61.8 years. The incidence of non-urologic disease was similar for both potent and impotent groups. The authors concluded that impotence in the elderly male is usually independent of physical condition.

320　Catalan, Jose, Hawton, Keith, & Day, Ann. (1990). Couples referred to a sexual dysfunction clinic: Psychological and physical morbidity. *British Journal of Psychiatry, 156,* 61-67.

The purposes of this study were to describe in detail the demographic characteristics, source of referral, sexual problems, general relationships, psychopathology and physical morbidity of the couples, to examine the relationships between the various sexual dysfunctions and general relationship difficulties, psychopathology and physical morbidity, and to study the types of treatment recommended, the factors associated with these recommendations, the extent to which patients took up the offer of sex therapy and the characteristics of couples who completed this form of treatment. Subjects were 200 couples referred to and assessed in a sexual dysfunction clinic over 2 years. Ages of males ranged from 20 to 68. Ages of females ranged from 18 to 57. The most common sexual dysfunction for males was impotence (60%) and for females impaired sexual interest (64%). Other male problems were premature ejaculation, impaired sexual interest, retarded ejaculation, and pain on intercourse. For females, other problems were vaginismus, dyspareunia, and orgasmic dysfunction. Treatment offered was sex therapy, marital therapy, brief counseling, and psychiatric referral. No comparisons of problems of older couples as compared to younger couples were reported.

321   Cogen, Raymond, & Steinman, William. (1990). Sexual function
      and practice in elderly men of lower socioeconomic status. *The
      Journal of Family Practice, 31*(2), 162-166.

      This article investigated the sexual activities by impotent
      men of lower socioeconomic background. Using physician-
      administered interviews, 87 men (mean age 72.6) attending an
      urban Veterans Administration geriatric clinic were studied to
      determine the prevalence of erectile dysfunction and the sexual
      practices and attitudes of this group. The group consisted of 50.6%
      white and 49.4% black males. The majority of the men had not
      graduated from high school. Their occupations were unskilled
      (14.3%), semiskilled (30.9%), skilled manual (27.4%), clerical/sales
      technicians (14.3%), and professional/semiprofessional (13.1%).
      For purpose of reporting, the authors divided patients into two
      groups. Group 1 men continued to practice coitus. Group 2 men
      had not practiced coitus within the preceding year. Among the
      Group 2 men some had used mutual masturbation with his
      spouse (N = 1), oral sex (N = 1), and self-masturbation (N = 11).
      Therefore, overall, 67% of the men interviewed engaged in some
      sexual activity. Among the Group 1 men, 30% had problems with
      an erection in 25% of their attempts at coitus. Others identified
      lesser difficulties with achieving an erection. In Group 2, 54%
      reported no longer experiencing erections spontaneously, on
      awakening, or during attempts at coitus or masturbation. Six of
      the patients were able to masturbate to orgasm but said they were
      unable to achieve vaginal penetration. None of the subjects said
      they practiced anal intercourse. Of these subjects, 59% were
      taking medications for hypertension and 29.7% had had a
      prostatectomy. The authors concluded that erectile dysfunction is
      very common and often associated with a decrease in self-esteem.

322   Cole, Ellen, & Rothblum, Esther. (December, 1990). Commentary
      on "Sexuality and the Midlife Woman." *Psychology of Women
      Quarterly, 14*(4), 509-512.

      This article is a response to Sandra Leiblum's article,
      "Sexuality and the Midlife Woman." The authors state that the
      article, as does nearly all scholarship in the field, uses the term
      "symptoms" to describe women's experiences during menopause,
      "foreplay" to describe sexual activity that precedes intercourse,
      and the terms "senile" and "atrophic" to describe physiological
      changes at menopause. They contend that these terms are unnec-
      essarily limiting, incorrectly describe sexuality and development,
      and offer alternative descriptive terms that do not pathologize

women's normative and natural experiences. The article also describes research by the authors that was drawn from a nonpatient sample of 41 lesbians (mean age = 51.1) at menopause. They reports that 31 (76%) of the women did not feel they had a sex problem.

323 Deutsch, Stanley, & Sherman, Lawrence. (November 28, 1980). Previously unrecognized diabetes mellitus in sexually impotent men. *Journal of the American Medical Association, 244*(21), 2430-2432.

The purpose of the study was to determine whether there was any difference in glucose tolerance among three groups of men and whether the diabetes or impaired glucose intolerance was associated specifically with secondary impotence (SI) or if it occurred nonspecifically in men with sexual dysfunction. Investigators have found a high frequency of SI (50% and higher) in overt diabetics. Subjects were 58 men with SI, 69 men who suffered from premature ejaculation (PRE), and a control group of 63 healthy men with normal sexual functioning. The subjects underwent a series of laboratory tests. Data analysis showed that 12.1% of the SI subjects had diabetes but none of the men in the other two groups had that condition. This difference was highly significant. Four of the SI subjects (6.9%) were impaired glucose intolerance, compared with two of the healthy men and five of the PRE subjects. Differences were not significant. The writers comment that undiscovered diabetes or "early" diabetes could be involved in cases of male impotence.

324 Ephross, Paul H. (February, 1989). Sexuality. *Maryland Medical Journal, 38*(2), 140-141.

This brief article discusses sexual dysfunction in older adults. The author recommends that evaluation of sexual dysfunction should consider the following factors: (1) the availability of a desirable partner; (2) the general level of mental health of the patient; (3) gynecological and urological evaluation; (4) the presence of disease processes known to have a negative effect or sexual function; (5) the effects of disfiguring surgery and of chronic symptoms that interfere with the older person's self image as sexually desirable; (6) the potential effects of the use and abuse of "recreational" drugs; (7) the potential effects of prescription drugs; and (8) for those living in congregate settings, the cognitive, attitudinal, or behavioral patterns that prevent healthy, satisfying sexual expression.

325   Freeman, Joseph T. (September, 1970). John S.—Widower. *Journal of the American Geriatrics Society, 18*(9), 736-742.

The purpose of the article was to discuss the historical desire of men to maintain sexual prowess into old age. The author cites the Biblical accounts of Sara and Abraham and King David. He presents the story of John S. from the notes of a surgeon writing in 1886 about a procedure he used to help his patient regain his ability to sustain erections. Freeman says that "all too often, even today, repotentiation is equated with rejuvenation."

326   Gupta, Krishan. (February, 1990). Sexual dysfunction in elderly women. *Clinics in Geriatric Medicine, 6*(1), 197-203.

The author says that sex and sexuality in old age has traditionally been viewed as immoral, inappropriate, and even sinful. The author examines the different aspects of female hormones, aging, frequency of sexual activity, illnesses, and sexual preference. It is only in recent years that the sexual function of aging men and women has been recognized as an integral part of the total well-being of elderly individuals. The author concludes that changing attitudes of the society and better understanding of the aging process have helped us to understand the sexual needs of the aging population. Continuing sexual well-being in senescence can be one of the few remaining pleasures of life for the older person.

327   Hsueh, Willa A. (June, 1988). Sexual dysfunction with aging and systemic hypertension. *The American Journal of Cardiology, 61* (supplement), 18H-23H.

In this article, the author focused on the role of the endocrine, neurologic, and vascular systems in normal male sexual function and emphasizes alterations that may lead to sexual dysfunction in the elderly and hypertensive patient. The endocrine system primarily regulates libido and maintenance of genital tissue. The autonomic nervous system and blood flow play important roles in the physiology of the male sexual response, especially penile erection. Vascular disease may be the main factor contributing to the sexual dysfunction that occurs with aging. Hsueh noted that hormonal alterations probably play less of a role and says that the importance of neurologic abnormalities remains to be determined. Specific diagnostic testing can be useful in defining abnormalities in each of these systems. The author concluded that treatment of sexual dysfunction in the setting of hypertension in the elderly patients remains a challenge.

328 Kaas, Merrie Jean. (1981). Geriatric sexuality breakdown syndrome. *International Journal of Aging and Human Development, 13*(1), 71-77.

The author applies the basic outline of Social Breakdown Syndrome (SBS), a cycle in which an older person internalizes negative attitudes of society and perceives himself or herself as useless, to sexual dysfunction in old age. This Geriatric Sexuality Breakdown Syndrome (GSBS) may be an explanation of diminished sexual activity among older people. The author suggests that older people may be predisposed to reduced sexual activity by this breakdown, and describes six stages according to the SBS outline. The author suggests that changing society's negative cues toward the sexual behavior of older people and helping the elderly person cope with negative cues are effective interventions to break this cycle.

329 Kaiser, Fran E. (February, 1991). Sexuality and impotence in the aging man. *Clinics in Geriatric Medicine, 7*(1), 63-72.

Decreased sexual function commonly occurs with aging but should not be considered a normal event. This article discusses normal physiologic changes and the pathologic events that can lead to erectile difficulties. Proper evaluation can lead to a more appropriate choice of therapeutic agent or device and can benefit the quality of life of the older man and his partner.

330 Kaiser, Fran E., Viosca, Sharon P., Morley, John E., Mooradian, Arshag D., Davis, Susan Stanik, & Korenman, Stanley G. (1988). Impotence and aging: Clinical and hormonal factors. *Journal of the American Geriatrics Society, 36*(6), 511-519.

A study of 216 impotent men ages 40 to 79 years was conducted to determine if there were age-related changes in clinical and hormonal extents in an impotent population. The authors noted a slight increase in the degree of sexual dysfunction with age, with complete erectile failure occurring in a larger percentage of the 60- to 70-year-olds than in younger patients. They found there was a marked age-related alteration in the concentration of testosterone (T) and bioavailable testosterone (BT). An increase in the prevalence of eugonadotropic hypogonadism with age was found. This suggested an increased prevalence of hypothalamic pituitary dysfunction in this patient group. Both vascular and hormonal changed the greatest after the age of 50. These data supported the multifactorial nature of impotence in the elderly with prominent vascular and hormonal factors. They stressed the need for careful assessment and evaluation of these problems. They provided strong support for the impotence of organic components in males over 50 years of age.

331   Kaplan, Helen Singer. (1983). *The evaluation of sexual disorders: Psychological and medical aspects.* New York: Brunner/Mazel.
    In this book, Kaplan states that a careful evaluation of sexual dysfunction in older persons should include consideration of at least the following factors: (1) the availability of a desirable partner in the light of the total social situation of the patient; (2) the general level of mental health of the patient, with particular emphasis on the presence of depressive symptomatology; (3) gynecological and urological evaluation, sometimes hormonal studies; (4) the presence of disease processes that are known to have negative effects on sexual function of some persons such as diabetes and various neurological conditions, as well as the presence of debilitating symptoms, such as chronic pain; (5) the effects of disfiguring surgery and of chronic symptoms such as limited mobility that interfere with self-image of the elderly person as sexually desirable; (6) the potential effects of the use and abuse of "recreational" drugs, most notably alcohol, on sexual function; (7) the potential effects of prescription drugs, several classes of which can have negative effects on one or more phases of the sexual desire-arousal-orgasm progression; (8) for patients living in congregate or institutional settings, the effects of sex-negative and often personally degrading policies and procedures that can dehumanize and therefore desexualize older persons; and (9) specific dysfunctional cognitive, attitudinal, or behavioral patterns that operate to prevent healthy and satisfying sexual expression.

332   Kaplan, Helen Singer. (Summer, 1990). Sex, intimacy, and the aging process. *Journal of the American Academy of Psycho-analysis, 18*(2), 185-205.
    The author cites evidence from the literature demonstrating that the loss of sexuality is not an inevitable aspect of aging, and the majority of healthy people remain sexually active on a regular basis until advanced old age. However, the aging process does bring with it certain changes in the physiology of the male and the female sexual response. These changes, along with medical

problems that become more prevalent in the mature years, play a significant role in the onset of sexual disorders of the elderly. The author has made observations on over 400 patients with sexual complaints over a time period of 10 years. The typical patient over 50 has only a partial degree of biological impairment that has been escalated into a total sexual disability. The author explains that this overexaggeration of sexual dysfunction stems from a variety of cultural, intrapsychic, and relationship ideals. She concludes that these problems can frequently be dismissed by an integrated psychodynamically oriented sex therapy approach that emphasizes the improvement of the couple's intimacy, and the expansion of their sexual flexibility.

333   Kofoed, Lial, & Bloom, Joseph D. (July, 1982). Geriatric sexual dysfunction. *Journal of the American Geriatrics Society, 30*(7), 437-440.

This study examined questionnaire data obtained from a group of older persons with sexual dysfunction. Subjects were people responding to a newspaper column that referred to a fictitious 76-year-old man who had problems with impotence. Subjects sent a letter to the Department of Psychiatry of the Oregon Health Sciences University asking for more information. The authors returned a letter and questionnaire to complete. They received responses from 35 people (28 men, 7 women) ages 43 to 82 with systematic sexual problems, and a willingness to write about them. The group consisted mainly of men who had varying degrees of erectile failure and were negatively affected by the development of their problems. Two thirds had consulted a physician. The older subjects were more likely to be abstinent, to have total erectile failure (if men), to have known their physicians only a short time, and to describe their physicians as uninterested or pessimistic. Couples involving a medically ill wife, married for a long time, and who defined sexuality in a nonaffective way were less affected by the development of sexual difficulties. A small group of older men had become impotent because of prolonged abstinence related to lengthy illnesses of their wives. These findings indicate that some physicians show an age-related bias in treating such patients. The authors concluded that the data collected may help clinicians in their counseling of such patients and in the identification of certain at-risk subgroups.

334   Leiblum, Sandra, Bachmann, Gloria, Kemmann, Ekkehard, Colburn, Daniel, & Swartzman, Leora. (April, 1983). Vaginal atrophy in the postmenopausal woman: The importance of sexual activity and hormones. *Journal of the American Medical Association, 249*(16), 2195-2198.

This research was undertaken to determine the effects of sexual activity on the vaginal status of postmenopausal women. The question to be answered was whether sexually inactive postmenopausal women have more senile changes in their vaginas than comparable women who are sexually active. A related question was whether differences in vaginal status reflect differences in the hormonal milieu. Subjects were 52 postmenopausal women ages 50 to 65 who were not receiving estrogen therapy who were recruited between January 1980 and May 1981. Subjects were free from any major physical or mental disorders and not taking medications known to affect sexual response. Each subject was examined by a gynecologist who completed a vaginal atrophy index (VAI). Blood was drawn to determine a hormone level. Subjects were divided into two groups: sexually active N = 25 (those who had intercourse at least three times a month over the preceding year, and sexually inactive N = 23 (those with intercourse frequency of less than ten times yearly.) Sexually inactive women were heavier than active women and had lower mean gross incomes. Inactive women reported lower frequency of physical affection, giving and receiving manual genital stimulation, giving and receiving oral stimulation, and masturbation than the active women. Current coital activity was not significantly related to hormone levels. There was a positive correlation between ideal frequency of intercourse and androstenedione levels but not with testosterone or other hormone levels. Ideal intercourse referred to how often a woman would like to have intercourse. As predicted, there was significantly less vaginal atrophy in sexually active women than in inactive women. The researchers noted that mean frequency of sexual activity was not much different between the active and inactive women. The results of the study suggest that androgens rather than estrogens are critical in terms of maintenance of sexual interest both before and after menopause.

335   Leiblum, Sandra Risa. (December, 1990). Sexuality and the midlife woman. *Psychology of Women Quarterly, 14*(4), 495-508.

This article reviews some of the myths, issues and controversies surrounding the sexuality of the midlife woman.

Leiblum discusses changes in female response related to menopause associated with reduction in estrogen, changes in genital appearance, anatomical changes, and related psychological reactions. These changes, she says, do not mean that a woman cannot maintain an active sexual life. Hysterectomy prior to 1981 was the most common surgical procedure performed in the United States. In 1990 it ranks as the second most performed surgery. About 30 to 40% of American women will undergo this operation. Leiblum discusses both the physical and psychosexual aftermath of hysterectomy. The effect of which on sexual interest and behavior is varied and can result in both sexual impairment or sexual improvement. Common problems are painful intercourse, negative changes in orgasmic quality, reduced sexual sensation, and reduction or cessation of sexual desire. Postoperative sexual problems are often associated with removal of the ovaries as well as the uterus. This surgery catapults women into early menopause. Leiblum explains dyspareunia and effects of estrogen replacement therapy (ERT). She reports findings of studies in 1977, 1978, 1981, 1983, 1989. The article concludes with a brief discussion of common sexual difficulties and their remediation. The author concludes that menopause and postmenopausal changes differ across women but do not foreclose pleasurable physical relations. Hormone therapy can be useful in facilitating sexual interest and comfort. For women for whom ERT is contraindicated, alternative interventions are available.

336 Levine, Stephen B. (1976). Marital sexual dysfunction: Erectile dysfunction. *Annals of Internal Medicine, 85*(3), 342-350.

This comprehensive, practical article written by a physician for other physicians, provided a good overview of erectile dysfunction (impotence). Many important topics are discussed, including: history taking, how to determine whether impotence is physiological or psychological, drug review, physical and laboratory examinations and treatment considerations. The history taking should include four questions: (1) What is the physiologic impairment? (2) How firm does the penis become? (3) Is the impairment constant or episodic? and (4) What life events were occurring when the dysfunction initially appeared? Psychological impotence is usually related to either interpersonal factors (alienation from partner) or intrapsychic factors (anxiety at being sexual). Anxiety, fear, anger, and guilt are factors associated with psychological impotence. Depression can lead to impotence. If physiologic impotence is indicated, it could be related to diseases of the nervous system, diabetes, or endicrinopathies such as hypothyroidism or hyperthyroidism. Postoperative dysfunction often results from surgical procedures; and many commonly prescribed medications such as central nervous system depressants, antihypertensives and others cause impotency. A glucose tolerance test should be done to check for diabetes. The determination of testosterone level is important. Aortography should also be considered. The author provides several case illustrations of erectile dysfunction to highlight the points made. The last section of the article is devoted to therapeutic considerations. The physician needs to discuss the problem with the patient and his wife. The doctor can play a role as sex educator, suggesting sensate focus techniques and other strategies to combat impotence. In the case of psychological impotence, the physician should provide reassurance that erection is possible. He or she may want to suggest that the couple see mental health professionals.

337   **Maddock, James W. (July, 1975). Sexual health and health care.** *Postgraduate Medicine, 58*(1), 52-57, 68-72.
    This article presents a definition of sexual health and a list of criteria by which a health care professional can assess sexual health. The four components are: a sense of comfort about one's gender and sex role, the ability to carry on an effective interpersonal relationship with members of both genders, the ability to respond to erotic stimulation in a way to be involved in positive, pleasurable sexual activity, and the ability to make mature judgments about sexual behavior. The author then identifies and discusses components of sexual health care. They are: awareness, information, enrichment, counseling, therapy, clinical services, and community support. He describes sex-related programs in Minnesota as a means of illustrating one approach to organizing a sexual health care delivery system.

338   **Martin, Clyde E. (1977). Sexual activity in the aging male.** *Handbook of Sexology, 10*(5), 313-324.
    In data obtained from interviews with married, upper-middle-class males ages 60 to 79, frequency of sexual expression proved to be independent of such factors as marital adjustment, sexual attractiveness of wives, sexual attitudes, and demographic features of the marital history. However, former levels of sexual functioning, as revealed by retrospective inquiry, appeared as

highly significant correlates of current functioning in accordance with the hypothesis that males generally maintain relatively high or low rates of sexual activity throughout their lives. Of particular interest was the finding that, in the male, sexual frequency, erotic responsiveness to visual stimuli, and time comfortable without sex are closely interrelated phenomena, suggesting that all three variables are strongly commensurate with degree of motivation. Finally, those subjects found to be less than fully potent at report were also found to be virtually free of performance anxiety, feelings of sexual deprivation, and loss of self-esteem. This is consistent with lack of motivation being responsible for lower sexual functioning.

339   McCoy, Norma L., & Davidson, Julian M. (1985). A longitudinal study of the effects of menopause on sexuality. *Maturitas, 7*(2), 203-210.

The authors investigated changes in sexual interest and coital frequency, longitudinally, following the same women from up to two and a half year premenopause to one or more year after cessation of menses. Menstrual and sexual data were obtained continuously throughout the whole period of study. Sixteen subjects from the initial study group of 43 met the requirements and provided complete data. None of the subjects were on estrogen replacement therapy or had had a hysterectomy. Each month subjects completed a 10-item questionnaire. They also completed a modified version of the *Kupperman Test of Menopausal Distress*, and blood samples were drawn. Although the number of subjects limited the study, the authors say it was the first longitudinal study of its kind. They found that coital frequency decreases after menopause, sexual interest declines, and sexual responsiveness decreases. Changes were not extensive enough to constitute sexual dysfunction.

340   McKeon, Valerie Ann. (1988). Dispelling menopause myths. *Journal of Gerontological Nursing, 14*(8), 26-29.

This article examines myths about menopause with the aim of helping nurses assist their older female patients in achieving PMZ (postmenopausal zest). Among the myths discussed and dispelled are: that menopause ends a woman's sexual life, that it can cause mental illness or insanity, and that it causes or is accompanied by cancer. McKeon says that cultural factors and attitudes toward aging exert a powerful impact upon women's emotional responses to menopause. She points out that many of the books written for the general public about menopause are "paternalistic and patronizing" including David Reuben's popular book *Everything You Always Wanted to Know About Sex but Were Afraid to Ask*. Recent literature, McKeon notes, is providing a more positive view of menopause due in part to the women's movement and increased interest in women's health. She recommends that nurses play an important role in assisting women to appreciate and enjoy their menopausal years.

341   Mooradian, Arshag D. (February, 1991). Geriatric sexuality and chronic diseases. *Clinics in Geriatric Medicine, 7*(1), 113-131.

The author describes several age-related changes in sexual behavior that result from chronic diseases or illnesses. He discusses factors that can affect sexuality in elderly patients such as chronic diseases, prescribed drugs, hormonal changes, or psychosocial factors. He notes that the elderly are also more likely to undergo surgical procedures that may result in bodily disfiguration and that are often accompanied by psychological trauma that prevent the patient from achieving sexual satisfaction. Along with psychosocial trauma of chronic illness, many diseases alter sexual activity by interfering with vascular or neural integrity of the genitalia and brain. The author suggests that limitation in cardiovascular and pulmonary functions may force the patient to avoid sexual contact. The author concludes that many elderly patients would benefit if they receive instructions on alternative sexual techniques or positions. In many, referral to a specialized sex therapist may be helpful. The author suggests that optimization of elderly underlying physical condition will help in sexual activities along with regular day activities.

342   Morley, John E. (May, 1986). Impotence. *The American Journal of Medicine, 80*(5), 897-905.

The purpose of this review was to outline modern concepts of erectile dysfunction with particular emphasis on its occurrence in older men. An underlying tenet of this review is that sexual intercourse is a normal behavior that should continue throughout the life span. The development of impotence at any age should be treated. Impotence is defined as the inability to obtain and sustain an erection that is satisfactory for intercourse. The author provides a comprehensive, scientific discussion of penile erection, the prevalence of impotence, causes of impotence, instructions on how to evaluate impotent patients, how to manage impotent patients. Some of the causes listed by Morley are endocrine disorders, diabetes, alcoholism, systemic disease, medications, psychiatric, and psychogenic. Morley also provides a list of drugs commonly associated with impotence. The article includes illustrations, tables, and a lengthy reference list.

343   Morley, John E., Korenman, Stanley G., Mooradian, Arshag D., & Kaiser, Fran E. (November, 1987). Sexual dysfunction in the elderly male. *Journal of the American Geriatrics Society, 35*(11), 1014-1022.

The purpose of this article is to discuss the misconception that sexual dysfunction is normal process of aging. The authors cite evidence that shows that the ability to maintain healthy sexual activity depends on the person not the person's age. Sexual dysfunction can come from physical problems of the body, mental condition of the patient, medication the patient is on, hormones, or a combination. The authors suggest that treatment for these conditions can be obtained by consulting a doctor about health problems. If no medical problems exist, a psychiatrist should be consulted. The authors conclude that modern medical therapies of male sexual dysfunction have led to a major improvement in the quality of life for both the dysfunctional male and his spouse.

344   Morokoff, Patricia J. (December, 1988). Sexuality in perimenopausal and postmenopausal women. *Psychology of Women Quarterly, 12*(4), 489-511.

This article investigates the psychosocial and biological aspects of the effects of menopause on sexuality. Sexuality has multiple dimensions including desire, arousal, and orgasm. Population studies have revealed that postmenopausal status is associated with decline in these components of sexual functioning. While it is probable that psychological response to menopause affects sexual functioning, it is also possible that the relationship between sexuality and menopausal hormone changes. Low estrogen levels are associated with diminished sexual response and estrogen replacement produces enhanced sexual response. Testosterone level is more clearly related to at least some measures of sexuality. The author concludes that as women's life expectancy increases, it is increasingly important to understand determinants of sexuality in older women such as menopause.

345   Mulligan, Thomas, & Katz, P. Gary. (January, 1988). Erectile failure in the aged: Evaluation and treatment. *Journal of the American Geriatrics Society, 36*(1), 54-62.

This fairly technical medical article directed at physicians specifies many age-related physiological changes that lead to erectile failure; discusses the relationship between certain medications and erectile failure; recommends laboratory tests to determine diseases and other causes of impotence; and discusses several treatment strategies and techniques currently available. Age-related changes in the autonomic nervous system, cardio-vascular system, and local neurotransmitters can cause erectile failure in older males. For example, generalized neural changes that occur with aging include decreased nerve conduction velocity and a decline in autonomic function and neural changes specific to the penis such as loss of vibratory sensation and decreased sensitivity to light touch, which may contribute to impotence. Also, the arterial changes that occur with aging such as changes in penile arterial inflow and penile arterial occlusive disease contribute to erectile failure. To determine if erectile failure is physiologic, a detailed medical and sexual history should be obtained. Questions should be asked about libido, sexual activity and erectile function. A drug history should be obtained because certain medications cause erectile failure. Medications to be alert for include: diuretics, cimetidine, and any agent with anticholinergic, endocrine, or genital disorders related to erectile failure. Specifically, physicians should look for visual field defects, gynecomastia, abdominal or femoral bruits, testicular atrophy, penile plaques, diminished peripheral pulses, and peripheral neuropathy. A fasting blood glucose should be obtained because diabetes is a major cause of impotence. Testosterone level should be measured, also. Treatment consists of the following: testosterone supplementation, penile prosthesis implantation, elimination of adverse drug effects, sex therapy, pharmaco-therapy, external suction devices, intracavernosal injections, vascular surgery, penile prostheses, and smoking cessation.

346   **Mulligan, Thomas, & Katz, P. Gary. (June, 1989). Why aged men become impotent.** *Archives of Internal Medicine, 149*(6), 1365-1366.

This cross-sectional study of aged impotent men was designed to gain insight into the disorders associated with erectile failure in the elderly. The authors evaluated 121 impotent male veterans ages 60 to 85. Data were obtained using a 74-item sexual history questionnaire, a complete medical history, and a physical examination. Most of the subjects (85%) were married. The remainder were divorced, single, or widowed. The authors found that in most cases, erectile failure was gradual and progressive despite intact libido and orgasmic ability. The study had four major findings. First, aged men suffering from impotence are unlikely to suffer from psychogenic impotence. Second, impotence among elderly males is most often due to neurovascular disorders. Third, in this study 15.7% of the cases were caused by potentially reversible disorders. Fourth, 31.5% of the subjects suffered from disorders that respond penile self-injection of vasoactive substances and therefore do not require surgical intervention.

347 Mulligan, Thomas, & Moss, C. Renee. (February, 1991). Sexuality and aging in male veterans: A cross-sectional study of interest, ability, and activity. *Archives of Sexual Behavior, 20*(1), 17-25.

The authors studied male veterans' sexuality and interest in sexual intercourse to determine differences associated with age and potency. Veterans surveyed were from the ages of 30 to 99. The study consisted of a mailed survey with 88 questions to veterans along with a pretest on potent males (mean age = 31) and aged impotent males (mean age = 70) from the McGuire Veterans Affairs Medical Center. The questionnaire consisted of questions dealing with erectile function including frequency, rigidity, and duration of erections during intercourse. Eight hundred and six replies returned to the researchers. The results showed that sexual interest (maximum score = 5) decreased from ages 30 to 39 (mean = 4.4) to 90 to 99 (mean = 2.0). The researchers noted the respondents preferred vaginal intercourse. However, intercourse frequency diminished from once per week in 30- to 39-year-olds to once a year in 90- to 99-year-olds. Frequency, rigidity, and duration of erections have a downward slope through the age cohorts. The authors concluded that these facts should demonstrate the need for a greater focus on sexuality and aging.

348 Mulligan, Thomas, & Schmitt, Brian. (September, 1993). Testosterone for erectile failure. *Journal of General Internal Medicine, 8*(9), 517-521.

The authors critically reviewed existing medical literature to determine the association between testosterone and erectile function. The authors limited their analysis to adult men with low serum testosterone levels. They found 12 studies with data regarding testosterone efficacy for erectile inadequacy. None of the studies identified their sampling methods and most samples were small. The subjects were relatively young. Most subjects seeking treatment for erectile failure are older and have diabetes mellitus or peripheral vascular disease so the absence of data regarding aged subjects impairs the generalizability of the available data. Based on their examinations and analysis of the studies, the authors concluded that testosterone replacement in men with low serum testosterone levels results in enhanced sexual interest. They also concluded that testosterone replacement leads to an increased frequency of sexual acts and that testosterone increases the frequency of sleep-associated erections but may have no effect on either fantasy-stimulated or visually stimulated erections.

349   Nadelson, Carol C. (1984). Geriatric sex problems: Discussion. *Journal of Geriatric Psychiatry, 17*(2), 139-148.

This article is a discussion of elderly sexuality. Because society equates sexuality with youth, the sexual needs of the elderly are often seen as inappropriate. The second half of life is also seen as a period of androgyny and changes in sexual roles. Studies of aging and sexuality have found that the elderly maintain sexual interest throughout later life, but declining physical capacity often makes couples adapt their sexual activity. The issue of elderly homosexuality is rarely addressed, but research seems to indicate that older gays and lesbians also continue to have satisfying sex lives.

350   Nambudiri, Draupathi E., Shamoian, Charles A., & Jain, Hira C. (June, 1987). Sexuality after menopause. *The Female Patient, 12*(6), 20-21, 23-24, 26.

The authors studied a common myth that the elderly lack sexual desire and do not enjoy sexual activity. They point out several ways for women after menopause to become more sexually active if there are no adverse physical, medical, cultural, or psychological factors. Many older women believe that menopause inevitably marks the beginning of the decline in sexual desire and activity, but they are misinformed. The authors indicate that several health factors can lead to the loss of sexual activities. They suggest that counseling on different positions for intercourse, alternatives to intercourse, and timing of intercourse relative to taking certain medications can do much to alleviate these problems. The author concludes that with the right counseling and education of physiological and psychological factors, older women can continue to enjoy an active sex life.

351 Norton, G. R., & Jehu, Derek. (April, 1984). The role of anxiety in sexual dysfunctions: A review. *Archives of Sexual Behavior, 13*(2), 165-183.

The purpose of this article was to review selected research relevant to the role of anxiety and sexual dysfunctions. Three types of studies were considered: (1) studies that had compared anxiety reactions of normals with people who had sexual dysfunctions; (2) studies in which anxiety reduction procedures had been used in the treatment of sexual dysfunction; and (3) studies that had experimentally manipulated variables related to anxiety to determine their effects on sexual behaviors. Based on their review of literature, Norton and Jehu drew three conclusions. First, studies that have evaluated anxiety and psychopathology of people with sexual dysfunctions have produced inconsistent findings, with some showing that people with sexual dysfunctions have more anxiety and others indicating that when sexual dysfunction exists "at least part of the psychiatric disturbance is the result of sexual difficulties and marital discord, and not the cause." Second, several studies, but not all, have demonstrated that systematic desensitization is an effective treatment procedure for some components of sexual dysfunctions. Third, under some circumstances, induced anxiety can either inhibit or enhance sexual arousal; and some activities that distract attention away from erotic cues can reduce sexual arousal. The authors call for more basic and clinical research on the relationship between anxiety and sexual dysfunction and methods that can treat sexual dysfunctions more effectively.

352 Perez, E. David, Mulligan, Thomas, & Wan, Tom. (March, 1993). Why men are interested in an evaluation for a sexual problem. *Journal of the American Geriatric Society, 41*(3), 233-237.

The purpose of this study was to understand why men were interested in an evaluation of a perceived sexual problem. The subjects were male veterans ages 30 to 99 who were registered at a Veterans Administration medical center (N = 427). Of those, 136 men mean age = 59.6 were interested in an evaluation. The independent variables were emotional state, physical state, and/or demographic characteristics (marital status, race, and age). The dependent variable was interest in evaluation of a sexual problem. Men were asked how strong their current interest in sexual activity was and how often they felt a loss of sexual interest or pleasure. They were also asked about their erectile and orgasmic functions. They were asked how often they felt lonely, had feelings of worthlessness, or had lack of interest in activities. They were asked if they cried easily or had suicide ideation. The analysis found that men seek evaluation of sexual dysfunction for complex reasons. First, men who perceived their erectile rigidity to be inadequate are likely to want evaluation, but erectile function alone does not adequately predict interest in an evaluation. Age and race also effect interest, age and non-white status were both negatively associated with interest. Chronic illness does not appear to lessen the negative effect of age on interest in evaluation. After statistically controlling for all variables, the researchers found that the characteristics of the men who were least interested in an evaluation for a sexual problem were those who were never married, nonwhite, and elderly.

353   Philo, Susan W., Richie, Mary Fern, & Kaas, Merrie J. (November, 1996). Inappropriate sexual behavior. *Journal of Gerontological Nursing, 22*(11), 17-22.

The authors identify inappropriate sexual behavior (also called sexually aggressive behavior) such as making obscene gestures, touching body parts of another person, hugging, exposing body parts, disrobing, masturbating in public. They say that inappropriate sexual behavior is a problem that occurs in all types of facilities accommodating the elderly and one that involves both males and females. The incidence is highest with demented patients. They identify several causes such as an indicator of underlying physical problem, an aggressive response to the stressors of institutionalization, physical alterations in the brain, the need for intimacy, nonsexual age-related changes in the ego and superego, and panic associated with death. The authors also discuss consequences of inappropriate sexual behavior both appropriate and inappropriate and suggest ways to manage inappropriate behavior according to its cause. A detailed case study, a figure illustrating nurse-patient dynamics, and a figure showing a detailed decision tree for inappropriate sexual behavior which presents both general interventions and interventions by cause.

354   Renshaw, Domeena C. (1984). Geriatric sex problems. *Journal of Geriatric Psychiatry, 17*(2), 123-138.

The author discusses issues related to sexuality and sexual problems among the elderly and suggests ways that physicians can help the elderly with their sexual questions and problems.

The physical, social, and emotional changes associated with aging can have an impact on sexual functioning. Disability, substance abuse, and drug interactions can also cause sexual problems in this age group. The author describes specific ways for physicians and nursing facility personnel to handle elderly sexuality and sexual problems in clinical and nursing facility settings.

355 **Renshaw, Domeena C. (February, 1978). Impotence—Some causes and cures.** *American Family Practitioner, 17(2)*, **143-146.**

This article discusses the causes and treatments for impotence. The first task is to establish etiologic factors. Renshaw discusses organic causes such as acute prostatitis, urethritis, excessive alcohol consumption or drug use. Sometimes organic and emotional factors are both contributing to the problem such as in the cases of diabetes, stroke, myocardial infarction, or major surgery which results in severe anxiety or depression. Emotional factors alone may be the cause including anxiety, anger or clinical depression. Aging may cause dysfunction only if it causes anxiety. Sexual problems may be linked to deliberate sexual control, simple ignorance, the "madonna complex," homosexual fantasies and other unconscious sexual fantasies. Renshaw recommends brief sex therapy and sex education. Renshaw provides an eight step plan for the physician or sex therapist to use as therapy. She also describes penile plethysmography and penile prostheses, and discusses unproved remedies.

356 **Renshaw, Domeena C. (December, 1982). Sex education: Why the physician must help.** *The Female Patient, 7(12)*, **33, 37-38.**

In this article, Renshaw expresses the need for the physician to help with sex education. She says that sexual feelings, sexual problems, and sexual ignorance cross all boundaries of race, religion, and age, from infancy to old age.

357 **Rieve, Janice E. (March, 1989). Sexuality and the adult with acquired physical disability.** *Nursing Clinics of North America, 24(1)*, **265-276.**

This article discusses the effects of disability on sexuality. One theme of the article is that sexuality is a broad concept that includes perception of one's self as male or female as well as sexual drives and behaviors which are influenced by personal, societal, and cultural factors. The author discusses psychosocial factors and sexuality, the role of sexual counselors, assessment, and interventions, and disability-specific information (e.g., arthritis, traumatic brain injury, and spinal cord injury). Interventions include providing assistance with personal care and appearance, providing information about contraception and family planning, and providing counseling regarding human sexual response. Other issues that the author feels deserve further attention are alternative sexual preferences, sexual abuse and/or exploitation of the disabled, and partners of persons with disabilities.

358   Schumacher, Dorin. (1990). **Hidden death: The sexual effects of hysterectomy.** *Women, Aging and Ageism, 2*(2), 49-66.

The author describes the sexual and emotional effects of hysterectomy and oophorectomy (surgical removal of the ovaries). Hysterectomies and oophorectomies are performed as "cures" for a variety of ailments, including premenstrual syndrome, abdominal pain, and benign fibroid tumors, and as a prevention of cancer even where no symptoms of cancer are present. It has been estimated that only 10.5% of all hysterectomies performed in the United States between 1970 and 1984 were necessary and medically indicated. The author views the prevalence of these treatments as a sociopolitical phenomenon that reflects cultural denials and reveals the tragic consequences of such denials for middle-aged and older women. This surgery results not only in sudden menopausal changes but in some of the most extreme changes that can be brought about by sexual aging, occurring in a matter of days and weeks rather than gradually over a period of many years. Without ovarian testosterone and without a cervix or uterus, Schumacher says, a woman lacks the major tissues and hormone levels needed for sexual desire and a strong and complete orgasm, or perhaps for any orgasm at all. These issues are dysfunctional after hysterectomy as purely psychological. The loss of something that women experience alone and without validation; their doctors and lovers do not believe them and there are no support groups for them to turn to. Eighteen sociopolitical factors are postulated for the "ongoing epidemic of surgeons hysterectomizing women."

359   Snowdon, John, Miller, Robert, & Vaughan, Rosemary. (June, 1996). **Behavioural problems in Sydney nursing homes.** *International Journal of Geriatric Psychiatry, 11*(6), 535-541.

This study investigated the prevalence of significant behavioral disturbances among residents of nursing homes in one part of Sydney, Australia in order to recognize the extent to which these problems pose difficulties for nursing home staff. Data were collected from Directors of Nursing in 46 of the 47 nursing homes in one health district of Sydney. Nurses completed the *Cohen-Mansfield Agitation Inventory* (CMAI) to assess the resident they knew best at the home. The CMAI consists of 30 behaviors which nurses rated on a 7-point scale of frequency from never to several times an hour. They also used the *Rating Scale for Aggressive Behavior in the Elderly* (RAGE), a scale consisting of 19 behavior items rated on a 4-point scale from never to more than once daily. Of the 2,445 residents, 1762 were assessed with the *Mini-Mental State Examination* (MMSE). Restless, repetitive, demanding, or odd behaviors reported in 100 or more cases were general restlessness, pacing, repetitive sentences, constant calls for help, repetitive mannerisms, complaining, and strange noises. Aggressive, injurious or sexual behaviors reported in 100 or more cases were cursing, verbal aggression, grabbing, and screaming. Verbal sexual advances were reported for only 12 of the 704 cases and physical sexual advances were reported only nine cases. Odd behaviors were reported far more than aggressive behaviors. The study showed that most CMAI behaviors were more likely to be displayed by cognitively impaired than by cognitively intact individuals. People who were cognitively in tact, however, were more likely to be rated as often calling for attention. The authors conclude that their study demonstrates the extent of behavior problems and a need to seek solutions. They recommend involving more mental health professionals in nursing homes.

360 Sternberg, Steve. (November 5, 1996). **Impotence treatment keeps urologists busy: Erectile problems are a common side effects surgery for prostate cancer.** *Washington Post, Health News, 12*(45), 8.

The author discusses the guidelines for treatment for impotence released by the American Urological Society. This problem has become a common complaint among aging men and they are seeking treatment due to improved prostate cancer tests and an increase in diagnosis of prostate cancer. The author describes new treatments such as vacuum pumps and penile implants. The guidelines warn about methods with questionable effectiveness such as blood vessel surgery and a plant extract known as yohimbine offered at some clinics. Sternberg also includes a discussion of emotional reactions, anxiety, and conflict between marital partners related to impotence.

361   Tsitouras, Panayiotis D., Martin, Clyde E., & Harman, S. Mitchell. (1982). Relationship of serum testosterone to sexual activity in healthy elderly men. *Journal of Gerontology, 37*(3), 288-293.

This study investigated the relationship of sexual activity to testosterone. Subjects are members of the Baltimore Longitudinal Study on Aging. The subjects were 183 men, ages 60 to 79, who were free of significant physical or mental disability, and married at the time of study. Each subject completed a personal interview, physical, and hormone tests. The researchers' findings showed that serum testosterone did not decline with age, but sexual activity decreased in a highly predictable fashion. They also found that those with higher levels of sexual activity, for their age, had significantly greater levels of serum testosterone. Although they found an inverse correlation between testosterone and percentage of body fat, there was no relationship between percentage of body fat and sexual activity. They also found no correlation between testosterone or sexual activity and smoking or coronary heart disease. Subjects drinking more than four ounces of ethanol per day were more likely to have decreased sexual activity but not diminished testosterone concentration. The data suggested that, although serum testosterone level and ethanol intake may affect sexual activity in older men to some degree, age itself still appears to be the most influential variable.

362   Van Arsdalen, Keith N., & Wein, Alan J. (October, 1984). Drug-induced sexual dysfunction in older men. *Geriatrics, 39*(10), 63-67, 70.

This article, written by two medical doctors, explains drug-induced sexual dysfunction in older men and presents a review of the literature on how frequently prescribed medications can affect sexual processes. Two widely prescribed medications to older people, antihypertensive and psychotropic agents, are the drugs most often associated with sexual dysfunction. The effects of antihypertensive drugs which are discussed, include diuretics, vasodilators, sympatholytic agents, depletion of neurotransmitter substances, alpha-adrenergic blockers, and beta-adrenergic blockers. Psychotropic drugs discussed are major tranquilizers, antidepressants, antianxiety agents. Also discussed are anti-cholinergic drugs, other prescription drugs such as clofibrate, cimetidine, metoclopramide, and estrogens. The authors also discuss the potential adverse affects on sexual functioning of alcohol, narcotics, and nicotine. They point out that drug interactions may impair sexual function as well but the true incidence is largely unknown and that effects of drugs may be more pronounced with aging because of altered pharmaco-dynamics. The authors provide several tables listing drugs with potential affect on sexual functioning.

363 Walbroehl, Gordon S. (October, 1988). Effects of medical problems on sexuality in the elderly. *Medical Aspects of Human Sexuality,* 22(10), 56-66.

Most people can remain sexually active throughout their lives. Brief counseling may help those who are unaware of the normal changes that accompany aging, and others who must learn to live with chronic illness. This article discusses normal physiological changes in men and women that affect sexual activity. Although the decline in sexual functioning is gradual, most men will experience changes between the ages 60 to 70. Changes include smaller testes, changes in erection, less urgency to ejaculate, less sensation in the genital region, and a longer refractory period. Women also experience physiological changes such as smaller ovaries, thinner vaginal lining, and decreased genital sensation. Refractory period does not change for women. Psychological changes are less well known. The author discusses medical problems related to sexuality such as diabetes, heart disease, hypertension, cancer, and arthritis. He concludes that the need to express sexuality continues throughout the process of life and that physicians need to help patients understand those needs and changes related to sexuality.

364 Weiss, Jeffrey N., & Mellinger, Brett C. (February, 1990). Sexual dysfunction in elderly men. *Clinics in Geriatric Medicine,* 6(1), 185-195.

The purpose of this article is to discuss the incidence of sexual dysfunction increasing with age and possible treatments. The authors discussed key factors that affect sexual activity: normal age-related physiologic changes which primarily affect arousal and orgasm, medical causes of sexual dysfunction such as diabetes, hypertension, and several others. They note that medication-induced sexual dysfunction is the most frequent cause of sexual dysfunction and is difficult to distinguish from medical problems. The authors discuss options and procedures that physicians can use to help men deal with their current condition. The authors concluded that sexual dysfunction should be investigated and treated in a manner acceptable to the patient.

365   Williamson, Marvel L. (January-February, 1992). Sexual adjustment after hysterectomy. *Journal of Obstetric, Gynecologic, and Neonatal Nursing* , 21(1), 42-47.

This article discusses the impact of hysterectomy on sexual identity and relationships such as altered body image, depression, and marital dysfunction. Williamson also discusses the sexual impact of hysterectomy on physiology and anatomy including hormonal effects, structural changes, sexual dysfunction, physical sexual response, and tissue damage. The author concludes with a discussion of implications of these effects on nursing. She recommends initializing discussion of sex with patients to prevent misconceptions as well as to promote accurate understandings of physical and emotional changes.

366   Zimmer, James G., Watson, Nancy, & Treat, Anne. (October, 1984). Behavioral problems among patients in skilled nursing facilities. *American Journal of Public Health*, 74(10), 1118-1121.

The authors surveyed a 33% random sampling of 3,456 patients in 42 skilled nursing facilities (SNFs) in upstate New York. The study found that 64.2% had significant behavioral problems. Of these, 22.6% had what were defined as serious problems. Serious problems included physical aggression, behaviors endangering self or others, disturbing others, and behaviors which concerned staff such as exposure of the genitalia and masturbation. The authors analyzed the details of the problem behaviors among this group, their previous history, current management, frequency of psychiatric consultation, and adequacy of documentation. The median age was the same as the general SNF population, a slightly lower proportion was female, and, while 66.5% had diagnoses indicating organic brain syndrome, very few had specific psychiatric diagnoses, and only 4.7% had been admitted from a psychiatric facility. The attending physician noted the behavioral problem in the record in only 9.7% of the cases and had requested psychiatric consultation in 14.8% of the serious cases. The authors suggest that staff needs more training in mental health care and that patients need more consultation from physicians and psychiatric professionals.

14

Impact of Health and Disability on Sexuality

The elderly have increased risk for many health problems that have an impact on sexuality. One of the most common of these is the increased use of medications for hypertension, arthritis, and other chronic health problems. Each health problem, also impacts on the ability to engage in sexual activities and sexual desire.

Among the many other health problems that impact on sexuality are diabetes, Parkinson's disease, Alzheimer's disease, dementia, strokes, heart attack, stress, depression, colostomy and ileostomy, lung disease, obesity, and cancer. Injuries such as head injuries and other fractures also affect sexuality.

Articles offering suggestions for overcoming sexual problems related to health issues are included in this chapter. The most frequent suggestion is exercise. Other suggestions are providing social support and rehabilitation therapy. Articles discussing the health benefits of sex are also included in this chapter.

367 Blackerly, W. F. (1988). *Head injury rehabilitation: Sexuality after traumatic brain injury.* Houston: HTL Publishers.

This book provides guidelines for creating and ensuring a permissive environment for rehabilitation patients to discuss sexual issues. Steps outlined are: ensure that the individual has privacy when feasible and appropriate; when necessary, redirect the individual either verbally or physically, depending on the person's level of cognitive functioning; describe the inappropriate behavior (e.g., what you are doing now makes other people feel..."; and describe an appropriate behavior to replace the inappropriate one.

368   **Blake, Daniel J., Maisiak, Richard, Alarcon, Graciela S., Holley, Howard L., & Brown, Sam. (1987). Sexual quality of life of patients with arthritis compared to arthritis-free controls. *Journal of Rheumatology, 14*(3), 570-576.**

The purpose of the study was to investigate the sexual satisfaction, sexual concerns, sexual activity, and receptivity to sexual rehabilitation of patients with arthritis compared to matched, arthritis-free controls. Subjects were 169 outpatients with arthritis who completed a personal interview and 130 controls. Patients differed from controls in their greater loss of sexual satisfaction over time, but they were comparably satisfied with their current sexual adjustment. The authors reported similar reductions in frequency of intercourse over time. Joint symptoms and fatigue disturbed the sexual adjustment of patients more than controls, but damaged body image, worry about partner interest, loss of libido and loss of lubrication did not. There was receptivity to a program of sexual rehabilitation among patients and controls that was not dependent upon sexual dissatisfaction. The authors concluded that a counseling program within the rheumatologist's field should be considered to help patients with sexual activities.

369   **Bray, Grady P., DeFrank, Richard S., & Wolfe, Terri L. (June, 1981). Sexual functioning in stroke survivors. *Archives of Physical Medicine and Rehabilitation, 62*(6), 286-288.**

The paper presents the initial data concerning libido, physical function, and sexual attitudes from a sample of stroke survivors (N = 35). Patients participated by responding to a sexual history questionnaire during an interview. The results showed that, before and after a stroke, subjects revealed no significant changes in sexual interest or desire for either men or women. The results did show that men experienced significant decrease in ability to achieve erection and to ejaculate. All of the women (N = 5) who were premenopausal at the time of stroke reported major alterations in menses. Only one woman reported orgasm after a stroke. Nineteen of the men and eight of the women reported sexual function to be of importance to others of their age. The authors' findings from this small sample indicated that although the majority of stroke survivors maintain consistent levels of sexual desire and believe that sexual function is important, most will experience sexual dysfunction following stroke. The authors concluded that the sexual problems experienced by poststroke patients appear to be of sufficient magnitude and frequency to warrant further investigation.

370 Brecher, Jeremy. (1977). Sex, stress, and health. *International Journal of Health Services, 7*(1), 89-101.

This article discusses the benefits of sex on the health of males. One link between increased health and sex is that sexual arousal elevates testosterone and increased testosterone has health-promoting effects such as increased strength, immune response related to increased testosterone, and reduction of cortisol reduction. Brecher also presents evidence that sex promotes exercise, relaxation, and sense of well-being. The author also discusses the effects of sexual dysfunction on health. A primary effect is increased stress. He found several types of stress that affect sex: stress about sex, stress from the sexual relationship, and general stress. Other topics covered in this article are sex therapy techniques as stress reduction, social roots of sexual dysfunction, and social change as sexual prevention medicine. Information for this article was derived in part from a review of the literature and in part from interviews with sex therapists.

371 Butler, Robert N., Barber, Hugh R. K., Lewis, Myrna I., Long, James, & Whitehead, E. Douglas. (March, 1989). Sexual problems in the elderly, part 1. The use and abuse of medications. *Geriatrics, 44*(3), 6164, 66, 71.

This article is a summary of a panel discussion of professionals in the geriatric field discussing medical personnel/patient relationships. The article focused on doctors talking to elderly patients about their sexual activities before prescribing a medication that will hinder such activities. They discussed the assumption that conversation about sexual activity is off-limits with health care professionals and often prevents informed clinical intervention and leads to needless suffering. Panelists defined a broad role for primary care management of sexual dysfunction in the elderly. The panelists also discussed how certain drug side effects affect sexual activities and appropriate use of estrogen to help women in their later life problems.

372   Butler, Robert N., Finkel, S. I., Lewis, Myrna I., Sherman, F. T.,
       & Sunderland, T. (May, 1992). Aging and mental health:
       Primary care of the healthy older adult. A roundtable discussion:
       Part I. *Geriatrics, 47*(5), 54, 56, 61-65.

       Dementia, depression, alcoholism, and suicide are some of
       the most important mental health issues for the aging population.
       Among the factors that affect the physician's ability to evaluate
       and manage these disorders are: drug-induced side effects, the
       ability and willingness of patients to communicate their feelings,
       the level of caregiver cooperation, and limitations imposed by
       federal regulations and reimbursement policies. In this first of
       three installments of a panel discussion, experts in geriatrics and
       geropsychiatry discuss healthy aging, age-related memory and
       sensory loss, sexuality in the elderly, and side effects of common
       psychoactive medications.

373   Dacher, Joan Elise. (March, 1989). Rehabilitation and the geriatric
       patient. *Nursing Clinics of North America, 24*(1), 225-237.

       In this article the author defends the concept of geriatric
       rehabilitation as a means of reducing dependency and its related
       costs among the elderly. She begins by presenting a
       developmental framework with which to view the geriatric
       rehabilitation patient, citing Erikson's 8-stage model with its
       options in old age as integrity versus despair and disgust. She
       identifies major treatment issues in geriatric rehabilitation
       including cerebral vascular accidents, depression and cognitive
       impairment, amputation, hip fractures, and incontinence. The
       author also discusses the success of rehabilitation and future
       concerns especially related to Medicare requirements and other
       government policies. In her view keeping elderly people
       functioning successfully in the home and community is beneficial
       both to the individual and to society. She calls for a specialization
       in geriatrics within the field of rehabilitation.

374   Deamer, Robert L., & Thompson, John F. (February, 1991). The
       role of medications in geriatric sexual function. *Clinics in
       Geriatric Medicine, 7*(1), 95-111.

       As the authors point out in this review of literature, one of
       the effects of medications and drugs is to inhibit or impair sexual
       function. Older adults take the most prescription and over-the-
       counter drugs. The first part of this article focuses on the sexual
       physiology of aging men and women outlining changes in the
       endocrine system, central nervous system (CNS), peripheral

nervous system, and vascular system. The next section discusses psychotherapeutic agents taken by older people that negatively affect sexual function. Among the drugs discussed are: antidepressants, neuroleptics, anxiolytics, diuretics, other anti-hypertensive drugs, sympatholytics, and other cardiovascular drugs. They also discuss the effects of alcohol, tobacco, chemotherapeutic agents, opioids, and anticholinergie agents. the last part of the article outlines various medications for treatment of impotence in males (e.g., hormone therapy, bromocriptine, and intracavernous regimens) and females (e.g., estrogen, K-Y jelly for lubrication).

375 **Dlin, Barney M., & Perlman, Abraham. (June, 1971). Emotional response to ileostomy and colostomy in patients over the age of 50.** *Geriatrics, 26*(6), 113-118.

This article investigated the effect of colostomy and ileostomy on a patient's perspective of life and those around them, with an accent on sexual activity. Subjects were 164 people ages 50 and older in a psychotherapy program for ostomy patients who completed a questionnaire and a personal interview. The researchers found that patients continued their interest in sex and their concerns about it. The authors noted that the decreased amount of sex in the patients was the result of advanced aging or the attitude of the patient. They concluded that a well-adjusted ostomate copes with the physical and emotional problems of aging as well as their healthy counterparts.

376 **Fooken, I. (July, 1994). Sexuality in the later years: The impact of health and body image in a sample of older women.** *Patient Educational Counseling, 23*(3), 227-233.

Research on sexuality in the elderly is still rather scarce. Quite often, there is an underlying assumption that health problems function as main constraints against sexuality in the later years. This article tries to challenge this view and proposes that health aspects tend to be—at least among women—quite overestimated. The data presented here are from a study on sexuality and aging. Sixty West German women, born between 1907 and 1936 had been interviewed on their psychosexual development in the context of their life histories. The results show that health variables are of rather little significance in explaining the development and/or maintenance of sexual interest and activity in old age. More general aspects of the so-called body-image seem to be more valid in shedding some more light on the determinants of psychological well-being and of keeping sexuality alive in old age.

377   **Harris, Raymond. (January, 1988). Exercise and sex in the aging patient.** *Medical Aspects of Human Sexuality,* **22(1), 148, 153-156, 159.**

The author recommends exercise to overcome a deteriorating sex life in older men. In this article he explains sexual changes in aging men and women, benefits of physical exercise program for older people, and how to have a safe exercise program. He offers suggestions for types of exercise suitable for older people including stretching and relaxation exercises, walking, and conditioning aerobic exercise. He recommends exercises that improve specific body areas such as weak muscles, body and bone mass, and hand and forearm strength. He recommends a warm-up and cooldown period each time someone exercises. He says that walking is the best and safest exercise for people ages 60 and over. The article includes a chart listing the "Daily Dozen" warm-up and stretching exercises.

378   **Hellerstein, Herman H., & Friedman, Ernest H. (June, 1970). Sexual activity and the postcoronary patient.** *Archives of Internal Medicine,* **125(6), 987-999.**

The purposes of this questionnaire study were to compare the sexual activity of postcoronary and normal highly coronary-prone subjects to identify some of the modifying factors, to evaluate the physiologic changes in heart rate and electrocardiogram (ECG) during daily living activities and during coitus, and to provide a sound basis for counseling patients. Subjects were 91 white, middle-aged, middle and upper class, predominately Jewish males who were randomly selected from a larger population who had participated in the Case Western Reserve University (CWRU) physical-fitness evaluation program. Subjects completed a questionnaire concerning their sexual activity and cardiac status at the beginning of two regularly scheduled exercise sessions. Data regarding a detailed cardiovascular history, results of physical examination, ECG monitoring, ergometric testing with the patient on a bicycle was performed, and others were obtained on subjects on intake and at 6-month and two yearly intervals. A psychological exam was also conducted using the *Holtzman Inkblot Test* and the *Minnesota Multiphasic Personality Inventory.* A complex data analysis was performed. The authors concluded that even those postcoronary subjects with a reduced aerobic capacity over 80% were able to participate in sexual activity without symptoms or evidence of significant strain and that they were able to resume this activity safely.

379   Jacobson, Linbania. (January, 1974). Illness and human sexuality. *Nursing Outlook,* 22(1), 50-53.

If nurses are to care for the whole patient, then sexuality must be considered in the care plan, since many disorders and their treatment create sexual problems, sequelae, and conflicts in patients. Many common health disorders such as heart disease, lung disease, and obesity affect a patient's sexuality through indirect means. Other conditions cause deterioration in bodily processes and diminish or destroy the usual forms of sexual functioning. An example is cancer of the rectum and colon in men which can cause direct effects to a person's sexuality because of the surgery technique used to treat the cancer. Women also may have surgery that affects their sexual activity. The author suggests that the best way to deal with these problems is patient counseling and educating the medical staff. Most patients are not told what a surgery or a disease will do to their sexual functioning until after it has taken effect. This lack of knowledge causes stress on the individual as well as the medical personnel that have to deal with the individual. The author believes that the traditional nursing education often denies nurses the right to acknowledge their sexuality and also that of their patients.

380   Leviton, Dan. (Summer, 1973). The significance of sexuality as a deterrent to suicide among the aged. *Omega: Journal of Death and Dying,* 4(2), 163-175.

The author argues that there is an inverse relationship between sexuality and the desire for death among the elderly. He cites M. Farber's theory of suicide as support for his hypothesis. The author cites data showing the sharp rise in the rate of suicide for older people, especially for white males. He also cites data showing the age-related decline in sexual activity which is related to both physical and psychological causes. He points out that previous studies showing a sharp decline in sexual intercourse did not include other types of sexual activity such as masturbation and homosexuality. When data did include other forms of sexual expression, activity rates were higher. In Leviton's view, therapy should include help for sexual dysfunction. He recommends letting older people know they are still attractive, encouraging participation in sports to improve physical fitness, and encouraging human relationships in all environments including nursing facilities and hospitals. He calls for empirical testing of his hypotheses, teaching medical personnel about healthy sexuality at all ages, and including questions about sexual functioning in any medical examination.

381   Lichtenberg, Peter A., & Strzepek, Deborah M. (1990). **Assessments of institutionalized dementia patients' competencies to participate in intimate relationships.** *The Gerontologist, 30*(1), 117-120.

This paper outlined the assessment the authors developed to determine the competency of patients to participate in intimate relationships. The study was conducted at the Western State Hospital in Virginia, an intermediate care facility for psychiatrically-impaired elderly. Thirty-four patients, 18 women and 16 men (mean age = 74), in the dementia unit made up the subject population. Subjects completed five 2-part interviews in a year. Part one was a one-on-one interview with a person of the same sex. Part two was a team interview with a patient consisting of nursing, recreational therapy, psychiatry, psychology, dietary, and psychiatric aide staff. After each session the interviewer(s) tallied the responses and scored them on the *Mini-Mental State Exam* (MMSE) to determine the patient's cognitive functioning. The researchers' data showed that in the ward four out of five patient couples that formed did not know that they had formed any relationships. Two case studies are presented. The first case was about a woman who wanted companionship with anyone, man or woman. The problem was she would do anything with a person as long as they were near her including participating in sexual activities. The researchers removed this female from the ward. The other case was about a couple who had a relationship that grew over time. Both parties were aware of what was going on so the researchers decided that they would allow the relationship to continue. The researchers did not make any claims of the reliability or validity of this study because of too few cases. However they do feel that the assessment test is worth using for now to determine its usefulness. They concluded that by giving practitioners this assessment tool they will be better able to consider carefully the sexual needs of their patients.

382   McIntosh, William Alex, Kaplan, Howard B., Kubena, Karen S.,
      & Landmann, Wendall A. (1993). Life events, social support, and
      immune response in elderly individuals. *International Journal
      of Aging and Human Development, 37*(1), 23-36.

      This research focused on the relationship between stressful
      life events and immunocompetence in a sample of free-living
      elderly men and women. The sample consisted of 192
      Houstonians randomly selected from random digit dialing and
      members of the American Association of Retired Persons (AARP).
      The subjects took part in an investigation to determine if recent
      life events, psychological adjustment, and social support on
      lymphocyte count. The subjects are screened for nutritional status,
      age, education, income, and the presence of lymphocyte-altering
      drugs. A blood sample was taken from each subject and
      analyzed. For elderly males, recent sexual dysfunction lowered
      lymphocyte count, whereas psychological adjustment and
      percentage in intimate network elevated it. For elderly females,
      family or legal problems elevated count as did frequent
      interaction with members of an intimate network was noted. The
      authors' results suggested that life events have very different
      effects on elderly men and women's immune systems. They
      concluded that social support has direct but mediating effects on
      lymphocyte count for both genders.

383   Morley, John E., Mooradian, Arshag D., Rosenthal, Mark J., &
      Kaiser, Fran E. (September, 1987). Diabetes mellitus in the
      elderly: Is it different? *American Journal of Medicine, 83*(9), 533-
      544.

      This review of the literature discusses the prevalence of
      diabetes among the elderly, the nature of the condition, and the
      prognosis of diabetes in elderly patients. Other topics include
      glucose counter-regulation, acute diabetic complications, ocular
      complications, nervous system complications, depression and
      impotence, foot complications, renal complications, infectious
      complications, thermoregulatory disturbances, and nutrient status.
      The authors point out that impotence occurs commonly in diabetic
      patients and that diabetes appears to be responsible for impotence
      in 10 to 20% of the cases. Treatment of diabetes in elderly patients
      is discussed.

384   Murray, Barbara L. S., & Wilcox, Linda J. (December, 1978).
      Testicular self-examination. *American Journal of Nursing, 78*(12),
      2074-2075.

This short article provides a step-by-step approach to doing a self-examination of the testicles. Like breast self-examinations, self-examinations of the testicles is important for early detection of any changes, particularly lumps in the testicle. Testicular lumps may or may not be cancerous. X-rays are usually taken to determine if the lump is cancerous. Urine tests may also be done to aid in diagnosis. Surgical biopsy, a more invasive procedure, is one sure way to determine malignancy. If the lump(s) is/are malignant, the testicle, spermatic cord, and inguinal lymph nodes are removed through inguinal incision. Chemotherapy and/or radiation treatment follows. Even after testicular surgery, a man can have an erection and experience orgasm. If the appearance of the genitalia is a concern, gel-filled testicular prostheses can be implanted. The article concluded by telling readers how to order the film, *Self-Examination of the Testes.*

385　**Papadopoulos, Chris. (October, 1986). Sexual problems following a stroke. *Medical Aspects of Human Sexuality, 20*(10), 39-40.**

This article is an interview with Chris Papadopoulos on the effect of a stroke on sexual activities. The article starts off with a basic look at how patients are concerned with the effects of a stroke. The interview then goes on to talk about how a stoke can effect sexual activities and contributing factors that help make the problem worse than it already is. The interview concluded with ways to regain sexual activities for the patient with help from doctors and, if any, spouses.

386　**Paulson, George W. (March, 1983). Sexual aspects of parkinsonism. *Medical Aspects of Human Sexuality, 17*(3), 271, 274-275.**

This article discusses Parkinson's disease and its effects on sexual activities in a patient. Paulson suggests that it is up to the doctor to help the patient overcome this difficulty. The disease attacks older people and it can affect, in some cases, an already weakened sexual state because of patient's age. A physician's attitude toward a patient who has the disease and complains about decreasing sexual activity needs to be positive. Unfortunately most doctors will examine this problem as minor and not related to the disease. Most doctors are unable to help the patient because they do not think the patient should be sexually active in the first place because of his or her age. In some people the disease affects the mobility of muscles, so sexual activities may become difficult or impossible for some patients. Parkinson's does not just affect the muscular system, it also affects other body systems that affect sexual activity, such as the circulatory and cerebral systems. The author concluded with several suggestions for ways that a physician can comfort and help the transition to the disease be more comfortable and easier.

387   Relf, Michael V. (November-December, 1991). Sexuality and the older bypass patient. *Geriatric Nursing, 12*(6), 294-296.

This article, addressed to geriatric nurses, provides advice on counseling individuals who have undergone coronary artery bypass grafting (CABG) and their spouses about sexual relationships after surgery. For patients suffering from coronary artery disease (CAD), sexual relations may change for several reasons, including fear of recurrent myocardial infarction or sudden death, or fear of precipitating, angina, dysphnea, or palpitations. The article recommends counseling the patient and spouse individually and together to provide them with accurate information about normal physiological changes with aging that may affect sexual performance; effects of the surgery and the disease process; how to distinguish incisional pain from anginal pain; and the fact that sudden death attributed to sexual activity is extremely low. The author provides a useful table of counseling guidelines. He also provides a table outlining commonly prescribed medications and their compromising effects on sexual function.

388   Renshaw, Domeena C. (March, 1988). Sex and cognitively impaired patients. *Consultant, 28*(3), 133-137.

In this article, the author discusses steps that caregivers can apply to cognitively impaired persons displaying inappropriate or open sexual behavior. These steps can foster more productive management, reduce fear of sexual assault, and avert crises. She recommends that caregivers anticipate the range of sexual behaviors that occur when patients have cerebral impairment. Coercive sexual behavior is rare from cognitively impaired elders. More common behaviors are verbal obscenities or sexual overture to staff or other patients. Patients may also undress in public. Learned sexual controls are no longer operative. Management, Renshaw says, consists of evaluation, behavior modification techniques, and teaching consequences. She provides a list of 14 points of advice for family and staff members. Renshaw concludes by saying that sexual misbehavior associated with cognitive impairment is less alarming if understood by caregivers. Sometimes normal sexual urges are misunderstood and in those cases the caregiver should provide privacy. The behavior needs to be understood and the appropriate response should be made.

389   Renshaw, Domeena C. (August, 1978). Sex and drugs. *South African Medical Journal, 54,* 322-326.

The purpose of this article is to discuss the effects of drugs on sex. The author says that despite myths, aphrodisiacs cannot be clinically shown to increase arousal. She says the brain and mind are much more important in sexuality than the penis or vagina. In this article Renshaw describes the promises and scientific knowledge of several aphrodisiacs, hormones, stimulants, antidepressants, tranquilizers, hypnotics, lithium, L-dopa, antihypertensive drugs, antihistamines and anticholinergic drugs, marijuana, and psychedelic drugs. She concludes that there is no magical alchemy for sexual joy. There are side effects from needed medications that should be studied by physicians.

390   Renshaw, Domeena C. (November, 1981). Sexual problems in old age, illness, and disability. *Psychosomatics,* 22(11), 975-977, 981,985.

This review describes how several common illnesses and disabilities interfere with sex and how the knowledgeable, compassionate family physician or psychiatrist may help both patients and their spouses to cope with their sexual problems and how to compensate for them. Renshaw discusses common sexual problems associated with aging, such as: arthritis, alcoholism, cancer, cardiac disease, paralytic stroke, diabetes, renal dialysis, and spinal cord injuries. She says that physicians need to retain sensitivity to all patients, including the disabled. Adequate sexual information and advice can restore optimum functioning and self-esteem. She says that a sexual history should be a routine part of the medical history for all patients, including the disabled and chronically ill.

391   Woods, James S. (1984). Drug effects on human sexual behavior. In Nancy Fugate Woods (Ed.), *Human sexuality in health and illness, 3rd ed.* (pp. 434-456). St. Louis: The C. V. Mosby Co.

The purpose of this chapter is to consider recent developments from biomedical and clinical research, as well as some of the more traditional concepts and misconceptions regarding the effects of drugs on sexual behavior in humans. Woods discusses oral contraceptives, drugs that decrease sexual activity and functioning, antihypertensive drugs, antidepressants, antihistamines, antispasmodics, sedatives and tranquilizers, ethyl alcohol, barbiturates, sex hormone preparations, saltpeter, cantharis, yohimbine, strychnine, narcotics, and psychoactive agents. Other drugs which the author says can affect sexual behavior are L-Dopa, PCPA, Amyl nitrite, caffeine, Vitamin E, selenium, clomiphene citrate, bromocriptine mesylate, cimetidine, clofibrate, disulfiram. He concludes that while many drugs have an adverse effect on sexual functioning, some actually enhance sexual behavior. This article includes a detailed chart listing all of the drugs or drug categories discussed in the article with their effects, and probable mechanism of action.

15

AIDS and the Elderly

In recent years, researchers have begun to consider the risk of AIDS in the older population. People over age 50 comprise 10% of new cases annually. Risk factors of older people include: infrequent use condoms, rarely being tested for HIV by physicians, and a higher than average incidence of transfusion. Since AIDS can develop many years after HIV exposure, prevention among the elderly needs to be considered. Also, as apparent by the findings in other chapters, the elderly continue to be sexually active and many must seek new partners after the deaths of their partners. The risk of HIV infection is there for both elderly heterosexuals and elderly homosexuals.

Other risk factors for HIV which exist for people at any age are having multiple sexual partners, receiving a transfusion between 1978 and 1984, hemophiliacs, using drugs by injection, and having a risky sexual partner. Little information is available to determine how many of the growing number of sexually active elderly population is at risk since these variables have not been included in recent studies of elderly sexual behavior.

392 Catania, Joseph A., Stall, Ron, Coates, Thomas J., Pelham, Anabel O., & Sacks, Celia. (Fall, 1989). Issues in AIDS primary prevention for late-middle-aged and elderly Americans. *Generations, 15*(3), 50-54.

In this article, the authors discuss the kinds of AIDS programs that are needed and whom the programs should be targeting. The authors present information about the prevalence of AIDS among elders; approximately 10% of cases occur among people ages 50 and older each year. They describe risk factors for AIDS and discuss program content. The article also includes a discussion of intervention elements and delivery modes designed to reduce AIDS risk.

393   Catania, Joseph A., Turner, Heather, Kegeles, Susan M., Stall, Ron, Pollack, Lance, & Coates, Thomas J. (June, 1989). Older Americans and AIDS: Transmission risks and primary prevention research needs. *The Gerontologist, 29*(3), 373-381.

The focus of this paper is on primary prevention of AIDS among late middle-aged and elderly people. Primary prevention refers to prevention of HIV transmission. Data are presented which show a continual increase of AIDS cases among adults ages 50 and older including an increase in cases among heterosexuals. They discuss ways in which AIDS is transmitted, including blood transfusions and through infected sexual partners. The authors compare transmission risks among heterosexuals and homosexuals. They conclude that AIDS has permeated all facets of society, including middle-aged and elderly people, both heterosexuals and homosexuals. They say that among older individuals, HIV sexual transmission may be limited if most older sexually active individuals are in long-term monogamous relationships. Since little is known of the sexual practices of older people regardless of their sexual orientation, the limits of HIV transmission in these populations cannot be predicted.

394   Catania, Joseph A., Turner, Heather, Kegeles, Susan M., Stall, Ron, Pollack, Lance, Spitzer, Sherry E., & Coates, Thomas J. (1989). HIV transmission risks of older heterosexuals and gays. In Matilda White Riley, Marcia G. Ory, & Diane Zablotsky (Eds.), *AIDS in an aging society: What we need to know* (pp. 77-95). New York: Springer Publishing Company.

This chapter deals with the primary prevention of HIV infection in the older population. Two sources of transmission important to older people are blood transfusions and heterosexual relationships. Older people, because of their experiences with chronic diseases and disabilities requiring transfusions, have frequently received infected blood. Because of the long period of time required for symptoms to manifest themselves, these people may infect their sexual partners. Since the majority of older adults in their 50s and 60s remain sexually active, their risk of contacting

HIV continues unless prevention measures are taken. This chapter also discusses the processes through which sexual behaviors and attitudes can lead to infection. The authors point out that certain biological changes with aging may increase the efficiency of HIV transmission among older individuals. Age-related behaviors may also be risky but little information is available about sexual behaviors of older adults. The authors also discuss older gay men as a source of transmission. Although most older gays have tended to reduce their high-risk behavior, some risky behavior continues. The article concludes with a conceptual model of AIDS risk reduction and a research agenda for primary prevention. The model includes three stages: recognition of the risk, commitment to changing behavior, and seeking and obtaining strategies to achieve that goal. Needed areas of research are information about the behaviors of older individuals and couples, about older people's knowledge and beliefs about AIDS, and about the prevalence and characteristics of older people engaged in high-risk sexual activities.

395 Centers for Disease Control. (September 18, 1987). Recommendations for prevention of HIV transmission in health-care settings. *Journal of the American Medical Association*, *258*(11), 1441-1452.

This article discusses the precautions that should be taken routinely in the care of all patients. Standard sterilization and disinfection procedures for patient-care equipment currently recommended for use in a variety of health-care settings is adequate to sterilize or disinfect items contaminated with blood or other body fluids from persons infected with HIV. The article then presents several experiments on the survival of HIV in the environment involving drying of fluids affected. The next section discusses HIV testing in patients and management of patients and health-care workers infected with the virus. The authors discuss the importance of telling all parties involved in a case with a person infected with HIV. The article concluded with a section on management of exposure of the virus to health-care providers. Examples of procedures are illustrated in the article.

396 Kendig, Newton E., & Adler, William H. (1990). The implications of the Acquired Immunodeficiency Syndrome for gerontology research and geriatric medicine. *Journals of Gerontology*, *45*(3), M77-M81.

This article discusses the clinical expression of AIDS in older patients. The authors report that there is an age-related increase in disease progression with a shorter survival rate. This increase is based on two factors. First, AIDS attacks the immune system and blocks it from working correctly over a period of time. So if a person is HIV positive, there is a higher than usual chance that the person will die from another disease or virus such as a common cold. Second, older people have an already diminished immune system and greater chances of obtaining diseases than the young. These two factors working together considerably decrease the time it takes the AIDS virus to completely block the immune system. Researchers are starting to look at older AIDS patients to examine the impact of the virus. The authors concluded that health providers as well as society need to learn about AIDS so as to help those with the virus. Also, researchers need to learn to combat other diseases and viruses inside an AIDS patient so they may improve the quality of life of the infected individual.

397   **Rogstad, Karen E., & Bignell, C. J. (September, 1991). Age is no bar to sexually acquired infection.** *Age and Ageing, 20*(5), 377-378.

The authors investigated the risk and prevalence of human immunodeficiency virus (HIV) and sexually transmitted disease (STD) among elderly patients visiting a genito-urinary department of a hospital in England. The case notes of 242 patients ages 60 and over were reviewed for disclosed sexual activity and results for STD and HIV. STDs were diagnosed in 58 patients (47 men, 11 women), and included gonorrhea, non-gonococcal urethritis, genital warts, genital Herpes simplex virus infection, trichomoniasis, and acute hepatitis B. Sexual activity with casual partners was reported by 68 patients, with the range in number of contacts being 1 to 30. Anxiety regarding HIV infection was the primary reason for the clinical visit in 22 men and 6 women, although none of these patients tested positive for the virus. Findings confirm that HIV infection and STD are issues for elderly people and should not be discounted as a cause of anxiety and illness.

398   **Stall, Ron, & Catania, Joe. (January 10, 1994). AIDS risk behaviors among late middle-aged and elderly Americans.** *Archives of Internal Medicine, 154*(1), 57-63.

This study describes the prevalence of AIDS risk among Americans ages 50 years and older. The authors present data from the National AIDS Behavioral Surveys (NABS), two large cross-sectional national surveys taken in 1990-1991. Data were collected between June 1990 through February 1991 by random-digit dialing telephone calls. Risk factors were defined as having multiple sexual partners, receiving a transfusion between 1978 and 1984, being a hemophiliacs, using drugs by injection, having a risky sexual partner. Respondents were also asked about condom use and sexual orientation. The authors found that about 10% of Americans ages 50 or older had at least one risk factor for AIDS. Very small proportions of Americans past the age of 50 used condoms during sex or had undergone HIV testing. At-risk Americans were one sixth as likely to use condoms during sex and one fifth as likely to have been tested for HIV as a comparison group of at-risk individuals in their 20s.

399 Talashek, Marie L., Tichy, Anna M., & Epping, Hugh. (1990). Sexually transmitted diseases in the elderly: Issues and recommendations. *Journal of Gerontological Nursing, 16*(4), 33-40.

This article discusses existing knowledge about the relevant issues regarding sexually transmitted diseases (STDs) in the aging population and recommendations for appropriate preventive health-care strategies. They cite data to support the increasing incidence of STDs in elderly populations. Under the category of primary prevention the authors discuss disease transmission and counseling. Under the topic of secondary prevention, they discuss sexual history, diagnostic findings, treatment, and counseling. Under the topic of tertiary prevention, they discuss counseling. The authors point out that despite antibiotics, STDs continue to escalate in scope and complexity. They believe nurses should be encouraged to implement primary, secondary, and tertiary prevention activities.

16

Effects of Training on Caregiver Attitudes and Knowledge

Many writers recommend educational intervention for people who work with the elderly to increase their knowledge of elderly sexuality and to rid them of negative stereotypes. This chapter describes such interventions and reviews their impact on staff knowledge, attitudes and practices.

Populations most commonly involved in study populations are nursing students. A number of researchers have examined the effects of various training programs and workshops on the attitudes and knowledge of elderly sexuality of this group. The PLISSIT Model and adapted versions of the model have been used in several studies. Studies have also looked at the effects of courses such as psychology of aging or human sexuality, entire curricula, curriculum changes, and clinical experiences, and a gerontology certification program. Results have been frequently disappointing but there is an overwhelming support in the literature for providing such training. Medical school students are also targeted for education in elderly sexuality. Attempts to improve their knowledge and change their attitudes toward elderly sexuality have met with mixed results.

Another popular study population is nursing home staff. Training methods have included films (explicit and implicit approaches), 6-week courses in human autonomy, the physiology of normal aging, and physical and psychosocial problems of the elderly.

While education has been shown to change knowledge and attitudes, the variable which may influence change more than education are religious beliefs and conservative beliefs of the caregivers. Very religious and conservative staff were less likely to change their attitudes after participating in an educational experience. In at least one study, education was related with a negative attitude toward elderly sexuality. Recent studies also suggest the existence of a cohort effect. The young-old have more positive attitudes toward their own sexuality and toward sexuality of others. Few studies have investigated the relationship between knowledge, attitudes, and practices.

Measures of aging and sexual knowledge used in these studies are White's *Aging Sexual Knowledge and Attitudes Scale (1982)*, the *Sex Knowledge Attitude Test (Lief & Reed, 1970)*, Rokeach's *(1960) Dogmatism Scale*, LTK *Attitude Rating Scale (Aja & Self, 1986)*, and the *Adjective Checklist (1972)*. Tests of attitudes and knowledge of aging (which usually contain one or more items about sexuality) are Palmore's *Facts on Aging (1977; 1988)*, the *Aging Semantic Differential*, Tuckman-Lorge *Attitudes Toward Old People (1953)*, and Kogan's *Old People Scales (1961)*.

400   **Aja, Anne, & Self, Don. (January, 1986). Alternate methods of changing nursing home staff attitudes toward sexual behavior of the aged.** *Journal of Sex Education and Therapy, 12(1), 37-41.*

The authors studied the effects of exposure to different levels of explicitness in sexual related materials on the perceptions, attitudes, and knowledge of adult nursing home staff. Staff of a nursing facility (N = 45) ages 18 to 62 were divided into two groups based on the scores obtained on *Rokeach's Dogmatism Scale*. Each group was then randomly assigned to three groups: Implicit, Explicit, and Control. Implicit and Explicit groups then took a 2-day Sexual Attitude Reassessment (SAR) formatted class. Implicit groups are shown nongraphically depicted sexual behavior material whereas Explicit groups were shown graphically depicted sexual behavior material. Between group differences in attitudes, knowledge, and perceptions of sexual behavior in the aged were tested using the *Sex Knowledge and Attitude Test* (SKAT), a 106-item multiple choice test. Subjects also completed the LTK *Attitude Rating Scale*, an 80-item Likert-type scale developed by Anne Aja. Data showed that those in the Implicit group scored higher than the Explicit and control groups on the SKAT. Data resulting from the *LTK Scale* showed no significant differences among the groups. The authors conclude that the SAR class needs to find more effective ways to facilitate exploration of sexual attitudes and values, increased knowledge of sexual behavior, and encourage the development of more tolerant sexual attitudes. The list of films shown in the course are included with the producer's address.

401   Almquist, Eleanor, Stein, Shayna, Weiner, Audrey, & Linn, Margaret W. (March, 1981). Evaluation of continuing education for long-term care personnel: Impact upon attitudes and knowledge. *Journal of The American Geriatric Society, 29*(3), 117-122.

   The authors' goal in this article was to provide the nursing staff with increased knowledge about long-term care, to improve their attitudes toward their elderly patients, and to determine the success of the program through evaluation of the impact of the training on changes in attitudes and knowledge of nursing personnel. Nursing assistants (aides, N = 29) and licensed practical nurses (LPNs, N = 52) from three proprietary nursing homes participated in this study. The program covered six weeks and covered knowledge about human anatomy, the physiology of normal aging, physical and psychosocial problems of the elderly, and for nurses, problems associated with cardiovascular accidents. The participants completed a pre- and posttest with respect to knowledge, life satisfaction (*Life Satisfaction Scale*), and attitudes toward the elderly. Results indicated overall favorable changes for both aides and LPNs, particularly in the areas of increased knowledge and more positive attitudes. The data suggested that continuing education is an effective means of influencing the knowledge and attitudes of personnel in long-term care facilities, and it should be a first step toward improving the quality of care for elderly residents. This study also found that happiness in one's work may be positively associated with favorable attitudes toward (and possibly also superior management of) those under their care.

402   Angiullo, Loren, Whitbourne, Susan Krauss, & Powers, Charles. (July-August, 1996). The effects of instruction and experience on college students' attitudes toward the elderly. *Educational Gerontology, 22*(5), 483-495.

   This study investigated the effects of instruction and experience on knowledge and attitudes toward the elderly. Researchers measured the attitudes of college students before and after enrolling in a psychology of aging class. The treatment group attended the psychology of aging class and participated in different types of projects. A group of students enrolled in a personality class served as controls. Data were gathered using Palmore's *Facts on Aging Quiz* (FAQ), a 25-item true/false questionnaire and the *Aging Semantic Differential* (ASD), a 32-item questionnaire used to measure subjects' perceptions and attitudes about older adults. Students' knowledge about and attitudes toward the elderly significantly improved over the course of the semester. There was no significant difference among the subgroups who participated in different types of projects.

403   Brower, H. Terri. (December, 1981). Teaching gerontological nursing in Florida: Where do we stand? *Nursing and Health Care, 11*(10), 543-547.

To determine the status of gerontological nursing education in Florida, the State Health Care Coordinating Council's Long-term Care Task Force decided to carry out a study to identify factors of preparedness for quality care. The survey instrument questions involved faculty preparation, curriculum content, and clinical experience in gerontological nursing. The survey was distributed through the mail to deans and directors of the diploma, associate degree, and baccalaureate nursing programs in Florida. The results showed that nurses were more likely to prefer to work with younger patients than older. They also demonstrated that the nursing programs did not place much emphasis on gerontological nursing. The results demonstrated that, with the population of aged individuals increasing in Florida, there needs to be a medical staff to take care of them. The authors conclude that nursing programs in Florida need to emphasize gerontology more or there will be a problem in the future.

404   Buschmann, M. B. Tank, Burns, Elizabeth M., & Jones, Faith M. (May, 1981). Student nurses' attitudes toward the elderly. *Journal of Nursing Education, 20*(5), 7-10.

In order to help student nurses attain a positive attitude toward the field of gerontology, a course was designed to provide student nurses with a fundamental knowledge concerning normal changes that occur during aging and to help them become more sensitive to the specific needs of the elderly. A questionnaire was given to students the first day of a junior-level nursing course. A total of 160 completed questionnaires was returned. The questionnaire examined a student's exposure to working with patients, attitudes of society toward aging, and students were then asked in which areas of specialization they would like to work. Most students at one point had dealt with older people and had had a positive experience. The society questions revealed that students thought that society was youth-oriented and was slightly biased toward older people. The area of specialization was open to some variance but about half said they would consider gerontology a field of study. The results showed that there is an interest in learning about aging and its effects. Nurses need to learn more about caring for the elderly because as the years pass the number of elderly grows considerably. The author concluded that it is more effective to produce nurses with positive attitudes early in their education than trying to change attitudes later in their schooling or careers.

405   Chaffee, Mary W. (November, 1984). The missing link in nursing education: Sexuality. *Imprint, 31*(4), 43.

This essay expresses the views of the author, a staff nurse in a general and gynecological surgery ward, regarding the need for including information about sexuality in nursing education. She expresses the view at all people are sexual, regardless of age, health, or involvement in a sexual relationship. All nurses, in her view, need to expand their knowledge of sexuality.

406   Chamberland, Gerry, Rawls, Betty, Powell, Carla, & Roberts, Mary Jo. (January-February, 1978). Improving students' attitudes toward aging. *Journal of Gerontological Nursing, 4*(1), 44-45.

The authors reported on their attempts to improve the nursing students' attitudes toward aging. Each semester they evaluated the effects of Fundamentals of Nursing class, the first quarter of the nursing sequence at Troy State University, on attitude using the Tuckman-Lorge *Old People's Questionnaire* as a pretest and posttest at the beginning and end of the quarter. Their program initially consisted of four hours of classroom content to explore attitudes toward the aged and to teach some psychosocial adaptations of normal aging in society. Students also were involved in clinical experiences in nursing facilities. At the end of the first quarter the authors reported that students' attitudes had become more negative. The second quarter they initiated a nursing home group project that would involve student initiative and creativity. This group of students demonstrated more positive attitudes at posttest. The authors concluded that the projects were useful in meeting their goal. No data are reported in this article.

407   Chandler, Jane T., Rachel, John R., & Kazelskis, Richard. (October, 1986). Attitudes of long-term care nursing personnel toward the elderly. *The Gerontologist, 26*(5), 551-555.

The purposes of this project included the assessment of attitudes of long-term care nursing personnel toward the elderly, to determine if differences were related to levels of nurses, and to determine if differences existed between staff of a nursing home and a nursing home with an intensive care unit, and to evaluate the impact of an adult experiential program on the attitudes of nursing personnel employed in two long-term care facilities. Subjects were 101 individuals consisting of RNs, LPNs, and nursing assistants. The group was divided into an experimental group (N = 51) and a control group (N = 50). Both groups completed the Palmore's *Facts on Aging Quiz* and Kogan's *Attitudes Toward Old People Scale*, twice. The experimental group completed a five session course on the aged before taking the tests again. The total group mean at pretest was significantly higher that Palmore's FAQ average. Posttest comparisons found that the training had no significant effect on the experimental group. The results from this project contradicted several of the popularly held beliefs concerning the attitudes of nursing personnel toward the elderly and education's potential role in changing attitudes.

408   Cook, Beth Ann, & Pieper, Hanns G. (Summer, 1985). The impact of the nursing home clinical on attitudes toward working with the elderly. *Gerontology & Geriatrics Education, 5*(4), 53-59.

This study evaluated the effect of a 2-week nursing home clinical on the attitudes of 70 second year nursing students. The clinical was an introduction of nursing students to actual nursing home patients. Each nursing student was assigned a patient at a nursing home for two weeks. The researchers used a 38-item questionnaire with a Likert-style answering format to assess students' general attitudes before and after the experience. A list of the items is included as a table but no information about the reliability of the instrument are included. The results showed that some student attitudes improved, but the overall group showed a negative feeling. The authors concluded that nursing students had a negative experience with the patients at the home. The authors suggested preparation for this experience was not complete. The overall impact of the study demonstrates that the students' preparation time to deal with older people was not complete. The results suggest that student introduction to gerontological nursing needs some revision in preparing nursing students.

409 Eddy, Diane M. (1986). Before and after attitudes toward aging in a BSN program. *Journal of Gerontological Nursing, 12*(5), 30-34.

This article reports the results of a study that tested the effects of curriculum changes on the attitudes of nursing students toward older adults. Subjects were 56 junior students enrolled in a baccalaureate nursing program. Curriculum content related to healthy aging was introduced. Students also visited at least five well elderly patients ages 60 to 91, kept a diary of the interactions during each visit, and submitted a term paper analyzing the aging experience. Attitudes of the nursing students were assessed before and after the treatment using the Tuckman-Lorge *Attitudes Toward Old People Scale* and a structured demographic tool. Analysis of variance revealed no significant change in attitude from Time 1 (before the curriculum change and visitation program) to Time 2 (after the curriculum change and visitation program). Forty-two percent of the students showed no change. Thirty-five percent showed an improvement in attitudes as demonstrated by a decrease in negative stereotyping. The author concluded that there were too few visits to bring about a change. The author also noted that the students reported that the experience was rewarding.

410 Frazer, Jo, Albert, Martha, Smith, Jamie, & Dearner, Jim. (March, 1982). Impact of a human sexuality workshop on the sexual attitudes and knowledge of nursing students. *Journal of Nursing Education, 21*(3), 6-13.

The purpose of this study was to determine the effectiveness of the University of Oklahoma College of Nursing's Human Sexuality Workshop by comparing the questionnaire responses of nursing students before and after completing the workshop. Subjects were 92 senior nursing students, a majority of whom were females ages 20 to 25. The authors found that participation in the workshop made significant changes in both the knowledge and attitudes of the participants. Two variables which appeared to have the most influence on change in attitudes were the degree of the subject's religious beliefs and the degree of political conservatism. Students who described themselves as very religious or politically conservative were less likely to report changes in attitudes. The authors suggest that future research determine how the workshop may be changed to address the constraints of religious and political beliefs on the degree of attitude change among nursing students who attend the workshop.

411   Garrard, Judith, Vaitkus, Aldona, & Chilgren, R. A. (October, 1972). Evaluation of a course in human sexuality. *Journal of Medical Education, 47,* 772-778.

The purpose of this paper is to describe an evaluation design and the instruments used in a seminar in human sexuality. A total of 215 people from the medical field and the community participated in the study. All participants were part of a 2-day seminar at the University of Minnesota Medical School held in three sessions. The subjects completed a pretest and posttest using the *Sex Knowledge and Attitude Test* (SKAT), *Adjective Checklist,* and *Attitude Rating Scale.* The latter two tests were developed from items developed by the National Sex and Drug Forum. The *Adjective Checklist* consists of five kinds of sexual behaviors. The subject was instructed to rate his usual reaction to reading, seeing a movie, or seeing pictures of each behavior by checking one of nine adjectives. In the *Attitude Rating Scale* 13 statements about sexual attitudes or behaviors are given and subjects indicate whether they agree or disagree on a 5-point scale. Data analysis indicated that all categories of participants showed a significant pretest to posttest change in the direction of a more tolerant attitude. Changes in knowledge were not significant. The authors attributed the lack of change to the high scores on the pretest. The authors compared their results to a separate control study conducted in October 1971. The SKAT was administered to 17 senior medical students as a pretest and a posttest. Control group data showed no significant differences on either the attitude or knowledge sections of the test.

412   Glass, J. Conrad, Jr., & Dalton, Jo Ann. (March-April, 1988). Sexuality in older adults: A continuing education concern. *The Journal of Continuing Education in Nursing, 19*(2), 61-64.

Glass and Dalton note that myths and stereotypes about sexuality and aging persist among older people, their family members, and health care providers. They call for continuing education of nurses about sexuality and aging as a way to dispel these myths and accurately inform members of society at all ages of the facts about sexuality and aging. Nurses need to learn about the physiological changes that occur with aging, and how those impact sexuality. For example, older males may experience some decrease in blood flow to the genitals and a disturbance of pelvic innervation; while older females experience a decrease in estrogen production and atrophy of the reproductive organs, as well as a decrease in vaginal secretions. In addition to the sexual response cycle (SRC) Nurses need to learn that older adults may experience some alteration in sexual response as a result of various medical and surgical therapies and/or as a result of taking certain medications such as sedatives, narcotics, antianxiety agents, and antidepressants. Pain and stiffness associated with aging of the muscular skeletal system may also affect sexual relations. Nurses should also know that social, psychological, and personal factors may also be damaging to the older adults' feelings about his or her sexuality. The authors argue that nurses are in a good position to be sex educators for society as a whole.

413   Gomez, Gerda E., Otto, Dorothy, Blattstein, Abraham, & Gomez, Efrain A. (January, 1985). **Beginning nursing students can change attitudes about the aged.** *Journal of Gerontological Nursing, 11*(1), 6-11.

This study investigated the impact of a 3-week, 8-hours-per-week clinical experience of caring for "ill" elderly in long-term care by baccalaureate students taking their first clinical course. The students completed the *Kogan Old People Scale*, which measured a person's attitude towards the elderly, before and after the clinic. The main finding was that there was significant increase in the positive attitude toward the elderly by these students after the course. An additional finding was that the older age group of students held a more positive attitude toward the elderly than did the younger students.

414   Gordon, Susan K., & Hallauer, Dean S. (August, 1976). **Impact of a friendly visiting program on attitudes of college students toward the aged.** *The Gerontologist, 16*(4), 371-376.

This article reports results of a study of the impact of course content in human development and a friendly visiting program in which students visited older people on the attitudes of college students toward older people. Four groups of undergraduate students at Geneseo State College, a liberal arts college in New York State, were studied: (1) child development course, no visiting; (2) child development course, visiting; (3) adult development course, no visiting; and (4) adult development course, visiting. The visiting was mandatory and consisted of weekly 1-hour sessions over a 10- to 12-week period. The majority of older people visited were residents of a health-related facility (HRF). Attitudes were measured before and after the class for each group using the *Kogan Old People Scale*, consisting of 17 positive and 17 negative items rated on a 5-point scale from strongly agree to strongly disagree. Results indicated that while the course content alone significantly altered students' attitudes toward the aged, friendly visiting in addition to course content had an even greater effect. Final reports done by students indicated that both students and older residents visited benefited greatly from the program. Eighty percent of the students said they would like to participate in the program again. Some problems of the program were noted such as logistics of transportation and the difficulties of ending the student/elder contact.

415   Gunter, Laurie M. (July, 1971). Students' attitudes toward geriatric nursing. *Nursing Outlook, 19*(7), 466-469.

In this article, the authors report and discuss some of the findings of a study of 162 students who took a gerontology course, particularly in terms of the effects of the course on the stereotypes and interests of the students in the care of older patients. The *Tuckman-Lorge Attitude Questionnaire* was used to measure stereotyped responses. Gunter found that nursing students showed higher negativity toward caring for elderly than before the course. The researcher concluded that one reason why nurses do not have positive attitudes toward sexuality of the aged and have limited knowledge about elderly sexuality, is, that nursing curriculums may not provide adequate geriatric nursing theory or sufficient positive "real life" experiences in this area. Nursing students may, therefore, not prefer the geriatric nursing role because of feelings of inadequacy about caring for the elderly.

416   Hammond, Doris B., & Bonney, Warren C. (February, 1985). Results of sex education for support persons working with the elderly. *Journal of Sex Education and Therapy, 11*(2), 42-45.

This article investigates one method for developing an understanding of the sexual needs and concerns of the elderly. Subjects consisted of a control group of 25 people and an experimental group of 28 people from a gerontology certification program. Both groups completed a questionnaire on elderly sexuality. Subjects in the experimental group then attended a 2-day class on sexuality and aging. After the course both groups completed a post-questionnaire to determine if there was a change. The experimental group showed a tremendous change in knowledge about sexual aging, whereas the control group did not. The authors concluded that nursing staff members have a limited knowledge about sexuality and aging and that if a course like the one used in this research were incorporated into nursing programs, nursing home staff might be more willing and able to help the elderly with sexual problems.

417   Hart, Laura K., Freel, Mildred I., & Crowell, Carolyn M. (August, 1976). Changing attitudes toward the aged and interest in caring for the aged. *Journal of Gerontological Nursing, 2(4),* 10-16.

       This study examined whether two courses in a nursing program which included contact with elderly people affected nursing students' attitudes toward working with the elderly. The first course was an introductory clinical nursing course, and the second was an elective gerontology course. Subjects were divided into five groups: non-nursing students, nursing students prior to the introductory course, nursing students after the introductory course, nursing students prior to the elective course, and nursing students after the elective course. Results of a questionnaire assessing attitudes toward the elderly showed that the guided instruction of nursing students including interaction with both well and ill elderly can have a positive effect on their attitudes toward older people. The authors suggest that this type of program may help workers in nursing facilities develop and maintain a positive attitude toward the people in their care. While this type of exposure has a positive effect on attitudes toward the elderly, it does not necessarily produce an interest in working with the elderly. The authors suggest that future research address the correlation between interest in working with the elderly and common stereotypes about the elderly.

418   Heller, Barbara R., & Walsh, Frederick J. (January, 1976). Changing nursing students' attitudes toward the aged: An experimental study. *Journal of Nursing Education, 15(5),* 9-17.

       The cognitive dissonance theory was used to design a study to test the hypothesis that nursing students' attitudes toward the aged and their preferences for working with the aged could be positively influenced by a program of study which emphasize the appropriate professional nurses' attitude toward old people and provide a series of positive experiences with "well" elderly. The study consisted of a 45-hour teaching unit developed to focus on the needs and problems of older people, especially about the maintenance of mental health. The study sample consisted of 110 senior students dived into two groups to form an experimental and a control group. Students completed the *Kogan Old People's Scale* (OP) and the *Modified Wilensky-Barmack Work Preference* questionnaires during preregistration in the class and the information pretest on the first day of class. After the class, students completed the OP, the *Modified Wilensky-Barmack Work Preference*, the *Information PreTest* and some demographic data questionnaires. The attitudes of the experimental group became more positive toward the elderly. Scores on the *Modified Wilensky-Barmack Work Preference* did not show any difference between pre- and posttests. A significant positive change was noted for the *Information PreTest* which resulted from the learning experiences. The findings showed that frequent contact and positive experiences with old people will influence positive attitudes toward old people. The authors concluded that attitudes of nursing students toward the aged as well as their preference for working with the aged can be positively influenced by selected learning experiences.

419   Hickey, Tom, Rakowski, William, Hultsch, David F., & Fatula, Betty J. (1976). Attitudes toward aging as a function of in-service training and practitioner age. *Journal of Gerontology, 31*(6), 681-686.

The authors investigated age differences in attitudes toward aging as a function of a 3-hour training program with 322 women ages 18 to 74 years from various geriatric health care and social service contexts. They used a quasi-experimental pre- and posttest design. Sites were randomly divided into initial experimental and control groups. All control participants received training following the research program. Their results indicated few instances of unfavorable attitudes toward aging in any age group, and slightly less stereotyping. Training appeared to result in less cynicism, stronger endorsement of family and public responsibility, and slightly greater anxiety. No age by Pretest/Posttest interactions could be found. The authors discussed implications of their findings for service providers-clients interaction, bringing about attitudinal and behavioral change, and appropriate instruments for assessing program impact.

420 LaMonica, Elaine L. (November-December, 1979). The nurse and the aging client: Positive attitude formation. *Nurse Educator,* 4(6), 23-26.

The purpose of this article was to share an experimental approach for helping caregivers develop an understanding of the aging process. The article focuses on the need for nurses to develop a personal understanding of their own attitudes toward the aging person, and discusses the need for nurses to develop a positive attitude toward the aged and the aging process. Nurses consistently rate geriatric units as the least desirable places to work. LaMonica argues that nursing education must focus on the development of positive attitude, motivation to reach positive goals, and an adequate knowledge base. LaMonica recommends an existential conceptual approach in which emphasis is placed on the importance of the individual's goals and values with attention directed towards understanding one's personal world and values. She comments that "nurses must be aware of their personal experiences in relation to the aging process, recognize them as valid and true, and respond to clients according to their (the nurses) own reality." In order to experience the world as an older person does, nurses need to participate in a learning experience in which the primary focus is on consciousness raising about aging and the aged and positive attitude development. At the end of the article a sample training exercise is presented step-by-step.

421 Megenity, Jean. (July, 1975). A plea for sexual education in nursing curriculums. *American Journal of Nursing,* 75(7), 1171.

This article makes a plea for including education in curriculums in nursing schools. As the author points out, at present, nurses are being graduated who are almost completely unprepared in the area of sexuality. The author recounts personal experiences in teaching situations and emphasizes the total lack of knowledge and many misconceptions in this area. She suggests that information on sexuality be offered within the maternity part of the curriculum in nursing schools.

422 Mims, Fern H., Brown, Louis, & Lubow, Robert. (May-June, 1976). Human sexuality course evaluation. *Nursing Research,* 25(3), 187-191.

The purposes of the study were to (1) determine how effective a 3-day concentrated human sexuality program would be in changing attitudes and increasing knowledge of human sexuality for the total group of students; (2) determine if and how each group would benefit from the experience; (3) compare medical and nursing students' pre- and postures performances; (4) compare results of the three-day with the five-day program that had been given the previous year; and (5) determine how each group of students perceived the experience. The goals of the program were to help participants increase sexual knowledge, help desensitize them against stressful and anxiety reactions to sexual stimuli, and resensitize them in the direction of a broader understanding of sexuality of self and others. The program covered a wide range of topics such as human sexual response, sexual value systems, adolescent change and sexuality, sexuality in the aging population, masturbation, homosexuality, sexual functioning associated with physical disability, and treatment of sexual dysfunctions. Films of explicit sexual behavior were shown. Subjects were 186 students; 86 sophomore medical students, 86 nursing students, and 14 graduate psychology students. The *Sex Knowledge and Attitude Test* (SKAT, form 2) was used in addition to an evaluation developed for the study. A copy of the 20 items on the evaluation is included with the article. The total group showed a significant gain between pre- and posttest mean scores on all SKAT items except the abortion attitudinal scale. The authors concluded that the program had been successful in increasing knowledge and moving attitudes from a more conservative to a more liberal viewpoint.

423   **Mims, Fern H., & Swenson, Melinda. (February, 1978). A model to promote sexual health care.** *Nursing Outlook, 26*(2), 121-125.

The authors point out in the first paragraph of their article that "now that human sexuality has become an accepted part of total health care, nurses have a responsibility to promote sexual health in their practice." They go on to note the many myths and misconceptions about sex and sexuality, which many nurses accept as true, and the lack of adequate education about sexual health received by most nurses. Mims and Swenson discuss their conceptual model, based on the PLISSIT Model developed for the behavioral treatment of sexual problems. Their model, which can be applied in nursing practice or nursing education, helps define the various levels of knowledge, attitudes, and skills needed in promoting sexual health. The model is composed of four ascending levels: life experience, basic level, intermediate level, and advanced level. The life experience level includes both destructive and intuitively helpful behaviors developed by living in our society. Many destructive behaviors are based on myths and stereotypes such as the belief that impotence in older men is nearly universal. The basic level is based on awareness composed of all one's cognition, attitudes, and perceptions of sexuality. In the cognitive area, for example, the nurse is aware of anatomy and physiology of the sexual organs, psycho-sexual development The intermediate level includes communication skills that facilitate permission and information giving. For example, permission-giving lets the patient know that a nurse sanctions his/her sexual attitudes or sexual behavior. At the advanced level nurses suggest particular sexual techniques or recommend various exercises or sexual positions. Sexual therapy may be recommended by a nurse at this level. The advanced level also includes participation in educational programs and research projects on sexuality. Authors provide many illustrations for each of the four levels of their model. They also include a helpful diagram of their sexual health model.

424 Mims, Fern H., Yeaworth, Rosalee, & Horstein, Stephen. (May-June, 1974). Effectiveness of an interdisciplinary course in human sexuality. *Nursing Research, 23*(3), 248-253.

The authors investigated the effect of a 5-day human sexuality program on a group of 70 medical students, 37 nursing students, 14 other students (non-medical) and 22 group leaders at the University of Cincinnati. The program consisted of the following goals: (1) supply accurate information; (2) encourage each student to question, explore, and assess his or her own sexual attitudes; and (3) help participants develop a more tolerant attitude toward sexual beliefs, attitudes, and behaviors of others. Participants completed a four part *Sexual Knowledge and Attitude Test* at the beginning and the end of the course. The authors found a significant difference between mean scores of the pre- and posttests. They suggest that this program has the potential of sensitizing people toward their own and others' sexuality.

425 Paul, Elizabeth A., & O'Neill, Jacquelyn S. (1983). A sexual health model for nursing intervention. *Issues in Health Care of Women, 4*, 115-125.

This article described and illustrated a conceptual model for nurses who wish to assist clients in attaining or maintaining sexual health. The Sexual Health Model for Nursing Intervention provided form and direction for nurses at all levels when they address client concerns or problems related to sexual health.

Interactions between the nurse and the client are the basis of all parts of this model. The model included four processes. The nursing process is the first and included all other processes and approaches contained within the model. The three other processes, communication, therapeutic, and teaching, define the role and skills of the nurse. The adaptation of the Permission, Limited Information, Specific Suggestions, and Intensive Therapy (PLISSIT) model, contained within the processes, is a hierarchy of interviews that guide the nurses' activities. The author concluded that the use of this model can assist nurses in making an important contribution to client sexual health.

426   Renshaw, Domeena. (September, 1977). Sexual therapist: Why not the family physician? *Consultant, 17*(9), 134A-134H.

In this article, the author argues her case for the family physician taking an active role in sex therapy. Sexual difficulties could be the cause of headaches, insomnia, and a host of other stubborn psychogenic ailments that patients bring to their physicians. Renshaw recommends that taking a sexual history be a part of the intake process. She offers nine practice suggestions for physicians to aid them in providing sexual therapy. Some of those involve using sex education aids, providing a sex reading list for couples, and seeing couples together. She describes the most common sexual problems that physicians encounter including impotence, premature ejaculation, orgasmic dysfunction, and loss of sexual desire. These usually respond to brief counseling. She recommends that a thorough physical examination be done. She describes sexual blocks and less common problems. Renshaw gives a brief description of the ideal sex therapist who can accept the ultimate intimacy with professionalism and is willing and able to discuss intimate details of sexuality. This article includes a list of educational material about sex for the physician, audiovisuals, films, and books for the patients.

427   Rienzo, Barbara A. (February, 1985). The impact of aging on human sexuality. *Journal of School Health, 55*(2), 66-68.

In this review of the literature, the author investigated the need for education for lay persons and professionals about the effects of the aging process on human sexuality by reviewing gerontological and medical literature. She suggested a primary prevention of psychosocial problems and sexual dysfunction could include accurate information about sexuality and aging. She also discussed the use of effective communication techniques in sexuality education programs, including those with young adults. The author concluded that professional preparation of health educators must include the skills and knowledge needed in this area.

428   Spence, Donald L., Feigenbaum, Elliott M., Fitzgerald, Faith, & Roth, Janet. (September, 1968). Medical student attitudes toward the geriatric patient. *Journal of the American Geriatrics Society, 16(9),* 976-983.

The purpose of this study was to explore, within the limitations of method, the interrelationships between general and medical socialization influences and the consequent medical student attitudes toward old people. Questionnaires designed to test attitudes toward old people were given to both the freshman and the senior class of students in the University of California School of Medicine. Data analysis showed that these two groups shared most of the general societal conceptions and misconceptions about the aged. They also found that these students adhered to a set of medical stereotypes about aging to a degree surprisingly unmodified between the two groups. The researchers discussed the lack of difference between the two student classes and the failure of 3 years of medical education to migrate attitudes about a major and growing segment of the population—aged patients.

429   Tarbox, Arthur R., Connors, Gerard J., & Faillace, Louis A. (July, 1987). Freshman and senior medical students' attitudes toward the elderly. *Journal of Medical Education, 62(7),* 582-591.

The main purpose of the study was to evaluate the attitudes expressed by medical students toward older adults. Another purpose of the study was to assess the specific effects of medical education on these students' attitudes toward older people. Questionnaires designed to measure attitudes were administered to freshman and senior classes of medical students in 1981 and 1984. To allow comparability, the questionnaire was the same one used by Spence and his colleagues in the 1960s. The questionnaire covered four areas: demographic characteristics and family background; definitional characteristics and traits attributable to old age, the students' attitudes toward different age and sex groups; and the students' attitudes toward the aged in medical situations. Analysis of data revealed that some prejudice against the elderly existed in both medical class samples (1981 and 1984), paralleling negative attitudes toward the elderly expressed by medical students in the 1960s. Compared to students surveyed in the 1960s, medical students surveyed in the 1980s saw the elderly as being economically productive for an additional 10 to 20 years. In both samples (1981 and 1984) seniors expressed more favorable attitudes toward older adults than did freshman medical students. In both years seniors also defined old age as beginning later than did freshmen. Seniors also viewed the elderly more positively in terms of productivity, social significance, and sexuality of the aged than did the freshmen. As the authors conclude, "Taken together, these results indicate that attitudes toward the elderly are becoming more favorable in society and in medical schools in particular and that the medical education process was responsible for the more favorable attitudes expressed by the senior medical students."

430   Tobiason, Sarah Jane, Knudsen, Frances, Stengel, Jean C., & Giss, Marilyn. (May-June, 1979). Positive attitudes toward aging: The aged teach the young. *Journal of Gerontological Nursing,* 5(3), 18-23.

This study evaluates a home visit program at Arizona State University designed to provide opportunities for students to develop interviewing skills, to learn about people from another age group, and to understand the process of adaptation to aging through sharing one individual's experiences. Both the students and the clients completed assessments of the experience. Both students and clients positively evaluated the program. The authors conclude that this program demonstrates one method of promoting positive attitudes of nursing personnel toward the elderly.

431   Tollett, Susan Morrison, & Thornby, John I. (June, 1982). Geriatric and gerontology nursing curricular trends. *Journal of Nursing Education,* 21(6), 16-23.

This study investigated the impact of education on the attitudes of nursing students toward aging. The sample consisted of 570 students from 12 baccalaureate schools of nursing accredited by the National League for Nursing. Researchers constructed an interview guide to gather information about the amount of geriatric curriculum content. Based on the data obtained in the interview with faculty from each school of nursing, the schools were classified as having low, medium, or high amounts of geriatric content. The *Tuckman-Lorge Questionnaire* (TLQ) consisting of 88 statements was used to measure the attitudes toward the elderly. Based on the findings of this study, the authors concluded that students' attitudes about the elderly are unrelated to the amount of geriatric content in their nursing curriculum. They also recommended specific content be included in nursing curricula in three areas: (1) social changes as well as physical changes that occur to elderly persons and adaptation patterns of these individuals; (2) usefulness of aged persons and the contributions they can and do make to society; and (3) characteristics of the well elderly as opposed to total concentration on the sick elderly.

432 Wilhite, Mary J., & Johnson, Dale M. (November-December, 1976). Changes in nursing students' stereotypic attitudes toward old people. *Nursing Research, 25*(6), 430-432.

The authors investigated student stereotype attitudes toward old people and whether they would diminish during an 8-week introduction to professional nursing course. They also investigated the relationship between in student attitudes toward the aged and the attitudes of the instructor toward the aged. The course featured laboratory and classroom components on health-illness ideas in the care of geriatric patients. The course consisted of 80 students randomly assigned to 10 groups, each having a different laboratory instructor. Kogan's *Attitude Toward Old People Questionnaire* was administered to the students at the beginning and end of the course. Instructors for each laboratory section completed the same questionnaire at the beginning of the course. The results suggested that the students' stereotypic attitudes declined during the course and that the amount of change in student attitudes was related to faculty attitudes toward the aged.

17

Effects of Education, Therapy, and Counseling on the Elderly

The effects of education, therapy, or counseling on elderly attitudes and knowledge related to their sexuality have received only a minimal amount of attention in the literature. A few educational interventions have been evaluated, mostly on elderly people attending senior centers, neighborhood centers, or senior day care centers, geriatric centers at hospitals. One study included here by White and Catania (1982) investigated the affects of a sexual psychoeducational intervention conducted and evaluated with a group of elderly residents of nursing homes. The intervention was also evaluated with adult family members and staff members.

The types of programs offered include short workshops on sexuality, 9-week seminars with sessions lasting 2 hours each, use of films followed by discussion, educational games, activity programs, and sexual enhancement programs for married couples. In some cases, programs on sexuality are presented within a broader topic area such as "Building Relationships" or within a comprehensive preventative health program. In almost every case, the subjects are volunteers.

Instruments used to evaluate effects of the training on the elderly subjects include the *Aging Sexual Knowledge and Attitudes Scale*, *Sex Knowledge and Attitude Test*, *Attitude and Knowledge Assessment*, and the *Sexual Behavior Questionnaire*.

Results, like those from caregiver populations, are mixed. For example, Adams and her colleagues (1990) found that while new information may be learned, attitudes about that information may be unchanged if the behavior is socially or personally unacceptable. Some researchers have found that elderly adults were curious about sexuality and lacked correct information about their sexuality. Problems in having the elderly participants complete the evaluation instruments, especially posttests, are reported.

Articles about sexual counseling and therapy interventions are also listed in this chapter including those written to present techniques and advice to therapists and medical doctors. One writer (Garetz, 1975) investigated the clients of psychiatrists and found differences between patients seeing older as compared to younger psychiatrists. A number of writers have argued that the family doctor should provide sexual counseling and have presented guidelines (Haffner, 1994; LoPiccolo, 1991; Morrison-Beedy & Robbins, 1989; Renshaw, 1978; Walbroehl, 1986). The need for sex education for the elderly is argued by Shomaker (1990). The need for sexual counseling and suggestions for presenting counseling to older people with specific health problems such as myocardial infarction is argued by Scalzi and Dracup (1978). Sexual help for men is the topic of Schover's 1984 book, *Prime Time: Sexual Health for Men over Fifty.*

433   **Adams, Mary Ann, Rojas-Camero, Cecilia, & Clayton, Kermeta (Kay). (November-December, 1990). A small-group sex education/intervention model for the well elderly: A challenge for educators. *Educational Gerontology, 16*(6), 601-608.**

The authors investigated the effects of an educational intervention on the knowledge and attitudes about sexual health on the elderly. The subjects are 10 healthy elderly people, ages 61 to 91, who attended a senior services day care center. Two graduate students conducted a 2-session education/intervention workshop on sexuality in the elderly person. Subjects completed the *Aging Sexual Knowledge and Attitudes Scale* (ASKAS) in individual interviews before and after the session. Data findings reported that the responses to attitudes about sexual behavior in nursing homes was negative in both pre- and posttests. Results indicated that although modeled judgments may be learned, they may not be expressed because they are socially or personally disfavored. The presumption is that modeling rewarded standards that are too discrepant with one's own moral judgment cannot be assimilated because of cognitive dissonance.

Suggestions are given for those who may desire to give similar workshops.

434   Boyer, Gerry, & Boyer, James. (September, 1982). Sexuality and aging. *Nursing Clinics of North America, 17*(3), 421-427.
        This paper is a review of the literature about sexuality and aging and a description of "Remaining Vital," a course for aging adults in a community setting that attempts to address that need. The authors summarize findings from studies by Alfred Kinsey, Eric Pfeiffer, Masters and Johnson, the *Starr-Weiner Report*, and writings of Alex Comfort, Robert L. Butler and Myrna Lewis. "Remaining Vital" was a nine week seminar series that was conducted with three different groups of aging adults in nine weekly two-hour sessions. The 111 participants ranged from 55 to 92. Written comments by the participants were evaluated. The authors found that the experience of the group member, past and present, varied significantly. Their lack of information about sex fostered many inappropriate fears and pain. Their curiosity about sex continued. The authors concluded that there was a strong need for adult education that includes information on sexuality.

435   Brower, H. Terri, & Tanner, Libby A. (January-February, 1979). A study of older adults attending a program on human sexuality: A pilot study. *Nursing Research, 28*(1), 36-39.
        This study investigated changes in older adults' knowledge and attitudes about human sexuality take place following a two-session course on the subject. Thirty subjects volunteered for the program after some discretion. All subjects attended a neighborhood center in Miami, Florida. Information was gathered before the first session and after the second session by use of pencil-and-paper questionnaire tests. Adapted test items originated from the *Sex Knowledge and Attitude Test and Attitude and Knowledge Assessment*. At the first session, small-group discussions followed a large-group instruction period; the second session consisted of a 20-minute film on human sexuality followed by group discussion. The authors report that of the 30 participants who took the pretest, only four completed the posttest, although most of the 30 attended the second session. The authors discussed several problems from miscommunication to misunderstanding of the study by both subjects and nursing home staff. The authors concluded that there is a need for sexual information for older adults and staff working with them.

436   Citron, Harry, & Kartman, Lauraine Levy. (Fall, 1982). Preserving sexual identity in the institutionalized aged through activities. *Activities, Adaptation, & Aging, 3*(1), 55-63.

The authors address ways to preserve the sexual identities of older people living in institutions. They say that the loss of feeling of sexuality in most older people is not related to the capacity for reproduction or intercourse. They describe activities at a geriatric center and hospital in Baltimore, Maryland. The facility sponsored a workshop for health professionals to help them accept and encourage self-expression including sexual expression. They describe an activity, enjoyed by the group, designed to honor fathers. The activity director arranged for belly dancers. Other activities to enhance sexual identifies of residents were men's and women's clubs, having a beauty shop on site, and musical activities. All of these activities were aimed at helping maintain and restore the ego strength essential for sexual identities of the residents.

437   Eckert, Jane W. (1984). Clinical perspectives on sexuality in older patients: Discussion. *Journal of Geriatric Psychiatry, 17*(2), 183-188.

The author discusses the case vignettes presented by Benjamin Liptzin in his article "Clinical Perspectives on Sexuality in Older Patients" in light of three phases of development in later life: ego differentiation versus work-role preoccupation, body transcendence versus body preoccupation, and ego transcendence versus ego preoccupation. Because sexual issues and problems can occur across many diagnostic areas and within a context of normal development, the author suggests that therapists may need to use a variety of interventions to learn about and treat the sexual concerns of their older patients.

438   Finkle, Alex L., & Finkle, Paul S. (November, 1977). How counseling may solve sexual problems of aging men. *Geriatrics, 32*(11), 84-89.

This study updates a previous report on the results of urologic counseling for male sexual impotence in which the authors demonstrated the therapeutic value of attentive listening and of offering psychologic support to men with sexual problems following prostatectomy. The authors reviewed the records of 138 men ages 45 to 90 who had sought urologic diagnosis and treatment. They found that most younger patients were sexually active and that activity declined slightly up to age 74. The researchers do not favor the use of testosterone for treatment of impotence. In their opinion, three psychologic factors account for most favorable responses to androgen therapy: prescription by a knowledgeable doctor of a purportedly useful drug to an expectant patient. Results of their counseling showed an increase in sexual activity and a reduction of sexual complaints. The authors present two case studies to illustrate counseling methodology and how they go about discovering if a patient has a biological problem, psychological problem, or both. The authors concluded that the understanding of the patient's problem both biological and psychological factors usually play a role in sexual impotence. If the doctor is able to determine which is causing the problem then he may be able to help the patient.

439   Garetz, Floyd K. (January, 1975). The psychiatrist's involvement with aged patients. *American Journal of Psychiatry*, 132(1), 63-65.

The author studied the relationship between the age of psychiatrists and the age of their patients and other variables. Subjects were members of the Minnesota Psychiatric Society. Subjects were asked to complete a questionnaire about themselves and their practices. The author found that the older psychiatrists saw a higher proportion of older patients, advocated more comprehensive treatment, and found older patients more interesting and gratifying than did the younger psychiatrists. Psychiatrists in general psychiatry and those who have a primarily inpatient practice saw the largest proportion of older patients.

440   Guarino, Susan C., & Knowlton, Carol N. (October, 1980). Planning and implementing a group health program on sexuality for the elderly. *Journal of Gerontological Nursing*, 6(10), 600-603.

The purpose of this article is to discuss the authors' experiences in developing and leading a health teaching group on sexuality for senior citizens. The article includes the objectives developed for the project which was named "Building Relationships." They conducted four weekly 1-hour sessions with an open group with voluntary members. The content for the four sessions was: (1) an introduction and establishment of an environment conducive to building relationships; (2) discussion of friendship, one's needs for friendship and desirable characteristics of a friend; (3) discussion of intimacy, the need to feel wanted and loved, ways of fulfilling intimacy needs; and (4) discussion of changes in sexual response and needs of the elderly. Based on their experiences the authors recommend that group leaders complete a course in sexuality prior to leading discussions with elderly people, the group should be closed after the first session to provide more stability, the physical environment should be intimate, the facility administration should be in support of the program, the group should meet at least six times with definite topics each time, strategies should include opportunities for touching, and effective follow-up procedure should be included in the planning.

441   **Gurian, Bennett S. (April, 1986). The myth of the aged as asexual: Countertransference issues in therapy.** *Hospital and Community Psychiatry, 37*(4), 345-346.

This literature review analyzed the findings of studies which have examined the frequency of sexual activity and the reasons for decline in activity among the elderly. The author reviewed the Kinsey studies, the Duke Longitudinal Study, and studies by Cameron, LaTorre and Kear, and Szasz. He concluded that the three latter studies support the view that sex for elders appears either unlikely or distasteful to both elderly and younger people as well as to those who care for the elderly. He pointed out that the Kinsey and Duke Longitudinal Studies focus on the frequency of orgasm, intercourse, masturbation, and degree of interest in sexual behavior, not on these behaviors as an expression of love or as one aspect of an integrated adult sensual life. He said that "all of the studies show an absence of data on the human experience and significance of sexuality in late adulthood." Gurian concluded that "sexual behavior does decline with aging, probably not because of age per se but because of issue of health and availability of partners. The elderly and their caregivers alike have attitudes that promulgate the myth of asexuality with aging." Gurian refuted the idea that society is responsible for creating a myth of asexuality, inferring that the elderly are sexual. He pointed out that psychotherapists in midlife grew up with the idea that sex was either a secret or it was wrong and that their feelings about sex probably resist adult rationality and continue as distorting influences to these therapists' view of patients who are their parents' age. He said that before therapists can help others learn that sexuality is part of life for older people as well as for younger people the therapists must also believe it. He concluded that much more substantive research is needed to explain the myth of asexuality among the aged than currently exists.

442   **Haffner, Deborah. (September, 1994). Sexuality and aging: The family physician's role as educator.** *Geriatrics, 49*(9), 26.

The author of this brief article argues that sexuality is a natural and healthy part of living and that sexual feelings, desires, and activities are present throughout the life cycle. She says that sexuality includes a person's sexual knowledge, beliefs, attitudes, values and behaviors. She recommends that sexual education should be provided for adults and that information is especially needed by older adults which addresses the biological, social-cultural, psychological, and spiritual dimensions of sexuality. She calls for physicians to play a role in making sure that older adults have opportunities for socializing, sexual expression, sexuality education, and sexual health care.

443   **Liptzin, Benjamin. (1984). Clinical perspectives on sexuality in older patients.** *Journal of Geriatric Psychiatry, 17*(2), 167-181.

The author uses specific cases to illustrate the variety of sexual situations that clinicians will encounter in evaluating and treating their elderly patients. Specific psychiatric disorders such as depression, hypomania, anxiety disorders, sexual delusions, paranoid symptoms, psychosis, and dementia have varying effects on elderly sexual behavior. Older people also continue to confront the same issues of intimacy, caring, guilt, and sexual identity in relationships as younger people do. The author suggests that mental health professionals become sensitive to listen and ask about the sexual needs of their older patients and also become more comfortable discussing sexuality with older people.

444   **LoPiccolo, Joseph. (February, 1991). Counseling and therapy for sexual problems in the elderly.** *Clinics in Geriatric Medicine, 7*(1), 161-179.

This article expresses the viewpoint that health professionals often fail to manage elderly patients' sexual concerns adequately. "Sexuality in the elderly," says LoPiccolo, "is a dark continent that most people, including physicians, prefer not to think about." The purpose of this article is to present information about sexual issues that could help health care professionals do a better job. Normal changes in men can cause problems even though they are minor and do not need to interfere with a full sexual life.

Some changes are slowed erection responses, an erection response which is more dependent on direct physical stimulation of the penis, a decline in the rigidity of the penis and angle of erection, need for more direct physical stimulation of the penis, increase in time needed for ejaculation, and a lengthened refractory period. Education and suggestions for adapting to changes will help. Hormone therapy is not effective for most men. In menopausal women, declining estrogen levels led to atrophy of the external genitals, changes in the size of the clitoris and the labia, and loss of pubic hair. These changes do not usually interfere with sexual activity. Estrogen losses also result in loss of skin elasticity, wrinkles, and sagging breasts which can be damaging to a woman's self-esteem and libido. Most of the changes in women respond well to estrogen therapy. The author discusses psychologic and cultural issues in aging and sexuality including sex and the elderly single person and the widower's syndrome. For single women there is a lack of partners. He says that older women were raised in a time when masturbation was extremely taboo and that even if it were acceptable to them, "most of us would agree that masturbation is not as rewarding, emotionally or physically, as is sex with a partner." He says that sexuality in long-term care is especially neglected and even suppressed. He believes the elder-care industry needs to reexamine this basic assumption. LoPiccolo describes the widower's syndrome as the situation that develops at the death of the wife when the widower becomes prematurely involved with another woman and cannot achieve an erection due to grief or guilt. Several diseases common among the elderly can interfere with sexuality. They are diabetes, coronary disease, renal dialysis, and prostatic disease. Medications also can affect sexuality by reducing sexual drive, interfering with erection, arousal in women, and orgasm in both men and women. Technology is providing aids for men with erectile failure such as penile prostheses and injections of vasoactive agents in the penis. LoPiccolo believes that proper counseling could eliminate the need for some of these technological "quick fixes." Low sexual desire in the elderly has become the most commonly reported problem in sex therapy clinics. Reasons include health problems, diminished sexual drive, problems in sexual function, use of some medications, cultural attitudes toward sexual attractiveness, and long standing marital problems. Clinicians need to be alert to a variety of causes. The author concludes with a case example which illustrates that stereotypes about aging and sexuality can be wrong and can negatively influence how elderly patients both think and act sexually. These stereotypes can also lead to errors in clinical management of the sexual concerns of elderly patients and to treatment of the elderly with less than humanistic concerns for their sexual needs. The author suggests that in the future, helping professionals will consider sexuality as a priority in their work with elderly patients.

445 Morrison-Beedy, Diane, & Robbins, Lorraine. (December, 1989). Sexual assessment and the aging female. *Nurse Practitioner,* 14(12), 37-45.

In this article, the authors discuss measures that will provide information about factors that can influence sexual relationships including personal and societal values. They recommend developing a sexual database which includes a complete gynecological history. The article includes tables with information about common myths associated with aging women and sexuality, common sexual response changes in the aging female, and common estrogen replacement therapy (ERT) guidelines. The article also provides information about sexual functioning in the elderly, guidelines for sexual counseling, a discussion of effects of illness on sexual ability, and tips on the management of sexual changes. The authors believe that health care professionals have a responsibility to assist interested elderly people in maintaining a satisfying sexual life and to communicate information in a non-judgmental and unbiased manner.

446 Poggi, Raymond G., & Berland, David I. (October, 1985). The therapists' reactions to the elderly. *The Gerontologist,* 25(5), 508-513.

The authors researched their reactions to elderly patients while leading a newcomers' group in a retirement home. They recorded notes after each hour-group session and discussed what they experienced as group leaders as well as in the group process. Using literature, peer supervision, and introspection, the researchers recognized their reactions, or countertransference, to the elderly in this situation encompassed sexual feelings, as well as the lack of these feelings, being "boys" to very elderly women, and providing medical treatment to avoid complex psychological concerns. The researchers believed that these issues prevail when workers and the elderly interact in a variety of helping situations.

447 Renshaw, Domeena C. (September, 1978). Sex and values. *The Journal of Clinical Psychiatry,* 39(9), 716-719.

In this article, the author discusses the importance of understanding that sex and values are inseparably related. This must be recognized and repeatedly dealt with in order to provide a complete therapeutic perspective. Renshaw describes morality and sexuality in the present and past centuries. She says that physicians are presented with people with sexual problems in their practices and that all but 6 of 110 medical schools in the United States in 1978 offered human sexuality in their curriculums. She points out that sexual dysfunction is learned maladaptive behavior that can be unlearned in brief treatment. She outlines the steps a physician can follow to provide treatment. In her view, physicians have a responsibility to provide education to patients regarding sexuality.

448   Rowland, Kay F., & Haynes, Stephen N. (Summer, 1978). A sexual enhancement program for elderly couples. *Journal of Sex and Marital Therapy, 4*(2), 91-113.

This study examined the effects of a group sexual enhancement program for elderly couples. Ten married couples ages 51 to 71 were placed in one of three sexual enhancement groups based on their scheduling preferences. All groups followed the same format, but each was conducted by a different pair of group leaders. The sexual enhancement program was divided into three 2-week phases: (1) a pretreatment period in which there was no contact with the therapists; (2) an education phase in which subjects were provided the information on human sexual functioning in aging people in particular; and (3) a communication exercises-sexual techniques phase in which subjects are provided with information on methods to improve communication and increase enjoyment of sexual contact. Following an initial interview in which the purpose of the study was explained, subjects completed a questionnaire assessing satisfaction and frequency of sexual activities and perception of partner's sexual satisfaction. The questionnaire was readministered after the pretreatment phase, after the education phase, and four weeks following the end of the program. The authors concluded that a significant increase in sexual satisfaction, frequency of certain sexual activities, and positive attitudes about marital and life satisfaction is found to occur over the course of the sexual enhancement program. The authors reported these significant increases occurred either during the pretreatment period or during some combination of phases.

449 Salamon, Michael J., & Charytan, Penny. (Summer, 1984). A sexuality workshop program for the elderly. *Clinical Gerontologist, 2*(4), 25-35.

This paper explores the development of a sexuality workshop for older adult community residents. The workshop was part of a comprehensive program, The Preventative Health Center (PHC), which provides a variety of both traditional and non-traditional health services. The design of the sexuality workshop consisted of both structured, semi-structured, and open-ended discussion sessions. Seven meetings were planned. Topics covered were: myths and realities of sex and aging, common medical problems, common emotional problems, and new patterns of intimacy. Three sessions were open discussions. The authors observed that participants were better able to discuss their sexual needs by the end of the program. They reported that the participants became more knowledgeable as measured by a self-report and an education-attitude scale. There was a slight but insignificant change in life satisfaction. Information about the instrumentation and specific data are not reported.

450 Scalzi, Cynthia, & Dracup, Kathy. (September-October, 1978). Sexual counseling of coronary patients. *Heart and Lung, 7*(5), 840-845.

This article, written by two clinical nurses, presents the need for sexual counseling for coronary patients, the factors to be considered, and the principles and the techniques of counseling. They cite studies which have found ineffective sexual counseling and its consequence to male patients. The most common consequence is a lasting reduction in sexual activity. The two major fears are fears of imminent death and the loss of physical capacity. The authors recommend that prior to counseling, the physician and the nurse need to know the physical status of the patient, the physiologic effects of sexual activity, and the psychological effects of an myocardial infarction (MI). They describe principals of sexual counseling which could help provide a sound foundation for sexual counseling of the MI patient and suggest techniques to follow. The article includes a detailed chart which can be followed by a physician or nurse in a counseling situation.

451 Schover, Leslie R. (1984). *Prime time: Sexual health for men over fifty*. New York: Holt, Rinehart and Winston.

The author, a sex therapist, discusses topics of interest to older men such as their ability to be a good lover as they age, whether there is a male menopause, sexual response and aging, and sexual health hazards. He includes a chapter titled "What do women really want" in which he says that men's confusion is caused by their childhood training regarding the expression of feelings. He discusses myths that men believe are true about women and their values. The author describes various health hazards that affect sexuality such as arteriosclerosis, hypertension, heart disease, diabetes, cancer, lung diseases, alcoholism, prostrate problems, and Peyronie's disease. He includes a chapter of advice to men who are single and dating which includes ideas about beginning a new sexual relationship.

452   Shomaker, Dianna McDonald. (June, 1980). Integration of physiological and sociocultural factors as a basis for sex education to the elderly. *Journal of Gerontological Nursing, 6*(6), 311-318.

The author expresses the need for sex education for the elderly. She says that nurses have a responsibility to advise and counsel their elderly patients on health matters, including sex. This paper examines change in sexual norms over time, sociocultural aspects of sexual behavior, and the impact of physiological change associated with age. It concludes with a model upon which nurses can incorporate their understanding of aging into a plan for sexual education for the elderly. Shomaker argues the case for people's right to continue functioning sexually into old age and expresses the view that sexuality fulfills human needs beyond procreation. She says that society perpetuates myths and taboos restricting sexual behavior among the nonproductive elderly and that those views are then accepted as valid. While she strongly supports the view that nurses should counsel the elderly on sexual matters, she warns against imposing values on the client and stresses the need to recognize the complexity and sensitivity of the subject matter when dealing with clients.

453   Walbroehl, Gordon S. (March, 1986). Sexuality: Advising the older patient. *Comprehensive Therapy, 12*(3), 35-38.

Walbroehl states that the need for sexual expression continues until death. He believes that society has denied older patients these feelings causing them to either cease to function sexually or to continue with guilt. He recommends that physicians change this situation by providing information about physical and psychological changes that occur with aging and about alternate means of sexual expression. He cautions about considering the moral views of the patient. The article includes information for physicians about physical changes, psychological changes, ramifications of these changes, societal views, and problems that can occur when an individual resumes sexual activity after a period of abstinence.

454 West, Helen L. (Fall, 1983). Sexuality and aging: An innovative educational approach. *Gerontology and Geriatric Education,* 4(1), 61-66.

This article describes a simulation game methodology to teach older people, their family members, and staff who provide care to elders about aging and sexuality. The innovative, non-traditional educational activity involved presenting to each group a short life situation narrative and asked to make a judgment about outcome or solve a problem. Information to help solve the problem was available from other people close to the situation, represented by labeled index cards (e.g., daughter). The simulation game provided heated discussions in all three groups. Data for evaluation of this educational approach were gathered through pre- and posttest interview scales used by trainee older adults. Findings indicate that this is a useful educational approach. Analyses revealed an increase in sexual knowledge, attitudinal changes toward more permissiveness, improved affect in regard to one's sexuality, increased sexual satisfaction, and for older people an increase in sexual behavior.

455 White, Charles B., & Catania, Joseph A. (1982). Psychoeducational intervention for sexuality with the aged, family members of the aged, and people who work with the aged. *International Journal of Aging and Human Development,* 15(2), 121-138.

The authors conducted a study on the sexual attitudes, knowledge, and behavior of elderly people. A sexual psychoeducation intervention was conducted and evaluated with elderly (N = 30), adult family members of elderly (N = 30), and staff members of nursing homes (N = 30). The elderly had an interview 1 month to 6 weeks prior to the experimental treatment. The elderly group completed the *Sexual Behavior Questionnaire* and the *Aging Sexual Knowledge and Attitudes Scale.* The other two groups completed the *Aging Sexual Knowledge and Attitudes Scale.* Data were collected by interview for all groups. The authors comment that older people are beginning to challenge society's tendency to measure sexuality solely through sexual performance and are expressing their desire for more information regarding sexual health. The study revealed that even if elderly people do not participate in sexual behaviors, they will become more tolerant of such behaviors after participating in workshops related to sexual issues.

456   White, Evelyn Joyce. (May-June, 1986). **Appraising the need for altered sexuality information.** *Rehabilitation Nursing, 11*(3), 6-11.

This study collected data from rehabilitation nurses on what they believed to be clients' behavioral indicators of readiness for information on altered sexuality. Subjects were 31 licensed registered nurses (2 men and 29 women, ages 20 to over 40) employed full time as rehabilitation nurses and providing continuous nursing service to spinal-cord injured (SCI) clients for at least 6 months. Data were collected by administering the *Behavior Checklist,* an instrument developed by the author for this study. The most common verbal and nonverbal behaviors were listed on the checklist. Nurses used the checklist to report their observations of behaviors they believed to be signs that clients were ready to learn about their altered sexuality. Tables with the lists of verbal and nonverbal behaviors are included in the article along with findings from this study. The study found that SCI clients communicated their needs for information in both verbal and nonverbal ways. The author recommends that nurses play an active role in promoting readiness behavior through tactful questioning on matters of sexuality which will enable clients to express their concerns.

18

Research Needs and Elderly Sexuality

$\mathbb{R}$ esearch articles generally end with suggestions for further research. The article, listed below, was aimed exclusively at identifying research needs in the area of elderly sexuality.

As evidenced by the 457 articles and books annotated in this collection, there is little information about the sexual behavior and sexuality concerns of the older population. Even more obvious is the lack of empirical data about the old-old population which is the fastest growing segment of the population in the United States. With men the major problem appears to be impotence; with women it is a lack of partners.

One generalization that is exceeding evident from reading these hundreds of articles is the similarity among those written in the 1970s, 1980s, and 1990s. Writers decry the same myths and stereotypes. Writers in each decade provide an overview of male and female sexuality using data from Kinsey and Masters and Johnson. They cite data about elderly sexual behaviors and sexual interest that resulted from the long completed Duke Longitudinal Studies. Little information, to date, about sexuality has been published from the on-going Baltimore Longitudinal Studies.

The most important question might be "What do the elderly want?" That question is not generally asked. What elderly people know about their sexuality and what they want to know is seldom investigated. Many writers feel strongly about the importance of sexuality in old age. Butler, Renshaw, and Waltz and Blum are among those who make strong cases. But as Eugene Thomas, the author of a 1982 article, "Essential Vitamin or Popcorn?" pointed out, how important is sexuality after all?

The di Mauro article (1996) reports a lack of empirical research, a need for comprehensive training for people in the health care field, and the continuing lack of academic and public acceptance of research in the area of elderly sexuality. The abstract of the executive summary is presented here. The address for obtaining the complete report is also provided at the end of the abstract.

457   di Mauro, Diane. (Summer, 1996). Executive summary of sexuality research in the United States: An assessment of the social and behavioral sciences. *Sexuality and Disability, 14*(2), 117-138.

The purpose of the project, which is the subject of this report, was to provide an overview of social science research about sexual behavior. It attempted to identify research trends and gaps, priority topics, and critical issues of sexuality research. The assessment revealed three primary concerns: (1) a need for fundamental research to expand the base on sexuality; (2) a need for comprehensive training for people in the field; and (3) the need to strengthen the sexuality research field to encourage greater academic respectability and public acceptance of research in the area. The summary report lists spheres of research in the field, gaps and needs in research, and major research topics. Topics discussed in the report are: gender, HIV/AIDS, adolescent sexuality, sexual orientation, sexual coercion, research methodology. The report discusses barriers in sexuality research which includes training and research dissemination. Another topic in the report is a discussion of government an private sector support. Recommendations include establishing an interdisciplinary task force concerned with advancing the field of sexuality research and establishing a formal network of grant makers to advance the philanthropic response to gaps in current sexuality research. This article is the executive summary of a full-length assessment report titled *Sexuality Research in the United States* which can be obtained through the Sexuality Research Fellowship Program at the Social Science Research Council (SSRC), 810 Seventh Avenue, 31st Floor, New York, New York 10019. The full report provides information about sexuality organizations and journals.

Author Index

Entries are keyed to page numbers.

Subject Index

Entries are keyed to page numbers.

About the Compiler

BONNIE L. WALKER is the president of a research and development firm specializing in developing training material for caregivers of the elderly. She is the director of two research projects sponsored by the National Institute on Aging, "Injury Prevention for the Elderly" and "Improving Staff Attitudes Toward Expression of Elderly Sexuality." Published works include *Injury Prevention for the Elderly: A Training Project* (1996), *Injury Prevention for Young Children* (Greenwood, 1996), and *Injury Prevention for the Elderly* (Greenwood, 1995).

ISBN 0-313-30133-6

HARDCOVER BAR CODE